ON BEING HUMAN

NOTES ON THE HUMAN CONDITION

Amardo J. Rodriguez

Copyright © 2013 by Amardo J. Rodriguez

All rights reserved. No part of this publication may be reproduced, distributed, or transmitted in any form or by any means, including photocopying, recording, or other electronic or mechanical methods, without the prior written permission of the publisher, except in the case of brief quotations embodied in critical reviews and certain other noncommercial uses permitted by copyright law. For permission requests, write to the publisher, addressed "Attention: Permissions Coordinator," at the address below.

Public Square Press
309 Fayette Drive
Fayetteville, NY 13066
USA

ISBN: 0615841260
ISBN 13: 9780615841267

FOR
JOSHUA AND JORDAN

CONTENTS

	PROLOGUE	IX
1.	ON KNOWLEDGE	1
2.	ON FORGIVENESS	9
3.	ON FEAR	15
4.	ON PURPOSE	23
5.	ON TEMPORALITY	31
6.	ON LANGUAGE	39
7.	ON GOD	47
8.	ON IMAGINATION	57
9.	ON NARRATIVE	73
10.	ON METHOD	79
11.	ON EXISTENCE	85
12.	ON PERCEPTION	97
13.	ON BEING AND TIME	101
14.	ON LAW	115
15.	ON MIND & BODY	121
16.	ON DISPOSABILITY	129
17.	ON DIVERSITY	133

18. ON BLASPHEMY	139
19. ON REDEMPTION	145
20. ON ACADEME	151
21. ON COMMUNICATION	155
22. ON COLONIALISM	163
23. ON CRIME & PUNISHMENT	175
24. ON BELIEF	195
25. ON VIOLENCE	199
26. ON POLITICS	205
27. ON MEDIOCRITY	209
28. ON CONFUSION	213
29. ON SEXUALITY	221
30. ON SOCIAL WORLDS	229
31. ON DOUBT	235
32. ON BUREAUCRACY	239
33. ON JUSTICE	245
34. ON TECHNOLOGY	255
35. ON METAPHORS	261
36. ON THE END OF CIVILIZATION	269
37. ON IDENTITY	279
38. ON EVOLUTION	283
39. ON MORALITY	289
40. ON REDUCTIONISM	295
41. ON CIRCULARITY	301
42. ON DESIGN	309
43. ON DISCRIMINATION AND HARASSMENT	315
44. ON TEACHING	325
45. ON THE GOOD LIFE	331
46. ON DEATH	337
47. ON MORAL PHILOSOPHY	345

48. ON LIBERTY	351
49. ON INTERCULTURAL COMMUNICATION	357
50. ON THE NATURE OF THOUGHT	371
EPILOGUE	377
REFERENCES	381

PROLOGUE

This book reflects my continuing search to understand what being human means. I am specifically interested in understanding the nature and scope of our potentiality to create more humane and just worlds. History, of course, conspires against my project. With so much misery, death, and destruction at the hands of our own doing, the narrative seems to be already written. We are a cruel and violent species. Without elaborate structures to control our destructive and violent proclivities, anarchy will supposedly reign. But is this the only story of the human experience?

I am, of course, by no means beginning from scratch. There are literatures emerging from different places that are speaking to the possibility of a fundamentally different story of the human experience that lends for much hope. There is the notion of us being relational beings rather autonomous selves. There is the new story of evolution that emphasizes cooperation rather than competition. But the status quo continues to have the momentum. The dominant narrative is still about us being beasts and savages. So the struggle continues. It now seems nearly certain that our day of reckoning will soon be upon us. After all, how much longer can we continue to create social worlds that appeal to our worst instincts and impulses before we become undone? We should no doubt have the power to create our own worlds on our own terms. Anything less would mean that we are merely subjects. But with such power to create our own worlds must come the attending responsibility. We should be ready to deal with the consequences and implications of our actions and lack thereof.

So as much as I believe that soon our day of reckoning will be upon us, I have no hope for divine intervention. Life should be our foremost concern, as in knowing what ethics, politics, and economics can promote all expressions of life. Only the rise of this kind of emergent ethics, politics, and economics will ultimately save us from ourselves. However, this is arguably where our downfall began. Somewhere we began to separate ourselves from the world. This separation eventually put us in conflict with the world. On the other hand, maybe we began in separation and our survival and prosperity require us to overcome our separation from the world. Either way, this separation from the world will eventually make for our undoing. It now pervades and shapes everything. Even our language is now mired in modes of separation that impede how we perceive and experience the world. Ending our separation from the world will mean dismantling all the social, rhetorical, ideological, and communicational practices that promote this separation.

Every day brings news that reflects our seemingly never-ending proclivity to inflict all kinds of misery upon each other. There is no let up. But such is also what makes for the urgency of my project. To believe that we possess this unrelenting capacity for evil ends any possibility for meaning. We would have to resign ourselves to be either witnesses or perpetrators of evil. My project is a search for meaning and the possibility of meaning. For without any possibility for meaning, what would become of any possibility for hope, grace, faith, mercy, compassion, joy, and love? Without such notions, what can being human *really* mean? Yes, the search for meaning can most likely be another expression of human folly. But I am specifically interested in the possibility of meaning. That is, I am interested in the *being* in being human. I view possibility as residing within our capacity to create meaning and believe that this capacity is potentially infinite. In this way, I view liberation in terms of meaning creation and oppression in terms of meaning suppression. Thus, I am interested in understanding how we can fundamentally enlarge our ways of being so as to promote meaning, creation, and ultimately, possibility.

In focusing on being I am assuming that this is a world of infinite ambiguity, mystery, and complexity. The possibility for meaning is infinite. What ultimately matters is which modes of being promote possibility. So as much as I understand the limits of my project, I also understand that the quest for possibility, however fraught with despair, is simply too important to be forsaken.

I

ON KNOWLEDGE

What is the value of any knowledge, and by that any academic enterprise, that separates knowing from doing? That is, what is the value of any knowledge that revolves around abstraction rather than action? Of course, many can conceivably argue that this is a false dichotomy. Reading, writing, and studying are all forms of action and doing. No doubt this kind of scholarly doing may differ from the vocational kinds—like plumbing, carpentry, auto-repair, and so forth—that Matthew Crawford (2009) celebrates in *Shop Class as Soulcraft: An Inquiry into the Value of Work*. Yet many would contend that the difference is merely qualitative. Still, Crawford claims that "modern science adopts an otherworldly ideal of how we come to know nature: through mental constructions that are more intellectually tractable than material reality, and in particular amenable to mathematical representations" (p. 80). He also claims that mathematics, like building houses, is constitutive, "every element is fully within one's view." In this way, "a mathematical representation of the world renders the world as something of our own making... the world is interesting and intelligible only insofar as we can reproduce it in ideal form, as a projection from ourselves" (p. 82).

Crawford's point is that modern science cultivates self-absorption and ultimately a knowledge that is divorced from the world, as well as people who are divorced from the world. We can no doubt challenge this division that Crawford is trying to establish between scholarly work and other kinds of work. We can even criticize Crawford's privileging of vocational work and devaluing of scholarly work. But there is arguably still a case to be made about the doing of modern science and the obsession with abstractions that seem to have nothing to do with the reality of our everyday world. What also of the division between teaching and scholarship? How could this division even seem plausible? For how could any person teach well without learning anything new? Just as well, how could any inquiry be of any value that pretends to be devoid of any moral direction and imagination? But such illusions and pretensions are the status quo in our institutions of higher learning. What results is education reduced to instruction, and inquiry devoid of any passion to understand the world in all its complexities, ambiguities, and uncertainties.

Most striking is the absence of any kind of imagination or ambition to fundamentally enlarge how we perceive the world, or to challenge others to do likewise. Repetition and reproduction are status quo. Nothing much is new, bold, or poses a threat to anything. Academics now run the place. Education, rather than being about challenging and enlarging our moral imagination, is increasingly about producing academics, as in, "How many publications do I need to have to get tenure and promotion?" But what is the value of this scholarship for the world? How did the doing of scholarship and the training of scholars become such disembodied processes? But such is the march of modernity. Quantity matters. The goal is to amass as much knowledge as possible, which means producing academics who are increasingly efficient and proficient in helping us amass this knowledge. As such, the number of publications does matter. Quantity reflects efficiency and proficiency. No doubt many would contend that quality of publications is what really matters, thereby a focus on publishing in the most prestigious journals and with the prestigious presses. But even such persons would contend that quantity of quality publications matters most. Either way, a good scholar must be productive and our productivity should be quantifiable and measurable. Yet all of this productivity has absolutely nothing to do with the condition of the world or with anything else.

I am always listening for the question. What is the question that drives a person's inquiry? Why is this question important? What is the value of this question? What will answering this question do for us? What will potentially change? What will become possible? Also, why is this question important to you? What brings you to this question? What does answering this question demand of you? But I never hear the question. All I usually get are endless papers about nothing. So I ask again, always wanting to believe that my phrasing is the problem. "*If you had only so many weeks to live, would your inquiry remain the same? Would you even be in academe? What would you teach? How would you teach?*" That I need to even ask these new questions is never a good sign.

The problem is our fear of dying. This is why our inquiry is devoid of any passion and urgency. This is also why our theories turn us inward and divorce us from the world and each other. To die requires courage, as in the courage to love, to believe, to imagine, to create, and most of all, to live. Inquiry begins with understanding our place in the world and recognizing all the forces that situate us accordingly. By recognizing the forces that situate us in the world we come to know the origins of our questions. This is why inquiry is fundamentally a process of self-exploration. Inquiring into the world is about inquiring into ourselves. Through inquiry, besides recognizing our location in the world, we also recognize our limitations. Inquiry is heuristic when we arrive at a new vision of the world and ourselves. It is an insurgent undertaking. It opposes the status quo as it aspires to achieve a new vision of the world that lends for new possibilities. But of course this kind of inquiry hardly occurs. Now inquiry serves the status quo. It poses no threats, and even proudly boasts of being neutral and apolitical. This is what happens when the questions I am listening for are absent.

But how did the matter of inquiry become so perverse and strange? How did we become such cowards, and how did this become the normal way of doing inquiry? Also, how could this kind of inquiry produce any kind of theory that poses a threat to the status quo? We merely get the same knowledge again and again, with the same cast of characters. Nothing is fundamentally new. So how are we to evolve and change? Herein resides the problem. We lack the courage to change and evolve, for to change and evolve requires the courage and resolve to experience the world anew. We must be ready to die. Only by being ready to die can we genuinely create a new knowledge of the world that will allow us to live with boundless passion, imagination, and conviction. Without the possibility of death, life is impossible, and the project of theory over.

To be human is to struggle with death and dying. This struggle never releases us. It is the most compelling and enduring existential struggle. Eventually a position is taken, a side chosen. In our case, or in the case of modernity, we have chosen to vanquish death. We aspire to live forever, which means imposing our will on the world. We will defy its constraints, rhythms, and tensions. We will be gods. Within modernity, knowledge, including how we define, relate, and acquire knowledge, is never assumed to be morally, historically, and culturally situated. The goal of knowledge is to conquer death. We are therefore of a consciousness that is averse and hostile to death and dying. That knowledge is always historically, morally, and culturally situated means that knowledge is always politicized. The notion of pure research or research for purely the sake of doing research is illusory. But what of the side that modernity has taken? What does this mean for us? What does it require of us? What does it make of us? How do we come to define, relate, and acquire knowledge in bold new ways when we lack the courage to die and have never been encouraged to learn how to die?

Modernity peddles in illusions. We cannot end death. We cannot impose our will on the world. We cannot defy the world's constraints, rhythms, and tensions. There will always be consequences. We cannot be gods. To oppose death is to oppose the natural order of the world. It is about opposing diversity and all diversity brings. It is also about being afraid of evolution, disruption, and innovation. It is also about being afraid of the world's mystery, ambiguity, and complexity, and thereby believing in the supposed necessity of various institutions, structures, and practices to bring order upon the world. In other words, to oppose death is to be hostile to chaos, ambiguity, and other such forces that presumably promise death. But to oppose death is really to oppose life, as both dwell within each other. Each nourishes and defines the other. That is, to understand death requires us to understand life, and to embrace one requires us to embrace the other. There is no meaning devoid of ambiguity, no order devoid of chaos, no knowledge devoid of ignorance. Yet we continue to believe differently, and what we believe shapes how we define, relate, and acquire knowledge. In fact, what we believe defines and shapes everything, including what we value, perceive, and experience. Thus the power of believing that the world is against us, as modernity propagates, is formidable. But such is the crisis of knowledge that is now upon us as the world pushes back against the ambitions of modernity. How can we cultivate a new set of beliefs?

Modernity has always sought to convince us that ontology (what we believe) has no purchase. It is a remnant of a previous evolutionary condition. We now supposedly have the capacity for complex rational, analytical, and computational thought. Thus the endless claims about our being at the end of history. We are supposedly now in the age of epistemology (knowledge), with our grand methodologies and technologies that will allow us to reveal the world's deepest secrets and also impose our full will on the world. There is no need to believe any more. Now we can know, and know with certainty. We can be gods. But modernity is yet to disabuse us of ontology. In reality, there can be no separation between epistemology and ontology. Ontology shapes everything, defines everything, locates everything, and permeates everything. It holds epistemology on a short leash. What we perceive begins with what we believe and are willing to believe. This in no way means that epistemology is at the mercy of ontology. It merely means that each must reckon with the presence of the other. Still, the everyday doing of inquiry and theory abides by the illusions of modernity. The focus is on epistemology, which includes learning how to employ various methods, how to test and develop hypotheses and research questions, and so forth. Ultimately, the focus is on developing a set of competencies and proficiencies that will supposedly allow us to make a contribution that will sustain a life in academe—that is, become productive academics.

There is simply no division between epistemology and ontology. For how can we separate what we believe from what we perceive? How is this humanly possible? Yet there is a serious fallout that comes from privileging epistemology and downplaying ontology. This tendency impoverishes the doing of inquiry and theory, beginning with separating each from the other. As with inquiry, we tend to view theory as an activity that happens outside of us. Presumably, a theory is a tool, a means of describing a set of relationships, or a relation amongst a set of variables. We focus on theory development, such as testing theory in new contexts, with new variables and new populations. As always, the focus is on learning a set of skills and techniques that will allow us to build more reliable theories, that in turn will ultimately allow us conquer the world's ambiguity. But there is no inside/outside divide, just as there is no divide between theory and inquiry.

The inside/outside divide is born out of efforts to mask the fact that our theories reflect our fragilities, vulnerabilities, and ambiguities. It is also about our unwillingness to look honestly and courageously within ourselves by failing to look honestly and courageously within each other. Such looking requires, most of all, the courage to engage all of the ambiguity, mystery, and complexity that come with being human. The inside/outside divide turns us outward and away from ourselves and each other. It also turns us away from the world. The turning away is what makes for our knowledge being foreign to the world. This is also why our knowledge tends to be devoid of flesh and blood, as in being devoid of any despair and misery, hopes and joys, desires and longings.

Our theories estrange and alienate us from the world and each other. In fact, our theories paralyze us by discouraging action, imagination, innovation. Even though there is now supposed to be a distinction between descriptive and generative theories, nothing much is fundamentally different. The problem begins with ontology. We have to find a way to believe that the world is laden with beauty and possibility. We also have to find a way to believe in our own potentiality. This is why we have no theories of love, grace, forgiveness, tenderness, compassion, and mercy. These theories require a different ontology. This is also why, for all our knowledge, the world remains fraught with peril and our own misery seems to be without end. Why is our knowledge yet to save us? Instead, only misery and peril seem to come from our knowledge. The problem, again, is with ontology. Our beliefs are conspiring against us, impeding our ability to forge a new knowledge and, ultimately, a new ethics and politics (axiology). Without a new ontology, nothing can be born anew. But how do we begin to believe in a world that makes theories of love, grace, compassion, and mercy? That is, how do we begin to believe in a new conception of what it means to be human? Also, how do we begin to do so when modernity seduces us again and again with an ontology that demands nothing much from us?

Ontology reminds us that our humanity exceeds our biology and physiology. There are many realms to our being, including the realm of the spirit, the soul, and the heart. In other words, besides the realm of the material, biological, and physiological, there is also the realm of the spiritual, existential, and sensual. Of course there is also the realm of the historical, cultural, and ecological. Modernity has always sought to mask our complexity. But to be born into a world of infinite ambiguity means that we have to create and abide by a set of beliefs. This in no way means that all belief systems are morally equal. We can always forsake those beliefs that prove to be destructive and cultivate more constructive beliefs. There is nothing inherently debilitative or restrictive about ontology. It is merely a matter of which beliefs we choose to cultivate and promote.

But modernity continues to insist that our prosperity resides in epistemology. We should be creatures of knowing rather than believing. To argue for ontology is really to argue for epistemology. To reclaim ontology is about improving the doing of epistemology. We should want knowledge, but we should aspire for a knowledge that will ultimately promote life. Only a new epistemology can give rise to such a knowledge. However, before such knowledge can arise, we have to be ready to believe in the possibility of a world that lends for this kind of knowledge.

2

ON FORGIVENESS

It is famously said that only the strong can forgive. But why can only the strong forgive? Who, exactly, are the strong? What does it mean to be strong? Is strength the only requirement necessary to forgive? Indeed, why should only the strong have the capacity to forgive? Why should this capacity be so exclusive when the world seems in need of so much forgiveness? What are the weak and feeble to do?

To forgive is an act of courage, an act of perseverance and resilience. This is why only the strong can forgive. For courage is about the ability to persevere and endure in the face of risk, peril, and even death. It is also about finding the resolve to believe in the possibility of redemption, especially when such possibility seems most impossible. In other words, forgiveness is an act of faith—faith in a possibility that seems improbable. Thus forgiveness is also an act of imagination—the courage to imagine a world that seems unimaginable. This, again, is why only the strong can forgive. For without courage, such imagination is impossible to sustain.

However, without such imagination, without such faith, all that remains is a world of vengeance and never-ending cycles of violence.

To forgive is to declare an end to this world, and the practices that create and perpetuate this world. This is hard to do. However, vengeance, in requiring nothing from us, is easy. Vengeance requires no courage, no faith, no imagination. It is devoid of any ambiguity and complexity. There is nothing extraordinary about vengeance. By releasing us of ambiguity and complexity, vengeance creates closed systems—systems that are averse and hostile to life. Vengeance therefore impedes our ability to change and evolve. It impedes life. It undermines possibility. For what is life? Ecologically, life is about the rise of possibility. Theologically, life is the promise of possibility, such as the promise of worlds that are yet to come. Either way, vengeance impedes life by impeding possibility. On the other hand, by sustaining possibility, such as the possibility to be born anew, forgiveness nurtures life. It appeals to the angels rather than demons in us. Moreover, forgiveness challenges us to believe in our own capacity to realize and actualize worlds that seem impossible. It calls us to look to each other for our redemption and prosperity. Through forgiveness we affirm the belief that we have within ourselves the ability to heal and move forward. This is why only the strong can forgive. In a world where so much brutality seems to affirm the reality of evil, only the strong can sustain such a belief, only the strong possesses the resolve to realize such a world. Without forgiveness, we are beholden to each other's hate, prejudice, and cruelty. So through forgiveness we choose and resolve to release ourselves of each other's demons and prisons. This, again, is why only the strong can forgive. The weak will demand vengeance, never recognizing that vengeance only begets vengeance.

But such is the nature of vengeance. It impedes our ability to view the world clearly and fully. It tunnels our vision and, in doing so, impedes our perception of things. In most cases, vengeance blinds us. It brings only darkness, and the demons that come from such conditions. Forgiveness is the path of light, the path of hope. There is nothing naïve about forgiveness. Forgiveness requires looking deeply at that which seems unforgiveable, for only that which seems most unforgiveable is deserving of forgiveness. Thus forgiveness requires us to reckon with evil. This is why only the strong can forgive. Only the strong can look deeply into the face of evil and walk away without promising to destroy the perpetrator. Forgiveness is about imposing our own reality on the world. We choose to forgive, and to do so unconditionally. Only such forgiveness is of any value.

Forgiveness is also an act of sedition. It challenges the status quo's belief in the necessity of retribution. Only the strong can take on the status quo. In challenging our foundational beliefs that legitimize retribution, forgiveness also opposes the institutions that are born of such beliefs, and the worldview that abides by such beliefs. To forgive is an act of resistance and defiance. It constitutes our unwillingness to submit to the will of the status quo. Forgiveness is always political. Through forgiveness we articulate our allegiance to a different worldview. In fact, forgiveness is an act of revolution. It constitutes a perilous undertaking. This is why only the strong can forgive. Only the strong possess the courage to die. Only the strong have the resolve to face such peril. We all want to live and save ourselves from peril and misery. The impulse is primal, even biological. To forgive is really difficult. It violates our most primal instincts and impulses. This is why only the strong can forgive. Only the strong possess the capacity to resist the pull of these instincts and impulses. To forgive is to affirm our capacity to function morally. We can exceed our biology. Forgiveness is an act of meaning, an act of becoming. This is why forgiveness is moral. Through forgiveness we demonstrate our capacity to create meaning and shape our worlds. In this way, forgiveness opposes the notion of evil being a natural force in the world. In a world of evil, forgiveness is impossible. For what is the value of forgiveness in such a world? What can forgiveness achieve? In a world of evil, we must vanquish evil. Only this recourse seems reasonable. Thus a world of evil limits possibility. Such a world is restrictive rather than generative. In short, a world of evil impedes the creation of knowledge. It also undermines imagination. As such, what kind of God would put evil in the world?

To forgive is to challenge any conception of God that claims that God is responsible for putting evil in the world. Accordingly, forgiveness is an act of heresy, and in the case of Jesus Christ, ultimately deserving of crucifixion by the will of the religious and supposedly righteous. Only the strong is ready to suffer the way Jesus Christ did for our sins and trespasses. Only the strong can resist being seduced by vengeance. But most of all, only the strong, and the very strong, can resist viewing the persecution and crucifixion of Jesus Christ as evil.

The world conspires against forgiveness. It makes nothing about forgiving easy. In nearly every way, the world favors vengeance. Vengeance is efficient. This is why vengeance is such a formidable force in human affairs. It seduces us by asking nothing from us. We merely have to submit to what seem our natural instincts and impulses. Moreover, vengeance conforms nicely to a conception of God that requires no imagination. For this God, redemption is merely a matter of submission. Vengeance exploits our seemingly natural aversion to ambiguity and complexity. Forgiveness, on the other hand, is difficult, even impossible. It is laden with all manners of complexities and ambiguities. Angst and anguish are always lurking, and there is no respite from doubt and confusion. Politically, forgiveness is difficult to sustain. It undermines the rule of law and the makings of a supposedly orderly society, for when everything is forgivable, everything seems tolerable. Forgiveness presumably threatens chaos, anarchy, and social devolution.

But what of this law and order that retribution supposedly makes possible? Is this really the case? Do the redundancy and pervasiveness of punitive systems make a community less deviant and violent? There should arguably be a correlation between the rise of such systems and civility. But there is no reality or period in history that supports such a correlation. In fact, the opposite is true, meaning that deviancy tends to rise with the proliferation of retributive and punitive systems. These systems tend to set off cycles of retribution, as the abused become the abusers. History makes plain that these systems only become more retributive and punitive. Only violence emerges in the end. Any perception of order is an illusion because incarceration often hides the increasing deviancy that tortures the community. The order that seems apparent is tenuous, for as soon as the threat of retribution disappears, the order collapses. Yet regardless of these illusions of order, we continue to believe that vengeance will save us from ourselves and each other. Such is an apt case of how vengeance can distort our perception of reality, even when the reality conflicts with our perception.

Forgiveness promises a different order and also a different conception of decency and civility. In a community that promotes forgiveness, order is emergent, with the focus being on developing our capacity to act democratically and compassionately. The focus is on developing our capacity to act with restraint by promoting relational responsibility and accountability, and enlarging our capacity for empathy by challenging us to experience and understand the world from the perspective of others. There is nothing about this focus that history ridicules. We are potentially capable of acting democratically and compassionately without the ubiquitous threat of retribution. But to believe this ultimately requires believing in a different worldview. Without this kind of belief, forgiveness is impossible. This is why only the strong can forgive. Only the strong is capable of believing in the possibility of new worlds. As what we believe shapes what we perceive, experience, and value, to believe anew is really to be born anew.

Change is always difficult. It involves reckoning with death and dying. Only the strong have the courage to die and be born anew. Changing is about learning, meaning that changing and learning are inseparable. Without being ready and willing to change, that is, without being ready and willing to die, learning is impossible. Learning is fundamentally about believing, as in being willing to believe that living and dying complement each other. Without being ready to believe anew, learning is impossible. Our knowledge is always a reflection of what we are ready and willing to believe. The courage we need to forgive is also the courage we need to learn, meaning that the relationship between forgiving and learning is also inseparable. Learning is about changing, evolving, and becoming. It involves all our being. Who is unwilling to believe anew can learn nothing, become nothing. This is why only the strong can forgive. Only the strong possesses the resolve and courage to believe anew.

3

ON FEAR

Fear is arguably the most destructive and debilitative force in the world. It impedes our ability to love, to imagine, to create, to explore, to trust, to learn. Yet in our society fear permeates, influences, and shapes everything. It shapes our conceptions of God, our relations to each other, our conceptions of self, and our relations to the world. According to one theory, fear comes from us being beholden to the past so as to avoid dealing with the unknown that comes with the present and the future. Indeed, peoples who are most beholden to the past, by insisting and preserving all kinds of rituals, traditions, and customs, do tend to reflect the most fear of the unknown.

Of course, to be afraid of the unknown (ambiguity) is really to be afraid of that which is new and different. Still, where does fear come from? What is the origin of our fear of ambiguity that makes for us afraid of the present and the future? Arguably, this fear comes from the fact that we are born into a world of ambiguity—one where the unknown will always exceed the known. To be human is to reckon with the reality that ambiguity is always present. It permeates everything. Every meaning, understanding, definition, action, relationship, decision is laden with ambiguity. Even trying to limit ambiguity is a tenuous project, for who would attempt to lessen the amount of water in the ocean, and is doing so even constructive? But who should stop a fool from trying? Yet this is the project of modernity—to fully conquer ambiguity and thereby rid us of all the fears that make for all kinds of superstitions, traditions, and religions.

Nothing good is coming from modernity. The death and destruction that surrounds modernity in the last century is staggering and remains unsurpassed. This new century promises no end to the misery and destruction. As modernity reaches every corner of the world, this new century even promises to be worse. On the other hand, in the face of all the carnage, the world's ambiguity shows no sign of yielding to our ambitions. As we learn more and more we seem to know less and less. We are also no less afraid as we profess to know more and more. In fact, we are increasingly afraid as we watch the collapse of many of modernity's ambitions and promises. We must now deal with the fallout and with what happens when we choose to believe in illusions. We will never conquer the world's ambiguity. In fact, our redemption resides in embracing this ambiguity.

We have to begin to find a new relation to the world's ambiguity. There is something profoundly sacred about being of a world with infinite ambiguity. Such a world lends for beauty, diversity, and creativity. Also, such a world lends for grace, love, and courage. In a world devoid of ambiguity, being human would be impossible. We would be nothing but machines. In a world devoid of ambiguity, God would be impossible. We would be devoid of faith and belief. There would nothing to inspire us, provoke us, excite us. This is why many scriptures view God as an act of imagination. This is also why every civilization possesses a conception of God. Without ambiguity, any kind of belief system would be impossible. To believe is to acknowledge our fallibility. Our perceptions, meanings, understandings, and conceptions of God are all incomplete. To believe is to be vulnerable to the possibility of a different perception, a different meaning, a different understanding, and even a different conception of God. In other words, to believe is an act of strength, an act of moral fortitude and courage. Only those who are strong can believe in a God that will always exceed our imagination. Without belief, submission would be status quo. Through belief we move between the world of the possible and that of the impossible. We should therefore strive to be a community of believers in which we cultivate the virtues of believing in a world of infinite ambiguity.

The origin of fear resides in our unwillingness to believe, or in our lacking the resolve and courage to believe. Without the resolve and courage to believe, fear pervades, distorts, and destroys everything. Through our resolve to believe we overcome fear. But belief is never devoid of fear. Fear can be generative. It can invite caution and challenge us to look anew. Fear can also inspire us, provoke us, and unsettle us. To believe is to embrace fear. Those who believe understand only too well the environs and forces that heighten our fear of each other and that of the world. There are no illusions about the destruction such fears can ferment. There is also no attempt to mask our own possession of these fears. What distinguishes us is merely our resolve to believe in the face of these fears. We resolve to believe. This is the essence of courage—the resolve to believe. This, again, is why only the strong can believe. This is also why only those who believe can imagine and conceive a God out of courage.

Our Gods are morally unequal. A God conceived out of fear is fundamentally different to a God conceived out of belief. A God born out of fear is devoid of any imagination. We are to be obedient and submit accordingly. Redemption is achieved through submission and the threat of retribution. This is the God that is always threatening us with damnation and retribution for violating any arbitrary stipulation. But again, this is still a God of imagination, or lack thereof. Our Gods come from inside of us. We conceive our Gods the way we conceive ourselves. We cannot conceive a God that is beyond our conception of self. Our Gods serve us by reinforcing how we conceive ourselves and the world. We serve only the Gods that serve us. Thus Gods born out of fear must legitimize our fears. Such Gods should help us to sustain a worldview that infuses our theology, psychology, anthropology, and communicology with fear. There should be no opportunity to doubt the veracity of our Gods. In any conception of God born out of fear, fear pervades everything. The goal of God is to protect us from doubt, which means that the price for fermenting doubt (heresy) is usually death.

But what exactly is doubt or the origin of doubt? Doubt comes from the world's ambiguity. It is the world reminding us that no meaning, no truth, no interpretation, no understanding is devoid of ambiguity. Ambiguity promotes doubt. Thus only those who have the resolve and courage to believe can doubt. Heresy is the measure of those who believe, and naturally the charge against those who believe. To believe is an act of sedition as doubt undermines the status quo. Such is the story of Jesus Christ's persecution and crucifixion. This is a compelling and enduring story about the perils and struggles of believing. Jesus Christ teaches us about believing and the obligations and tribulations of believing. Ultimately, to believe requires the resolve and courage to die. But as Jesus Christ demonstrates, to believe also requires the resolve and courage to love and forgive those who trespass against us. Those who conceive of Gods out of fear have no such resolve and courage, and, as a result, no way of making sense of love, mercy, and compassion. But for those who believe, love is the hallmark of believing. We love in spite of rather than because of. To believe is to recognize that love nurtures life. It is both redemptive and generative. Love nurtures life and cultivates possibility. Love is about believing that this world is blessed with possibility. This is why those who believe and love value mercy. We believe that people, even the worse amongst us, can change and evolve. Mercy is an act of possibility. We are by no means certain that redemption is possible for everyone.

But we believe that a world that promotes possibility is always more heuristic and humane than one that opposes possibility. We therefore strive to promote all the practices, such as love, hope, grace, mercy, and compassion, which promote possibility.

But the story of Jesus Christ is also about being unwilling to believe and what such unwillingness means. It means being hostile, even violently so, to the possibility of a new truth, a new understanding, a new message, a new revelation, even a new covenant. It also means having no compassion or mercy for the most vulnerable and despised amongst us. Such persons will receive no respite or refuge from us, for such persons are presumably being punished for violating God's will. The most we can presumably do for such persons is to instruct them to repent and plead to God for mercy. For those who are unwilling to believe, the focus is on allowing God's will to be done as God's love is supposedly only reserved for the righteous and chosen. The rest must suffer and perish for apparently refusing to follow the righteous path, or for simply never being chosen. Thus the persecution and crucifixion of Jesus Christ. In a world where we are unwilling to believe, the violent demise of any prophet who calls us to believe is inevitable. For in such a world, violence is the only recourse because love is impossible. But in a world where we are unwilling to believe, our redemption resides outside of us. We must look to Gods in the heavens for our redemption and prosperity, and be ready to submit accordingly. Submission is the origin of religion. Presumably, only through submission will our redemption or any prosperity be had. But again, what is the value of any redemption that merely requires submission? How great can any God be that demands merely submission from us?

For those who are willing to believe, our redemption resides elsewhere. It resides in community and in our relation to each other. We oppose religion because we believe that action is more heuristic than submission. Submission requires no moral imagination. Only a God born out of fear would demand so little of us. To believe in action means that our redemption will be found in our own doing or lack thereof. Our redemption is on us. We determine our heaven and hell. The new covenant that Jesus Christ speaks to embodies our struggles. We are to love each other even in the face of persecution and death. This means also finding the resolve and courage to do so. We believe that redemption is always an act of becoming, as our Gods will always exceed our imagination. We therefore believe that our becoming is laden with infinite possibility. We will never profess to know the mind of God or proclaim to be the chosen and righteous. We will never use our faith as a sword or as permission to destroy others. Heaven is any space that welcomes possibility. In a world of those who strive to believe, God resides in possibility. In cultivating possibility and the practices that promote possibility, God emerges. God is always within our potentiality. God never forsakes us. We are always of God. God dwells in the world's infinite ambiguity. How much resolve and courage we have to believe and imagine and love will determine how much of God we are. We locate God in possibility because only a God of infinite possibility can inspire us to believe and love, for any God that is deserving of our resolve and courage to believe should at least appeal to the angels in us. Locating God in possibility is also about us being made in the image and likeness of God. Just as much as the world is born out of possibility, and thereby out of love and grace, we too are capable of creating, through love and grace, worlds rich in possibility. In a world of possibility, besides love, hope, grace, and mercy, faith is also vital. We must be ready to believe in the impossible, or that which seems beyond our imagination and comprehension. Only in being ready to believe the impossible is possibility truly possible. To believe is most heuristic when we must, as Jesus Christ did, struggle to believe by finding the most resolve and courage to do so. Without such struggles, we compromise possibility, and ultimately our own prosperity. Such struggles exercise and enlarge our being by pushing us to find a new resolve to believe. For those who believe, there is always doubt. For who can believe in the possibility of a world without war when the world remains laden with war? Or who can believe in a world of plenty when so many continue to go hungry? But such is what believing requires of us. Without being ready to believe in the impossible, nothing great becomes possible or can ever become possible. We therefore limit God by being unwilling to believe the impossible.

4

ON PURPOSE

What is the purpose of life in a world of infinite ambiguity? Arguably, the meanings and purposes of life would be diverse and multiple. But what should we aspire to do? What would constitute the good life? According to Alan Watts, "People imagine that letting themselves go would have disastrous results; trusting neither circumstances nor themselves, which together make up life, they are forever interfering and trying to make their own souls and the world conform with preconceived patterns. This interference is simply the attempt of the ego to dominate life." In eastern thought, this ending of the ego is known as detachment—as in detaching ourselves from all affairs and practices that reflect our passions, interests, and yearnings. The focus is on detaching, as there will always be attachment. The good life is thus about cultivating detachment.

Without the ego, there can of course be no egotism, but also no ethnocentrism, narcissism, and chauvinism. Attachment limits us by narrowing our understanding and experiencing of the world. Eastern thought looks at the ego as the gateway to misery. But the ego is insidious and difficult to end. We want the world to unfold on our terms so as to allow us to avoid dealing with the angst that comes with the world's infinite ambiguity. This reality can be seen in us defining communication in terms of understanding. It seems a reasonable and plausible definition. But why should understanding be the goal of communication? Who declared this to be the goal, and upon what authority?

Viewing communication in terms of understanding is an insidious way of us interfering in the world so as to get others and the world to conform to our own preconceived notions. However, as with the world, communication is laden with infinite ambiguity, and removing this ambiguity is simply impossible. There is ambiguity in language as meaning resides within human beings rather than within words and symbols. There is also ambiguity within us. We often never know what we mean or what we are even trying to mean. We approximate. There is also ambiguity in our contexts and mediums. Our meanings change as our contexts change. That is, every context lends for a different meaning, a different understanding. There is simply no way to know or control what contexts will lend for what meanings as our contexts are born out of many different forces. Yet meanings and contexts are inseparable and inextricable. Also, the limits and constraints of every context and medium make ambiguity inevitable. We never have access to infinite time or space that could possibly allow us to remove all ambiguity. Finally, history shapes meaning, and history is ever changing. There is simply no way to know for certain what history will do to our meanings, and our meanings to history.

Viewing communication in terms of understanding or arriving at shared meaning is to deny the reality of all of these different ambiguities that undermine understanding. But defining communication in terms of understanding is purely of our own making. It is contrary to the world's natural rhythms. This is only the beginning of our problems. To view communication in terms of understanding assumes that communication is achieved by removing ambiguity, as in the ambiguity that produces Noise. Presumably, with enough feedback, this ambiguity is removable. What emerges is a conflict between communication and confusion, with confusion being cast as the antithesis of communication. We presumably achieve communication by vanquishing confusion.

What also emerges is a conflict between meaning and ambiguity. We supposedly achieve meaning by subduing ambiguity. Our fear is that without communication, social devolution will occur and even our survival will be in peril. We therefore believe that we have no choice but to interfere and impose meaning on the world and each other. We cannot leave the world to its own malevolent devices because to do so is to invite peril. But what only results from this enterprise is a deepening fear of the world and the rise of the ego. This vision of the world privileges our own role in the world as well as our own interference in the affairs of the world. The ego promotes self-interest and a vision of the world that perpetuates and legitimizes self-interest. It separates us from the world and each other by engendering conflict and division between us and the world, and us from each other. Simply put, the ego divides, separates, and balkanizes. It thrives by promoting division, separation, and fragmentation, and by making believe that such processes are necessary and even natural. It is self-fulfilling and self-perpetuating. Also, the ego emerges by releasing us of all the obligations and tribulations that come with being of the world and of each other. The division and separation that the ego creates allow us to lessen our obligation to the world and each other. In this way, the ego is primal. It encourages us to view the world dichotomously, dualistically, and simplistically—meaning/ambiguity, order/chaos, life/death, knowledge/ignorance, and so forth. Such false schisms lend for no complexity and ambiguity, and thereby make no moral demands on us.

But even the best illusions are still illusions. Trying to achieve communication by removing ambiguity is nothing but an illusion. Communication will always be laden with confusion, just as much as meaning will always be laden with ambiguity, order with chaos, and knowledge with ignorance. Ambiguity vitalizes meaning by keeping meaning in a quantum condition. By always destabilizing and unsettling our meanings, ambiguity promises that our meanings will always be open to change. That our meanings are always changing and evolving means that we are always changing and evolving. There is always the possibility of a new meaning, a new understanding, a new revelation, a new reality, a new vision of the world, even a new conception of God. Communication is always possible. We are ecologically bound up with each other. There is always something that we share or are capable of sharing that allows us to recognize our humanity in each other. It is the intensity and quality of this sharing that matter. But something is always shared.

Communication is about us enlarging what we share and are capable of sharing. Through communication we fertilize the possibility of new meanings in each other. In other words, communication is about serving others, as in encouraging others to have new meanings and experiences that reflect an expansion of our own capacity to mean, to experience, and, ultimately, to share. We achieve communication by encouraging our meanings to converge and diverge, evolve and change. Without allowing for this kind of quantum play, being human would be impossible. This is communication as a mode of being (ontology) rather than merely a means of sharing (methodology). Viewing communication in terms of being locates communication in our various ways of being. The world's becoming becomes our becoming, and the becoming of others also becomes our becoming. By allowing our meanings (and lack thereof) to organically change and evolve, merge and diverge, we allow the world to realize its own form. Yet this form, regardless of our doing, is always fluid and cascading. Change is inevitable as new meanings and experiences will eventually arise. But herein also resides the world's potentiality. In fact, herein resides our own beauty and potentiality.

A world born out of infinite ambiguity is also one that is laden with infinite possibility. However, every possibility is of a different value. The most heuristic possibilities are those that create other possibilities. So yes, slavery reflects a possibility, but this possibility impedes the rise of other possibilities, including more heuristic possibilities. Thus the demise of slavery was inevitable. Democracies are examples of heuristic possibilities. A world born out of infinite ambiguity is hostile to any possibility that impedes possibility. To impede possibility is to limit the world's ambiguity. Indeed, to impede possibility is to impede life. Such ambitions promise only misery and strife. A world born out of ambiguity possesses a moral persuasion. It encourages the rise of those practices, meanings, and experiences that promote possibility, and is hostile to those that do differently.

Truth is also of little purchase in a world of infinite ambiguity. For something can be true and still lend for no possibility. What then is the value of such a truth? On the other hand, something can be false but actually promote possibility. Also, the nature of something can be indeterminate, but still encourage possibility. In a world of ambiguity, consequences, implications, and outcomes matter. No action (or lack thereof) is morally neutral. We are always doing something to the world, doing something to ourselves. There is always doing, always being. Never is the world outside of being. What matters is whether our doing and being are encouraging possibility, and thereby affirming life. In a world of ambiguity, even this project is laden with ambiguity.

Knowledge can also be averse to possibility. Knowledge is laden with biases, prejudices, values, beliefs, assumptions, fears, and so forth. It is never ideologically neutral. There is always a cause or perspective that knowledge is serving, and this cause or perspective will determine how we will define, relate, and acquire knowledge. In the case of modernity, the goal of knowledge is to conquer the world's ambiguity, mystery, and complexity, and, in so doing, allow us to prevail in our supposed conflict with the world. In this vision of the world communication is merely a means of conveying knowledge. However, because knowledge is always ideologically laden, no knowledge system can undermine the dominion it serves. We will value only that knowledge we are ideologically capable of framing and understanding and, ultimately, answering. There is therefore no possibility of a new knowledge. What then is the value of knowledge? What also of the belief that through knowledge we will achieve progress and prosperity? In sum, why our obsession with knowledge, when knowledge is merely doing the bidding of ideology? Yet the obsession is what the ideology needs. It further legitimizes our interference in the world and our determination to make the world fit (and submit) to our preconceived notions. In this way, knowledge promises no possibility, or at least any that is truly profound. Our impulse is to understand only what we are ready and willing to understand.

To cultivate possibility constitutes a fundamentally different project as communication now emerges as a mode of being that promotes possibility. Through communication, possibility arises. It arises from us being unafraid of leaving our meanings and experiences and understandings in various states of confusion and ambiguity. We also have no desire to sacrifice convergence for divergence, believing that communication (and knowledge) involves the lessening of divergence. Possibility arises from us being vulnerable to others, including each other's ambiguities and complexities. It is about refusing to tidy up each other by putting ourselves and each other into neat arbitrary categories that subject us to all manner of expectations, distortions, and regulations. Possibility arises from us reclaiming our boundless complexity—the complexity that constitutes our diversity. We are also suspicious of any form of organization that arises from the need to organize our experiences and manage our diversity. Any such organization impedes possibility by reducing our complexity and diversity. To manage the complexity of others is to make those persons fit into our preconceived notions. This is egotism, even narcissism. This is also chauvinism, hegemonism, and ethnocentrism, as any determined effort to have others coercively fit our preconceived notions reflects the conviction that our own vision is deserving of this kind of submission. We are really demanding that others submit to our own fears, anxieties, and paranoia.

But why should others be willing to do so? Accordingly, coercion and retribution are usually necessary to limit the complexity and diversity of others. This is how violence emerges and is legitimized in human affairs. It is presumably necessary to save us from each other's complexity and diversity, which means that violence is necessary to deal with the world's ambiguity. But no amount of violence can end our complexity and diversity, much less the world's ambiguity and complexity. Because the world possesses too much diversity, complexity, and ambiguity, the limitations must eventually give way. Still, violence impedes possibility by seeking to limit ambiguity. It undermines the rise of new meanings and experiences, and, accordingly, the rise of new visions of the world. Violence always reflects a lack of moral imagination. It never constitutes an efficient and heuristic way of resolving any kind of human conflict. But when we assume that possibility is finite, violence becomes inevitable. That is, when we believe that our interference in the world is vital so as to presumably save us from chaos, violence becomes inevitable and morally acceptable. It even becomes kind of natural. We never recognize our own ordinary doing of violence. But to monologically and coercively and purposely impose our way on the world is violence. We perpetrate a lot of violence when we strive to impose our meanings upon others, either by trying to reduce the ambiguity in the world or the ambiguity between us. We also perpetrate violence by trying to scrub away the ambiguities that supposedly cling to our meanings and experiences. That no amount of scrubbing can remove these ambiguities forces us to increase our violence, yet to no avail. Such is how futile cycles of violence begin. We also perpetrate violence by striving to organize, manage, and reduce each other's complexities, ambiguities, and diversities.

To engage communication as a mode of being where the world is laden with infinite possibility is to save ourselves and the world from violence. Such modes of being assume that our interference impedes possibility. It diminishes us. We therefore aspire to release (and detach) others from our own ambitions, expectations, and aspirations. We also aspire to release others from our fears, anxieties, and paranoia so that we can allow each other to move in harmony with the world's quantum rhythms. Ideally, our goal is to want nothing, to be detached from everything. But even the noblest ideals can limit possibility. So as we aspire, we scrutinize, as we theorize, we interrogate. We believe this a world of boundless complexity, and as such being human involves constantly grappling with all the tensions, contradictions, and confusions that lend for no absolute or complete resolutions. Yet what would being human mean without all of this complexity? Where would life derive its texture and purpose?

5

ON TEMPORALITY

I am writing from my own struggles to resist western and European notions of temporality. This temporality supposedly reflects our civilizational superiority—our ability to manipulate the world through time. This is the origin of temporality in the western and European world. This is also what makes the clock the most seminal technology in the western and European world. But ultimately, the goal of time is to control us. For behind western and European notions of temporality is a deep distrust and suspicion of the human condition. We will presumably descend into savagery and strife without order and control. So modern notions of temporality are presumably a measure of our civility—our ability to control our savage impulses and passions and thereby allow for the creation of order. This temporality presumably saves us from being beasts and savages. It makes for superior kinds of coordination and organization, and in so doing, makes for the rise of complex civilizations where people are productive and efficient. Temporality supposedly creates progress. In allowing us to order the world, temporality allows us to order the human condition. For the western and European world, the conquering of time and space is a crowning achievement, an expression of our own power to control, order, and conquer the world.

This is where my struggles begin with western and European notions of temporality. That Third World and indigenous peoples have no comparable conception of temporality means that such peoples come with a lot of suspicion and distrust. Presumably, I lack the means to create a civil society and submit to the rigors of such a society. In other words, I presumably lack the capacity to be rational, mathematical, and analytical, and as a result, lack the capacity to reason carefully and develop arguments systematically. Ultimately, I presumably lack the capacity to develop great theories, methodologies, and sciences. This is the kind of burden that Third World and indigenous peoples must bear, and only because our temporal notions are different. We are supposedly at the mercy of our passions, emotions, and desires. We and our unruly bodies. We presumably lack a rigorous and rational mind to rule over our sensual, sexual, and spiritual impulses. This is presumably what makes us gullible and incapable of producing reliable knowledges. So whereas the music of Beethoven and Mozart is always cast as cerebral and rational, the music of the natives is always cast as sensual and spiritual. The latter will never be seen as comparable as there is no obligation for tedious and rigorous study, and presumably no capacity in the natives for high order rational thought.

Such are the struggles many of us face in a world that is increasingly ruled by western and European temporal notions. We are always positioned as being inferior. There is no such thing as temporal diversity. Such diversity would mean that there are other valid temporalities. But from a western and European standpoint, how could this be possible? What other temporalities can allow us to control the world and thereby control our destiny? That is, what other temporalities allow us to be gods—to order and control, submit and conquer? Thus these western and European notions of temporality increasingly control everything. There is no let up, which is why, for instance, the world's linguistic diversity is rapidly disappearing. No other force is more colonizing, more homogenizing. No other force is more insidious and therefore more difficult to resist.

This temporality even pervades our modes of writing. Developing rational arguments and positions supposedly require disciplining the body. Presumably, easy writing is poor writing. The process must be arduous. We must endeavor to achieve clarity of thought and expression by purging our thoughts of chaos and confusion. We must wrestle our arguments into submission. Presumably, writing is a contest between the forces of clarity and the forces of chaos, and temporality is a weapon that will allow us to prevail in this important contest. After all, what would be the possibility of a civilized society without our being able to achieve clarity of thought and expression? Presumably, the confusion we find in the world originates from inside of us. It supposedly comes from our own inability to be rational, analytical, and mathematical. Thus we see the relationship between mathematics and language, and why the western world continues to view vocabulary and language mastery as a measure of rationality, civility, and morality. Language mastery supposedly reflects the ability to control our savagery, and ultimately the savagery of others. For many Third World and indigenous peoples, especially those of us coming from rich oral traditions, this is the problem writing presents. We must cultivate a suspicion of our humanity. We must believe that at the core of our being is a struggle between competing forces. We must believe that achieving clarity requires the conquering of confusion. We must believe that confusion poses a threat to us and the world. In order to write well, we must believe all of this. In fact, as we endeavor to write well, this is what we come to believe. We come to embody a foreign cosmology. We become colonized. Trying to write (and speak) well should never be seen as merely a problem of technique.

So what are Third World and indigenous peoples to do? What is to become of writing for us? How do we develop, to use Audre Lorde's words, those tools that will build the house of the slave? To write out of the belief that clarity requires the conquering of confusion divorces being from understanding. This process weakens our thought system. We can never conquer confusion. We merely abide by the illusion of doing so. There is nothing inherently negative about what we define and experience as confusion. It merely reflects the world's infinite mystery. What we experience as confusion is of our own making. If we had no obsession with achieving clarity and ending the world's mystery, ambiguity, and complexity, we would have a different relation to the world's mystery. We would allow the world to come to us on its own terms. We would have no need to create elaborate illusions that mask the fact that the more we come to understand, the less we come to know. But we continue to strive for clarity, continue to believe that the world is in conflict with us. All of this comes from western and European notions of temporality. These notions are always putting us in conflict with the world, conflict with ourselves, conflict with each other. There is always the illusion of strife, always an entity that is threatening to impede our progress. So yes, the world will give us clarity, but a clarity that will always be laden with mystery.

We continue to believe that writing is purely a means we use to convey our thoughts. It is presumably devoid of any ideology, and by that, purely a creature of technique. But this, of course, is false. We can never separate how we articulate knowledge from how we define knowledge. We can also never separate what we believe from what we perceive. To write a certain way is to perpetuate a certain way of defining, framing, and experiencing knowledge. Nothing is inherently wrong about this reality. But this reality should push us to ask what is the value or purchase that comes with the way we are defining, framing, and experiencing knowledge, and the way we are articulating knowledge. Also, who is this knowledge serving, and on the other hand, who is this knowledge impeding? From a postcolonial standpoint, the matter comes down to which knowledge is enabling possibility. That is, which knowledge is enlarging our sense of what is possible? Or is the way I am articulating knowledge enabling this kind of knowledge? This is also why I am suspicious of so much writing that comes under the label of postcolonial theory. There is nothing different in the writing. It is as dense and opaque as any other. How can the knowledge be therefore any different? But what other ways can we experience writing and language to make for a knowledge that will build the house of the slave? Of course language plays an integral role in shaping our social worlds, but language can also create worlds, as in, first there was the Word, and the Word was God. That we are supposedly made in the image and likeness of God means that we are also of the Word and therefore also capable of creating worlds through our words. But just as much as we can use language to create worlds, just as much we can use language to destroy worlds. As such, the question that becomes paramount is how can we use and relate to language in ways that create just and decent worlds?

What kinds of worlds we create begins with how we relate to language, what kinds of beliefs we bring to language, as well as how we encourage and promote various ways of embodying language. In order to write differently, we have to view language differently, and this requires viewing the world differently. This is how we will begin to create the knowledge we need to create the worlds we need. In many ways, David Bohm understood this project. Seen by many to be one of the foremost theoretical physicists of the twentieth century, Bohm had much to say about the destructive nature of languages that engender division, separation, and fragmentation. Bohm believed that an emergent language mode is necessary to complement emergent understandings of the world. Such understandings point to a world of consciousness. All of the world belongs and evolves from consciousness. Consciousness depicts a world that ebbs and flows. It undermines the notion that the world is fixed, constant, and mechanical. Bohm believed that emergent language modes must be verb driven and without any kind of stridency that blocks spontaneity.

Bohm acknowledged that the possibility of an entirely new language mode is unlikely. He believed that what is provisionally possible is a new language mode that shifts the focus to the verb and away from the noun. He called this new mode the *rheomode* (from the Greek word *rheo* "to flow"). In *Wholeness and the Implicate Order*, Bohm (1980) contends that the rheomode stresses fluidity rather than rigidity:

We will now consider a mode in which movement is to be taken as primary in our thinking and in which this notion will be incorporated into the language structure by allowing the verb rather than the noun to play a primary role.... [T]he rheomode will be an experiment in the use of language, concerned mainly with trying to find out whether it is possible to create a new structure that is not so prone toward fragmentation as is the present one. Evidently, then, our inquiry will have to begin by emphasizing the role of language in shaping our overall world views as well as in expressing them. (pp. 30-31)

Bohm argued that the fragmentation that our common mode of language reflects and originates with a worldview—which is presently the dominant worldview—that holds to fragmentary notions—such as gender, race, causes and effects, forces and matter, and so forth—of the world:

[T]he dominant form of subject-verb-object tends continually to lead to fragmentation; and it is evident that the attempt to avoid this fragmentation by skillful use of other features of the language can work only in a limited way, for, by force of habit, we tend sooner or later, especially in broad questions concerning our overall world views, to fall unwittingly into the fragmentary mode of functioning implied by the basic structure. The reason for this is not only that the subject-verb-object form of language is continually implying an inappropriate division between things but, even more, that the ordinary mode of language tends very strongly to take its own function for granted, and thus it leads us to concentrate almost exclusively on the content under discussion, so that little or no attention is left for the actual symbolic function of the language itself. (p. 31)

There is also the matter of motive. Why should we write? Writing should be act of imagination. It should be creative and generative. It should change our relation to the world. This is how writing will give us a different relation to knowledge. But we continue to believe that our problems really spring from a lack of knowledge. This is false. Our problems are really about kinds of knowledge. We need no more knowledge that begins on a dualistic and mechanistic worldview. This knowledge will continue to put the world in peril. We need a different kind of knowledge—a knowledge that begins on a holistic and organic worldview. A different kind of knowledge speaks to a different way of embodying knowledge, as well as a different way of relating to knowledge.

We need to write in ways that end the divide between cognition and emotion, mind and spirit, being and knowing. Just as much as we create (and perpetuate) these divides in writing, just as much we can end these divides in writing. We can also write in ways that end the divide between truth and fiction. All of these divides are false. But besides being so, these divides are debilitative, as in they undermine our capacity to create knowledges that the world and we desperately need.

6

ON LANGUAGE

There is an inseparable relationship between how we perceive the world and the language we use to do so. What this relationship means is that to change the way we perceive and experience the world also involves changing the language we use to do so. It also means that the rhythms of languages are different, as different cultures do reflect different ways of experiencing and perceiving the world. Moreover, this relationship reveals that the rhythm of languages can change, and thereby we can always change the way we experience and perceive the world. Then there is the inseparable relationship between language and discourse, and how each shapes and influences the other. To change a discourse involves changing the language that constitutes that discourse. But discourses also mean outcomes and consequences, as there are always different interests with different goals. Discourses will always reflect different sides using and embodying different kinds of words and language to make for outcomes that favor one side. Language is never devoid of ideology. It is always laden with fears, biases, prejudices, beliefs, assumptions, and so forth.

Our own language in the western world reflects an ideology of separation, division, and opposition. This is why our discourses are always violently putting us at each other's throats. Yet such a reality is by no means inevitable. We can do differently, but doing so will involve changing everything. Besides the rhythms of our languages being different, our relations to our languages are also different. In the western world, we treat language as a method—a means of capturing and conveying our thoughts to others. We assume a divide between thought and language, where language is the conduit of thought. In this case, our relation to language is fundamentally mechanical. But in many indigenous cultures, the relation to language is different. We dwell within language. Our Gods dwell within language. Our worlds dwell within language. Language is sacred, and our relation to language no less so. We embody rather than merely use language. Our language runs over with passion and conviction as we experience language as a creative and generative activity. Through language we create rather than capture our worlds. Thus rather than using—really reducing—language to a tool "to find the available means of persuasion in a given situation," which is how the study of language is framed in communication studies, we focus on enlarging our capacity to embody language so as to allow language to be creative and generative, which in turn allows us to be creative and generative.

For Thich Nhat Hanh (2006), a prominent Buddhist monk, "The ultimate dimension cannot be described in words and notions that by their very nature serve to cut reality up into separate pieces" (p. 83). Ultimately, words and language impede our arriving at "true understanding." We must therefore evolve away from words and language. Thich Nhat Hanh claims that language is inherently divisive. It slices up the world into pieces, and in so doing, makes for a thought system that perceives the world in pieces rather than wholes. According to Thich Nhat Hanh, "concepts such as one and many, coming and going, collective and individual, above and below, even being and nonbeing, cannot be applied to ultimate reality" (p. 83). Moreover, "reality cannot be grasped by our discursive mind—the mind of imagination, discrimination, and discussion. We have to learn how to touch reality without using our usual patterns of thinking" (p. 85). This involves practicing and developing our capacity to find "the nature of interbeing of things" where everything is inside everything else.

So once again the notion reemerges that our redemption resides in our doing and being and less in our knowing. In this case the doing begins with us moving away from language. But what about numbers? Do numbers promote the experiencing and perceiving of the interbeing of things? That is, do numbers also slice up the world into pieces? What about our mathematical equations? It would seem that our numbers do what our words do, and also what our languages do, for interbeing begins with us. It begins with us recognizing ourselves in everything else. This recognition constitutes a consciousness that makes or perceives no division or separation between the world (and everything of the world) and us. We are inside the world and the world is inside of us. Interbeing enlarges our notions of being by challenging us to experience what the forests are experiencing, the oceans are experiencing, the mountains are experiencing, and so forth.

This is why language impedes the rise of interbeing. What kind of language can a mountain share with us? Or a forest? Or an ocean? But interbeing, involving no division or separation, requires nothing to be shared as there is no separation that makes sharing necessary. Instead, interbeing is about things being realized. Through interbeing we come to new realizations of things. Yet such realizations are like waves, always emerging and breaking, and like waves, every realization is different, reflecting a different contour, a different topography, a different power. But all of these realizations are emerging from within our states of interbeing. Such is the power that resides within and between us, but in a world of division and separation, such power is never realized. Indeed, nothing is realized. Nothing comes forth that gives us new visions of the world. Our lives are empty, devoid of any capacity to realize anything new. We are, like caged animals, trapped in the past, at the mercy of various divides that limit us. Our caging is as much spiritual, existential, and epistemological as it is physical, psychological, and ecological. As with any kind of caging, what results is us turning inward and upon ourselves and each other. Caging fosters violence and makes us desperate.

The absence of interbeing reduces us to savages. Through the cultivation of interbeing we become human, which means that being human involves recognizing ourselves in the oceans, the forests, the mountains, and, conversely, recognizing such things in us. Through such processes of recognition we become human. We therefore achieve being human by enlarging our mode of being. What also emerges from being human is an end of violence, for in a world where everything is inside everything else, to harm anything is to harm everything. Such is the futility of violence. We are never immune from violence. It always comes back on us. That we continue to believe, after already experiencing so much death and destruction from so many wars, that we can be immune from the violence we perpetrate on others is a compelling sign of our profound lack of interbeing. No less disturbing is how we continue to believe that we are immune from the violence we perpetrate on the world, as in our plundering of the world's natural resources. Such is the peril that the absence of interbeing poses to the world and us. Also, when such absence is status quo, communication becomes impossible. All that remains is persuasion, trying to coerce or manipulate or entice others to adopt our position. There is no recognition in persuasion that what we do to others we do to ourselves, as everything is inside everything else. Persuasion is about imposing our worldviews on others. It is an act of aggression. To impose a worldview upon others is really to reimpose a worldview on ourselves so as to remove any doubt and ambiguity from within us. The process imprisons us, cages us, and, ultimately, dehumanizes us.

Such is the status quo. We are always trying to impose our worldview on others. Through violence we create and shape our relations to each other. In sum, violence shapes our being. We are born out of violence. In many ways, violence is all we know. When problems arise, we assume that violence will remedy the situation. We have no doubts about the veracity of violence. We may argue about kinds of violence and when to use violence, but never about the necessity of violence. Thus the adage, "spare the rod, spoil the child." Our belief in the veracity of violence pervades everything. It is why our prison population is exploding, our military spending shows no sign of abating, and our foreign policy always insists on keeping all options—especially military options—on the table. We perceive anyone who questions the necessity of violence as foolishly naive. Presumably, such persons have no understanding of how the world really is. But of course how the world really is is about how we choose to be. In a world that is hostile to interbeing, violence is inevitable. It is all that seems plausible and available to us. In a world devoid of interbeing what emerges are stories and theories that perpetuate and legitimize violence. That is, stories and theories that reinforce our reality of the world and ourselves. Such is the origin of Darwin's theory of evolution.

The notion of survival of the fittest, strongest, and brightest assumes that competition makes for a natural distinction and division between human beings and within species. It also assumes that selfishness promotes prosperity. In addition, the theory assumes that the creation of this division is natural and necessary, and that competition makes for a natural culling of the species that improves the ability of the fittest to flourish. The fittest survives by demonstrating a superior ability—supposedly through competition—to adapt to changing environs. Supposedly, evolution begins at the level of genes, with genes presumably being selfish by nature. The selfish nature of our genes in tandem with competition for mates and resources is the calculus that constitutes evolution. The first and foremost motive is satisfying our self-interest to survive and reproduce, which can mean scheming, manipulating, and even eliminating others. In evolution, self-interest is vital. It is supposedly by no means our fault that the weak should perish. Such demise is presumably necessary so the strong can have the necessary resources to flourish and save the species. But what of this divide between the strong and the weak that allows the strong to exploit the weak for selfish gain? What also of this divide that reflects, in the form of competition for resources, a natural conflict between us? In a world of hardly any interbeing, this kind of division and conflict is inevitable as division always mean opposition. In such a world, empathy is absent. Apathy, distrust, and suspicion are status quo. Moreover, in such a world, natural forces are supposedly beyond our control. The best we can supposedly do is to understand and adapt to such forces. In this case, greed just happens to be good. In fact, everything about Darwin's theory of evolution just happens to mesh with a world of hardly any interbeing. We are to forget that no theory comes out of a vacuum.

Charles Darwin's theory of evolution is born out of Charles Darwin's belief system. It constitutes what Charles Darwin was ready and willing to believe, and thereby what Charles Darwin was ready and willing to understand. The theory's popularity and appeal reflects us also being ready to believe what the theory claims. Behind every theory is a vision of the world that constitutes a certain position and relation to the world. No theory is capable of describing how the world really is. Instead, theories describe our relation to the world, meaning that no theory is capable of explaining what we are incapable of understanding, much less believing. Theories describe what we are ready and willing to believe. This is why the world is laden with all manner of theories. This kind of variability reminds us that the world lends for multiple descriptions and explanations, all, of course, with different implications and consequences. There is no need to be beholden to any theory. This variability also means that even our best theories have constraints, and thereby are always susceptible to being revised and even replaced. Theories are fallible because we are fallible. However, because our theories are fallible, no theory can rule over us like gods. Theories are to serve us. But whose interests a theory serves is important to recognize. In the case of Darwin's theory of evolution, this question becomes important. Whose interests does this theory serve? On the other hand, whose interests are ill served by this theory? Also, how heuristically and constructively does the theory serve various interests? With regards to theory, these are the kinds of questions that matter. Darwin's theory of evolution is no doubt serving the interests of the privileged, and thereby such peoples have a vested interest in the promotion of the theory, and in the rest of us believing that the theory is truthfully describing how the world really is. But what about the rest of us? What theories can possibly serve us better and what do we need to believe in order to create such theories?

7

ON GOD

In an address given to *The Conference on Cosmic Design of the American Association for The Advancement of Science,* Nobel Laureate Steven Weinberg (1999) said the following:

I don't need to argue here that the evil in the world proves that the universe is not designed, but only that there are no signs of benevolence that might have shown the hand of a designer. But in fact the perception that God cannot be benevolent is very old. Plays by Aeschylus and Euripides make a quite explicit statement that the gods are selfish and cruel, though they expect better behavior from humans. God in the Old Testament tells us to bash the heads of infidels and demands of us that we be willing to sacrifice our children's lives at His orders, and the God of traditional Christianity and Islam damns us for eternity if we do not worship him in the right manner. Is this a nice way to behave? I know, I know, we are not supposed to judge God according to human standards, but you see the problem here: If we are not yet convinced of His existence, and are looking for signs of His benevolence, then what other standards can we use? (p. 7)

Weinberg raises a compelling point. The Old Testament does indeed make any belief in a loving and benevolent God difficult. We do find in this testament a God that is often petty, petulant, and cruel. God requires complete and obedient submission. Violators are dealt with harshly and cruelly.

But the LORD inflicted serious diseases on Pharaoh and his household because of Abram's wife Sarai.

Genesis 12: 17

For I, the Lord your God, am a jealous God, visiting the inequity of the fathers upon the children to the third and fourth generations of those who hate me, but showing mercy to thousands, to those who love Me and keep My commandments.

Exodus 20: 5-6

Moses stood in the entrance of the camp, and said, "Whoever is on the Lord's side—come to me!" And all the sons of Levi gathered themselves together to him.

And he said to them, "Thus says the Lord God of Israel: "Let every man put his sword on his side, and go in and out from entrance to entrance throughout the camp, and let every man kill his brother, every man his companion, and every man his neighbor."

So the sons of Levi did according to the word of Moses. And about three thousand men of the people fell that day.

Exodus 32:26-28

Weinberg (1999) contends that the "The Ten Commandments portray a deity who is self-centered, selfish, jealous, obsessed with his own importance; this is not a nice kind of person. The traditional teachings of religion are, from the point of view of the morality of most people share today, pretty immoral." We are to give up the "illusion that religion raises the moral level of society" (Weinberg, 2000). Weinberg contends that the moral persuasion of religions has been disastrous. For example, Weinberg challenges the claim that religious beliefs contributed to the ending of slavery. He argues that such beliefs actually legitimized slavery and that "most of the world's great religions coexisted very comfortably with slavery." In the end, according to Weinberg, "With or without religion, good people can behave well and bad people can do evil; but for good people to do evil—that takes religion."

Weinberg also contends that there is no need for any constructive dialogue between science and religion. Religion is simply nonsense. He believes that our future—or what future we can have—resides in science. He predicts "with fair confidence—that sooner or later we shall discover the physical principles that govern all natural phenomena." But such a final discovery will bring no redemption. According to Weinberg, "The more the universe seems comprehensible, the more it also seems pointless." In fact, the future of humanity is dismal and tragic. The physical principles of the planet apparently conspire against us. Eventually the planet will implode. We are to accept the reality these principles are impersonal and show no concern or purpose for human beings. Moreover, "science can never explain any moral principle." However, "one way we can find a purpose is to study the universe by the methods of science, without consoling ourselves with fairy tales about its future, or about our own." After all, the results (truths) of science are supposedly accumulative and objective.

Weinberg believes that the malevolent deeds of science result from our own malevolent motives and has nothing to do with the nature of science. "Of course, science has made its own contribution to the world's sorrows, but generally by giving us the means of killing each other, not the motive" (1992, p. 259). In other words, science is morally neutral. Apparently, religion can claim no such excuse. It is therefore "not safe to assume that religious persecution and holy wars are perversions of true religion" (p. 258).

We are therefore to believe from Weinberg that the conflict between science and religion is intractable and irreconcilable. We are also to believe that science is a stable and monolithic enterprise where all adherents share a common creed and temperament. But this is purely illusory. For example, about science's moral neutrality, David Bohm (1998) writes:

It is widely believed, for example, that in some sense, art, science, and mathematics are morally neutral. Thus, it is said that scientific knowledge may be used either for good or evil ends .... But such a separation between the content of men's work and its ultimate human significance is itself a result of the overall condition of fragmentation that has largely prevailed throughout the ages. Indeed, if men were generally considering knowledge as an unbroken whole (as is implied, for example, in the original meaning of philosophy as love of wisdom) they would understand that this whole has to fit in every aspect of life. So it would be clear that there is no meaning to such a notion of overall fitting if its end is not the good. (pp. 87-88)

Moreover, as for the ability of science to produce a definitive and cumulative knowledge through the employment of rigorous and objective methods and techniques, which Weinberg views as the hallmark of science, Bohm (1998) writes:

The notion of the necessary incompleteness of our knowledge runs counter to the commonly accepted scientific tradition, which has generally taken the form of supposing that science seeks to arrive ultimately at absolute truth, or at least at a steady approach to such truth, through a series of approximations. This tradition has been maintained, in spite of the fact that the actual history of science fits much better into the notion of unending possibilities for new discoveries, approaching no visible limit or end.... Indeed, physics is now in a state of flux, in which we expect the development of yet newer theories, again radically novel and different, in terms of which current theories will be seen as having only some relative and limited kind of validity. What has happened and is still happening in this respect suggests an indefinite and unending unfolding into a measureless unknown, rather than a better covering of some limited, measurable, and in principle completely knowable domain. (p. 71)

There is also hardly any unanimity among scientists that "nothing in science can ever tell us what we ought to value." For instance, Nobel Laureate Freeman Dyson (2000), who Weinberg regards as "one of the most perceptive and imaginative scientists" that he knows, would likely contend that science tells us that we ought to value diversity:

I do not claim any ability to read God's mind. I am sure of only one thing. When we look at the glory of stars and galaxies in the sky and the glory of forests and flowers in the living world around us, it is evident that God loves diversity. Perhaps the universe is constructed according to a principle of maximum diversity. The principle of maximum diversity says that the laws of nature, and the initial conditions at the beginning of time, are such as to make the universe as interesting as possible. (p. 3)

Indeed, all organic systems strive to promote diversity. When this striving is undercut such systems devolve and perish. On the other hand, however, Weinberg sets up religion as a monolithic enterprise where all adherents share a common creed and temperament. Nothing, of course, could be further from reality. Religion is just as pluralistic as science. As Abdolkarim Soroush, a prominent Islamic scholar, observes:

The essence of religion will always be sacred, but its interpretation by fallible human beings is not sacred—and therefore can be criticized, modified, refined, and redefined. What single person can say what God meant? Any fixed version would effectively smother religion. It would block the rich exploration of the sacred texts. Interpretations are also influenced by the age you live in, by the conditions and mores of the era, and by other branches of that knowledge. So there's no single, inflexible, or absolute interpretation of Islam for all time. (Wright, 1999, pp. 46-47)

In the end, Weinberg merely succeeds in further masking and eroding the tremendous complexity, diversity, and nuances that constitute our different views of the world. In so doing, however, he only further reinforces an array of false divisions that undermine our ability to find common ground with others who seem most different to us.

There are no doubt differences between many of us that are probably intractable and irreconcilable. However, there is also much we share. For instance, regardless of our theological and theoretical orientations, many of us believe that natural ecologies can teach us a lot about what we ought to value. We also believe in a progressive knowledge—one that allows us to work through the world's ambiguity, mystery, and complexity in ways that affirm life. We also believe in the rigorous pursuit of knowledge and in an inextricable relation between education and redemption. What merely distinguishes us from Weinberg is our suspicion of missions—found of course in both science and religion—that claim the power, either through god or man, to conquer the world's mystery, ambiguity, and complexity and thereby the authority to generate complete and absolute descriptions and interpretations.

Our reality is different. We find that the more we learn about the world, the more the world reminds us of how little we will ever know. Yet for us, this reality merely speaks to the magnificence of the world. We therefore in no way believe that the absence of knowledge constitutes a lack of knowledge. For us, what most threatens any knowledge enterprise is the belief—found in both science and religion—that the world is finite and therefore only lends for so many possibilities, and the forces that perpetuate this debilitating belief by either downplaying or simply possessing no understanding of our capacity to impact our worlds and thereby expand our realm of possibility.

IN SEARCH OF INCOMPLETION

There is arguably no notion more heuristic than that of incompletion—the notion that the world's mystery, ambiguity, and complexity will always exceed us and thereby we will never be able to produce absolute and complete claims. An incomplete world assumes a world that is boundless and laden with infinite possibility. Incompletion also promotes interpretation and reinterpretation by pointing us to a world where meaning is infinite, the reason being that "reality as a whole is vast and immense, so that anything that is known ultimately merges and shades into a measureless unknown in which the totality of what mankind may know, at any particular stage, has its origin, its sustenance, and its ultimate dissolution" (Bohm, 1998, p. 96). It also promotes the evolution of new ways of experiencing and embodying the world by forcing us to reckon with the world's infinite ambiguity, complexity, and mystery. In this way, incompletion undercuts the hegemony of forces, systems, and practices that aim to block our evolution and that of world.

But of course, most of us assume a complete world and a complete God. After all, how could God be any less? But a complete God allows for no collaboration, no creation, no evolution, and, most of all, no volition. Such a God gives us neither the ability nor opportunity to help shape the evolution of the world. We have no choice but to obediently love this God. What God would desire such a meaningless subordination? In fact, what would such subordination do for any God? Also, how can we truly love any God in the face of retribution? Indeed, a complete God puts no onus on us to love more, to care more, to give more, to tolerate more, and to forgive more. Our redemption merely demands our full submission to the wishes of an often petty and petulant God. We are released of any obligation to deal honestly and courageously with the world's complexity, diversity, and mystery—that is, all that makes the world fascinating and inspiring.

We should forsake the notion of completion and begin to demand more expansive descriptions and interpretations of the world and our gods. Our descriptions and interpretations come from within us rather than from our theories, methods, sciences, and even religions. Only in being ready to change how we embody the world can we change how we understand the world. So before we can bring forgiveness, mercy, love, and compassion into the world, we have to believe in worlds that have a natural place for these notions. Otherwise such notions remain nothing but empty doctrine. For example, the fact that Jesus Christ believed in love and forgiveness, even in the face of the most horrendous anguish and torture any person can suffer, signals that Jesus Christ's faith in an incomplete world was resolute. Indeed, the notion of incompletion pervades all of the world's great spiritual teachings, either in Judaism where God is one of possibility and imagination, or in Jainism, Hinduism, and Buddhism where God is infinite.

But of course, we are to believe from the likes of Weinberg that love, mercy, compassion, and forgiveness have no place in any rigorous knowledge enterprise. That is, matters of being have nothing to do with matter of knowing. Only in a finite and complete world would one dare operate so casually on such a false illusion, for knowing is really about framing, and framing is ultimately about being. For instance, if we come to the world believing that the world is a certain way, our knowledge of the world will fall within this vision of the world. If we therefore wish to change or even enlarge our knowledge of the world, we have to change our ways of framing the world, and this, of course, ultimately involves changing our ways of being. Any knowledge enterprise that claims to be committed to the creation of knowledge must ultimately be committed to promoting those forces that enlarge our being.

This is what love, mercy, compassion, forgiveness, empathy, and generosity constitute—practices that enlarge our being by demanding more from us. These practices in no way belong to a realm outside of science. Matters of knowledge and matters of morality are intertwined, which means that our knowledge of the world is and will always be an expression of our moral development. As such, the common notion that science is about knowledge and religion about faith is illusory. There is no foundation for this duality in the world's great spiritual teachings. Yet a complete and absolute knowledge we will never have. We will therefore never arrive at that point when our quest for knowledge is over. Such is the challenge of knowledge. But such is also the fact that knowledge, in being morally laden, will always be politically uneven.

We have long been made to believe that science saved us from the ravages of mysticism. Without science we would supposedly still be burning people on stakes and boring holes into the heads of others. But is science really bringing us the prosperity and progress that was long promised and remains ubiquitously advertised? Does the world have less anguish and suffering, even amongst those who have access to all the spoils of science? Is our survival and prosperity better assured as a species? Of course, the immediate answer that most of us would probably give to these questions is Yes. We would contend that though the knowledge science gives us is far from perfect, we are still better off with this knowledge than with the ignorance mysticism promises. We also still take comfort in the fact that science promises to do better. But we are operating on a false decision set. We have many more options to work with than we have been made to believe. That is, instead of simply choosing science and thereby unquestionably and passively accepting the fallout from the march of science, we need to find a way to begin asking why are we pursuing and even deriving from the world a knowledge that seems so perilous. What about the ways in which we are framing the world that is making for this knowledge? What about our ways of being that make for this way of framing the world? Regardless of how we come to discourses about knowledge, if we are truly committed to knowledge, we have to be open to the question of whether the world lends for a different knowledge, and therefore a different set of possibilities, including the possibility of much larger notions of gods.

The struggles found in all of the world's great spiritual texts are always about expanding our humanity—trying to love more, to give more, to care more, and so forth. We are always bearing witness to persons trying to be of a larger humanity in worlds that make it difficult and perilous to do so. We find, for example, in the New Testament Jesus Christ trying to love deeply in the face of betrayal, persecution, suffering, and death. In the Gita, we find Arguna struggling to be selfless. The struggle is always against those who wish to impose complete gods on us. As such, if we wish to believe in gods, which of course should be our prerogative, then let us believe in gods who will invite us to share in the completion of the world by seeking our devotion through knowledge rather than in ignorance. Any possibility for a more humane and just world requires us to remain open to the possibility that such gods are out there.

8

ON IMAGINATION

The story that pervades the sciences and humanities is that the origins of communication, and by that language, can be found in evolutionary necessity. Apparently, communication evolved so as to facilitate the accomplishing of more complex tasks that were necessary for survival in the harsh grasslands of Africa. This is the general story, but there are many versions. For example, in an essay titled *Primate Communication and the Gestural Origin of Communication*, Gordon Hewes (1992) offers this version that is based on the notion that our first language was primarily gestural, "We can generally agree that human language must have arisen through wholly natural processes, under completely describable environmental conditions, among creatures having less rather than more of the cognitive powers of modern man" (p. 66). Jean Aitchison (2000), author of *The Seeds of Speech*, offers this version,

Physically, a deprived physical environment led to more meat-eating and, as a result, a bigger brain. The enlarged brain led to the premature birth of humans, and in consequence a protracted childhood, during which mothers cooed and crooned to their offspring. An upright stance altered the shape of the mouth and vocal tract, allowing a range of coherent sounds to be uttered. (p. x)

For John McCrone (1991),

It all started with an ape that learned to speak. Man's hominid ancestors were doing well enough, even though the world had slipped into the cold grip of the ice ages. They had solved a few key problems that had held back the other branches of the ape family, such as how to find enough food to feed their rather oversized brains. Then man's ancestors happened on the trick of language. Suddenly, a whole new mental landscape opened up. Man became self-aware and self-possessed. (p. 9)

Michael Corballis (2002), author of *From Hand to Mouth: The Origins of Language*, offers this version,

My own view is that language developed much more gradually, starting with the gestures of apes, then gathering momentum as the bipedal hominids evolved. The appearance of the larger-brained genus Homo some 2 million years ago may have signaled the emergence and later development of syntax, with vocalizations providing a mounting refrain. What may have distinguished Homo sapiens was the final switch from a mixture of gestural and vocal communication to an autonomous vocal language, embellished by gesture but not dependent on it. (p. 183)

All of these versions generally assume that communication is fundamentally a linguistic and symbolic phenomenon. But this story about the origin of language and communication is much more than merely a story. It is a story about what being human means and our location and relation to the world. This story of communication and language reinscribes a vision of the world that presents a certain set of frames of what is possible and appropriate. In fact, this story perpetuates larger narratives that limit our understanding and experiencing of what is possible by perpetuating a narrow definition of what it means to be human. Presumably, we are merely evolved chimpanzees and apes and all that distinguishes us from our cousins is our evolved linguistic and symbolic capacity. We are supposedly in no way fundamentally and morally different. We therefore have no qualms about generalizing findings about apes, chimpanzees, and gorillas to us.

There are many ways to argue with a story. We can show how the story is wrong or deficient. For example, we can point to the fact that "no languageless community has ever been found," as well as no evidence of a pre-evolved or proto-language. We can also take issue with the motives behind the story, and even with the people who came up with the story. But probably the most constructive path is simply to present a different story of communication and language, and by that a different story of what being human means. If anything, what makes this emergent story more heuristic than others is that it constitutes a more expansive story of what being human means and, accordingly, fundamentally enlarges our understanding of what is possible.

FICTIONS AND STORIES

Every worldview constitutes a story of the world. Of course we are to believe that other worldviews have mythologies and we have sciences, which are presumably rational, rigorous, and objective. But at the foundation of every worldview is a set of fictions—positions that require a leap of faith. No worldview can end these fictions, which is to say that no worldview can escape our insecurities, anxieties, and paranoia. For example, we will never know how the world began and what set off the forces and motions that made for the big bang, or from where these forces and motions originally came. We will also never know everything about the universe. In fact, as for the origin of language, even linguists acknowledge that everyone is guessing. What all this means is that we will never have a knowledge of the world that is absolute and complete, a knowledge that can stand outside of history. Yet we should actually embrace such knowledge rather than trying to make believe our knowledge is empty of fictions. Fictions make our knowledge elastic. It allows our knowledge to change and evolve, and thereby incorporate new observations.

The problem with knowledge has nothing to do with the fictions that we find at the core of every knowledge system. The problem is with the kind of fictions that constitute our knowledge, and the anxieties, insecurities, and paranoia that make for our different fictions. For instance, how did we come to believe that we are merely *survival machines* who are doing the bidding of selfish genes? What anxieties, insecurities, and paranoia made for these beliefs, or from where did these beliefs arise? Moreover, what does it mean to believe that we are merely survival machines? How does such a belief enable or foreclose on knowledge and, ultimately, the making of the good society? On the other hand, to believe that our knowledge is superior is to believe that the formation of knowledge emerges through accumulation. Knowledge presumably constitutes those things that we can objectively know of the world. However, to embrace the reality that fictions are at the core of our knowledge is to recognize or define knowledge in terms of moral action. Knowledge is anything that enables moral action, meaning that fictions collapse the divide between knowledge and wisdom. Knowledge no longer emerges as an institution that is outside of us, meaning that knowledge is no longer seen to reside in books, journals, and other such entities. Instead, knowledge emerges from within us, by us continuously examining, scrutinizing, and challenging the beliefs, fears, anxieties, insecurities, and paranoia that make for our different fictions. It also involves the courage to change these beliefs, fears, and so forth so as to enable the creation of new fictions, which in turn make for new stories, and which in turn make for new ways of experiencing and understanding the world. In this way, fictions intertwine imagination with knowledge creation, and imagination allows us to defy spatial and temporal limitations.

In my emerging story of communication I begin with the fiction that the origin of communication is fundamentally spiritual rather than informational, meaning that communications situates at the center of the world and that the mission of communication is to form community. As much as I value and appreciate our linguistic and symbolic capacity, I believe that communication exceeds this capacity as evidenced by our ability to form rich and complex relations with persons with whom we share no linguistic and symbolic competence. Accordingly, I now define communication in terms of vulnerability. *Communication is about being vulnerable to the humanity of others.* Now the measure of communication is compassion. In being vulnerable we create knowledge, which in turn facilitates moral action. In other words, communication is integral to the formation of knowledge, and communication problems are really problems of knowledge rather than problems of clarity. So there is no possibility of knowledge, including knowledge of God, outside or separate from communication. Our capacity to be vulnerable is also what most makes us human and burdens us with a unique obligation to the world. After all, only humans possess the means to destroy the world.

But the story about communication being inherently linguistic and symbolic is hegemonic. In our quest to survive and evolve, we supposedly acquire knowledge to help us do so. Therefore the more knowledge we can acquire and accumulate, the better our chances of surviving and prospering. In this story knowledge emerges as a precious commodity that requires great investment, and communication emerges as purely the means to share and exchange knowledge (information). That is, knowledge and communication emerge as separate entities. Moreover, in this story, knowledge is about utility, and the measure of knowledge is determined by its ability to help us survive and evolve. Knowledge must therefore help us to be superior competitors as competition is supposedly the order of things. It must also help us conquer and defeat the various natural forces that threaten our survival and prosperity. In the end, knowledge must help us conquer the world so we can attain absolute control over our survival and prosperity. These ambitions define the sciences and humanities, and form the foundation of communication studies. Knowledge emerges as a weapon against the forces that threaten our survival and prosperity. As evidenced in our huge libraries, we now have great stockpiles of this kind of knowledge. We also have an elaborate infrastructure devoted to producing this knowledge and to training persons how to produce this knowledge. We are no doubt prevailing in our contest with the natural world.

But as the planet collapses under our unrelenting plundering, will victory be ours? Of course the status quo will contend that these problems have nothing to do with the nature of our knowledge. It is about to what uses our knowledge has been put. This is the argument that one should expect when we believe our knowledge is devoid of fictions. It is, after all, this illusion that allows our knowledge to be hegemonic. But when we recognize or embrace the reality that fictions are at the core of every knowledge system, we also recognize that we cannot separate ourselves from our knowledge. No knowledge can do something that is outside of the insecurities, anxieties, and paranoia that constitute that knowledge. If we are therefore now at a point in history where our demise is staring us down, our only recourse is to create a new knowledge, and this involves proposing a new story of the world with a new set of fictions.

COMMUNICATION AND KNOWLEDGE

No paradigm will ever willingly surrender its hegemony. Hegemony means that a paradigm has the means to perpetrate its fictions as truths. There are no longer any doubts or suspicions. Certainty is the order of things. Therefore in order to end hegemony, a paradigm must either face a violent outside force that it can neither contain nor seduce, or the conditions that support the paradigm must fundamentally change. So hegemony either goes the way of revolution or implosion, which is to say that hegemonies are inherently irrational. In many ways, the story that now pervades and rules our world, the one that posits that language and communication are products of evolutionary necessity, is facing the proverbial perfect storm. Besides the fact that the condition of the plant is on the brink of catastrophe, the world is less and less static and dualistic. Because our spaces and distances are increasingly collapsing and imploding, the world is increasingly dynamic and elastic, meaning that, among other things, our diversity is increasingly global and less racial (white and black). As much as we endeavor to simplify and keep human affairs neat and tidy, the world also seems no less determined to assert its complexity, mystery, and ambiguity. The problem is that our current models of communication, which are linguistic and symbolic based, have no means to negotiate this increasingly diverse and complex world. These models thrive in homogenous and stable environments, preferably ones where peoples share the same worldview and the same set of symbolic and linguistic codes. But such conditions are no more, or at least the illusion of such conditions is no more. Moreover, our paradigm can no longer deliver these conditions. This of course in no way means that we will stop trying to achieve these conditions. Again, no paradigm will ever surrender its hegemony without a struggle. But our determination to build new border fences, limit immigration, and make the English our legal and formal language will do nothing to beat back the many forces that are now upon us.

When we make believe our knowledge has no fictions we can avoid grappling with the origin of various forces that make for our fictions. But there is nothing heuristic in perpetuating this illusion. Before we know what we know, we know what we are ready and willing to know because we know what we are ready and willing to believe and experience. My experiences with humanity are by no means all positive. I too often wonder about the possibility of evil. But for one reason or another, I am still ready and willing to believe in a more expansive view of what it means to be human. That is, there is something about how I experience the world that makes me suspicious of the thesis that we are merely survival machines and communication is a tool of necessity. There is also something about how I experience my humanity that convinces me that communication is much more than the sum of our linguistic and symbolic practices, and through communication we are capable of forming knowledge. I am unable to isolate what specific experiences make for these stances. On the other hand, I am uncertain as to whether I need to know what these experiences were and whether it matters. But of course the status quo claims that we need to have something other than what we believe. We need evidence that is supposedly objectively verifiable, as our beliefs are seen to be fallible. However, what is fundamentally wrong with our beliefs being fallible? That our beliefs are fallible means that our beliefs can change and evolve.

What should concern us is how heuristic are our beliefs. Do our beliefs enlarge our worlds, enable us to imagine new ways of experiencing and understanding the world? Also, do our beliefs make us less afraid of the world and each other and thereby save us from various anxieties, insecurities, and paranoia? We should care about what people believe so we can understand how our beliefs shape and influence what we view as knowledge. Ontology and epistemology are inseparable just as much as epistemology and methodology are inseparable, and ontology, epistemology, and axiology are inseparable. But now we experience each as separate. Methodology is now its own discipline and subject. We have all kinds of method courses where we teach the techniques of executing different methods and knowing what methods are best for different research questions. Theory and method now belong to different universes and use different currency. Most research endeavors require an elaborate account as to why a certain theory is being coupled with a certain method. Such an account is supposedly necessary for rigor, but what we ultimately do in playing this out is perpetuate the notion that theory and method belong to different universes. But before we separated theory and method, we separated epistemology and methodology, and before we did this we separated epistemology from ontology, and before we did this we separated axiology from ontology and epistemology. Yet we continue to wonder why our research has no relevance or purchase in the real world. We continue to miss the problem. So now we have theory and praxis, pure and applied research, and pedagogy and research. There seems to be no interest as to why we perpetuate this fragmentation and whether this trend is heuristic. But why and how did the fragmentation begin? What made for the illusory decoupling of ontology, epistemology, and axiology? In other words, what made for this violence on our humanity? For this is what this fragmentation constitutes. It pits us against ourselves as we try desperately to keep different dimensions of our humanity in different compartments. So our supposed rational dimension goes under epistemology, and our supposed emotional, spiritual, and existential dimension goes under ontology, and our historical and cultural dimension goes under axiology. These divisions are illusory and destructive. Yet we persist in promoting this fragmentation. This persistence is evident in our stories of evolution that posit communication as a tool of necessity. It forms the bedrock of communication studies, and is arguably most responsible for perpetuating the fragmentation and separation that are the hallmarks of our worldview.

REDEFINING COMMUNICATION

The notion that communication is a tool of necessity begins on the fiction that our humanities are separate—no moral, spiritual, or ecological element binds us to each other. As such, in order for us to coordinate any action there is a need for us to devise a way to exchange our thoughts. Communication emerges as a bridge over which our thoughts and emotions move from one point to the next, and language constitutes the vehicle which carries our thoughts over the bridge. A communication problem therefore involves either something to do with the bridge or with the vehicle. But in this story of communication note the separation between cognition and emotion, cognition and communication, and, most importantly, that between communication and knowledge. Separation is ubiquitous. But the separation is also dangerous. One can possibly make the case for the possibility of cognition outside of communication, but can cognition really reside outside of communication? In fact, does this possibility reveal anything compelling? Cognition outside communication makes only for isolation, and isolation makes only for our demise. Consequently, by undercutting isolation, communication promotes life. But isolation never appears in our stories of communication and evolution. The problem is that these stories have no way to accommodate such a notion. This is the thing about stories—stories are inherently coherent. So isolation needs to go in search of a new story. However, because isolation is left out of our current stories of communication, we can continue to believe and even institutionalize the notion that communication is a tool of necessity that facilitates the exchange of our thoughts, and in so doing, ultimately makes for culture. We can also continue to propagate the notion that we are merely survival machines who are doing the bidding of selfish genes. Just as well, we can also continue to legitimize ideologies that assume no spiritual, moral, or ecological relation between us, such as ideologies that promote individualism, competition, autonomy, and greed. Indeed, if communication is meant to facilitate the exchange of thoughts and ideas, then the linguistic and symbolic component is vital. But if the origins of communication reside elsewhere, then the linguistic and symbolic component is secondary to communication.

There is no way to know for certain where the origins of communication reside. On this matter we are all in the fiction business. But we can analyze or determine which story of communication is more heuristic. When I posit or define communication in terms of knowledge creation, I am operating on the premise that we are relationships rather than separate entities. We are relationships to the world, the planet, and to each other.

We are fundamentally spiritual, ecological, and relational beings, meaning that we are never outside of a relationship. To be human is to be of a relationship and subject to all of the forces and implications that come with that relationship. For instance, no one in the U.S. is immune from the fallout of the deforesting of the Amazon forest. To be unaware of this relationship does nothing good for us. On the other hand, being aware of this relationship enlarges our humanity by pushing us to be more conscientious and responsible for all that is happening in the world. In this way, our destruction of the planet makes plain that we have yet to fully believe that we share a relationship with the planet. It also makes plain that our theories of knowledge are inadequate even to the most basic task, securing our own survival.

But who is ready to argue that we are better off for assuming otherwise? Evidently our fictions come with consequences and implications. In the face of all the dire warnings about the condition of the planet, we continue to believe and assume that we share no relationship to the planet. How do we begin to explain this matter? Why the unwillingness to enfold the planet into our humanity? Why also the unwillingness to enfold the world and each other into our humanity? Moreover, why do we hold steadfast to fictions that undermine such enfolding? To embody communication as a tool of necessity undermines such enfolding by denying any possibility of communication between the world and us, or between the planet and us. After all, can the planet or the world send messages or transact meanings with us? But what is the possibility of communication when communication has nothing much to do with language and symbols? In short, what is the possibility of communication when we define communication in terms of knowledge? In my view, the possibility would be great as compassion and knowledge formation, as seen in the recognition that we share a relationship with the planet, would make for a deeper and richer relationship to the planet, the world, and each other. Communication vitalizes these relationships, and in so doing, saves us from the anguish and torment of isolation. But what is isolation and why is isolation so rampant in our society? In my view, isolation is about our inability or unwillingness to form deep and rich relationships with the world, the planet, and each other. It is both ontological and communicational. Isolation is rampant because our worldview continues to deny our association with this trinity of relationships. What results is a society that has no deep regard for the well-being of the planet, the world, and most of all, for the human beings who constitute that society. In sum, what emerges is a society that is deficient in the most basic knowledge of all, the knowledge to save itself.

THE END OF KNOWLEDGE

What is it about our knowledge that is failing us? Why are we seemingly incapable of recognizing that our fate and that of the world are intertwined? For all the knowledge that we claim to have, how is it that we are unable to recognize this reality? I believe the answer to this question resides in the separation between communication and knowledge—that is, in the illusion that communication and knowledge are separate entities, and communication is merely the means we use to share, exchange, and frame knowledge. We therefore assume that knowledge is inherently linguistic, symbolic, and numeric. It is an entity we can share, exchange, and stockpile because of these traits. As such, we emphasize the sharing, exchanging, stockpiling, and even hoarding (such as nuclear technology) of knowledge. Knowledge emerges as this entity that our linguistic, symbolic, and numeric capacity allows us to draw from the world. The goal of science is therefore to develop more powerful equations, more rigorous theories, more elaborate experiments, and more powerful research technologies.

Evidently, our knowledge assumes a divide between the world and us, but one that our linguistic, symbolic, and numeric capacity allows us to breach. We therefore aspire to harness this capacity so we can draw all the knowledge we can from the world. Communication has been put in service of this story of knowledge. On the other hand, maybe communication plays a much more fundamental role in the formation of this story. Either way, communication plays an integral role in perpetuating and reifying this story, and this story of knowledge plays a vital role in rarefying the notion that communication is fundamentally linguistic and symbolic. What is also apparent in this story of knowledge is the omission of ontology and the various forces that shape and influence what we are ready and willing to understand. There is no recognition of the human element, meaning that there is no recognition of our sociology, anthropology, and psychology. But no human being drops out of the sky. There are always forces and systems that shape us and situate us in the world. No human being can ever escape these forces and systems. But as seen in string theory, for example, we continue to focus on how we can solve various equations rather than asking where within our anthropology these questions are coming from. That is, what is making for these equations? What forces are shaping and situating us now that we are producing these theoretical, conceptual, and methodological issues? There is of course no such emphasis, so our anxieties, insecurities, and paranoia face no scrutiny. But we can trace our anxieties, insecurities, and paranoia in our knowledge systems. Our own complexity, ambiguity, and mystery, and that of the world, continue to torment us to no end. We aspire for a knowledge that will release us of these anxieties, insecurities, and paranoia, one that will make the world stable, predictable, and even comfortable. This is what we want from knowledge. But why should this be the goal of knowledge? In fact, can any enterprise produce such a knowledge? Herein is where our problems begin.

No enterprise can grant such a knowledge as the world in no way lends for such a knowledge. On the other hand, maybe this is why our anxieties, insecurities, and paranoia now seem to be exploding. Maybe the illusion of finally arriving at a knowledge that will make the world stable, predictable, and comfortable is simply beginning to implode. This is what our current crisis of knowledge is fundamentally about. Our illusions are imploding. Hounds are no longer hunting. Eventually every illusion must deal with a world that is in every way real, and something has to give. However, after so many resources devoted to accumulating and stockpiling knowledge, we have no choice but to believe that the world should be stable, predictable, and comfortable by now. Of course it is anything but. There shall be no theory of everything, no unifying theory. But again, maybe such a theory was never meant to be. Maybe the world simply lends for no such theory. Just as well, maybe nuclear technology and cloning were knowledges that were never meant to be? What is the cost of pursuing such a knowledge—one that will supposedly allow us to achieve a stable and predictable world—and building a society on the pursuit of such a knowledge? Moreover, what is the cost of maintaining the anxieties, insecurities, and paranoia that constitute such a knowledge? In the end, axiology, epistemology, and ontology work in tandem to perpetuate each other. This is how paradigms behave, and also why every paradigm has its own logic and ways of making sense of things.

We are of a world where all signs of things to come point to something dire. Virulent fundamentalisms are now everywhere. Increasing number of nation states are collapsing and facing no end of virulent strife. The ice caps are melting and our destruction of the planet rolls on. New epidemics and pandemics are emerging as the gap between rich and poor continues to widen. We are also running out of fresh water as fertilizers and pollutants continue to contaminate our rivers, streams, and lakes. We also have the proliferation of weapons of mass destruction. Never before has the world been on the precipice of such catastrophe. The conditions are of such as to make people turn away from knowledge. Maybe this is what the rise of religious fundamentalism is about—our loss of faith in knowledge. We should therefore be in no way surprised by why books about the end of the world are now so popular. Neither should we be surprised by our growing intolerance. We are apparently in a clash of civilizations and even a fight for civilization. Communication is supposedly impossible. Presumably, the other side only understands aggression and military intimidation. But the communication that is being assumed is communication as transaction, where communication is inherently linguistic and symbolic. This model in no way helps us negotiate the dire situation that is now upon us. Everything this model requires for clarity actually damages knowledge and, ultimately, our own moral development. For example, to believe that communication is about the transaction of messages suggests that we achieve communication by removing or managing the ambiguity that inherently resides between peoples. Though in communication studies there is emerging recognition about communication as ambiguity management, there is still the overarching view in the humanities and sciences that ambiguity is an impediment to communication. We therefore generally strive to achieve clarity by limiting or ending ambiguity. But the problem with this goal is that ambiguity is actually vital for the creation of knowledge. Without ambiguity, there would be no knowledge, no possibility of communication. Ambiguity sustains inquiry by keeping the world open for possibility. Without ambiguity, there would be no reason or opportunity for inquiry. Inquiry and ambiguity share an inextricable relationship. Without inquiry, ambiguity would simply be empty space. In this case, however, inquiry is about how we engage and negotiate the world's ambiguity, including our own ambiguity. It constitutes a mode of being, a way of living, meaning that inquiry is communicational. Knowledge emerges through communication by us being vulnerable to the complexity, mystery, and ambiguity that situate and permeate us. It is something that comes from within, but in order for this to happen, we must become vulnerable. So what knowledge we come to will depend on how vulnerable we are willing to be, and how vulnerable we are capable of being will depend on how much courage we can muster to engage the world's infinite ambiguity, complexity, and mystery.

I believe a much more heuristic way to look at the origin of communication, and by that language, is in the fact that we are born into a world of infinite ambiguity, complexity, and mystery that will always exceed us. We can no doubt continue to promote the narrative that this ambiguity, mystery, and complexity is inherently in conflict with us, and as such, that we need to conquer and even end these entities. This of course involves waging war upon our humanity as we are laden with ambiguity, complexity, and mystery. We can also continue to believe that language evolved out of our need to conquer the world's ambiguity so we could survive the harsh grasslands of Africa. But how heuristic and constructive has been this master narrative? Can it in any way help us resolve the many dire problems that now bear down on us?

To look at the origin of communication from the stance I am suggesting is to look at communication as a mode of being and as a way of embodying language that moves us into the world's ambiguity, complexity, and mystery. This is how we achieve moral development, recognize our inseparable relation to the world, the planet, and each other, and ultimately, acquire knowledge. In other words, all communication practices are in no way morally, ecologically, or epistemologically equal. Whereas some practices move us into the world's ambiguity, complexity, and mystery, others undermine such movement, making only for isolation, aggression, and ultimately, our destruction. So whereas some practices promote ignorance, others promote knowledge. The onus is no doubt on us to cultivate and promote those that afford the latter.

9

ON NARRATIVE

To look at the notion of narrative as simply a way we make sense of the world or articulate our humanity depoliticizes our understanding of narrative. It poses no threat to the status quo, and thereby offers no new paths to understanding and experiencing the world. A much more heuristic way to look at narrative is in terms of being. Compelling narratives are about narratives as being in the world. Integral to this move towards compelling narratives is a rejection of the hegemony of truth. There is no purchase in the belief that truth is necessary for the good society. This belief assumes that the solution to our problems resides in the acquisition of truths, that the pursuit of truth is inherently constructive, and that we have the ability to find the truths of this world. Methodology comes to trump axiology. Instead, a compelling narrative stance focuses on the implications and consequences of different narratives. For example, do different narratives give us the possibility of new and different worlds, ones with less misery and suffering? Do the narratives stretch our humanity?

To view us as narrative beings who have the ability to create compelling narratives is to assume that we are incomplete rather than imperfect. We have a potentiality to construct deep and complex relations with the world. It is this quality that uniquely defines us as human beings. Our narrativity manifests our potentiality to construct such relations. Through our narrativity we therefore construct our understandings and relations with the world. As such, narrativity assumes that we are meaning-creation beings. We have a moral, existential, and spiritual striving to bring meaning to bear on the world. Through this striving we construct our different narratives and help with the completion of the world.

Compelling narratives are full expressions of our potentiality for deep and complex relations with the world. The deepest and most complex understandings of the world are found in compelling narratives. These understandings are often found in many of our most compelling narratives—the different spiritual teachings that abound the world. Compelling narratives lend for rich interpretations of the world. It is through interpretation that our narratives find meaning and prosperity. A narrative that undermines interpretation is one that forecloses on our ability and striving to forge deep and complex relations with the world. In doing so, such a narrative makes us less human. To be fully narrative is to be in the world in such a way that promotes interpretation, as only through expanding our potentiality for meaning creation do we become fully human. Herein reside the origins of the relationship between narrative and ethics.

To be fully narrative assumes that our redemption is intertwined with the quality of our being in the world. The world will become what we become. In other words, the condition of the world is inextricably intertwined with the condition of our humanity, with the condition of our narrativity. Narratives that undercut interpretation and meaning creation undermine the condition of the world by blocking the evolution of different ways of being in the world. Such narratives make for closed systems, those that are certain to perish. We need only note the increasing degradation of the world's natural systems with our increasing determination to expunge the world of the elements—ambiguity, mystery, diversity, and complexity—upon which our narrativity strives. We are also of a world that is openly hostile to our narrativity and peoples throughout the world who have deep narrative traditions. It is the inextricable relation between the condition of the world and the condition of our own humanity that most intertwines our narrativity with ethics.

To view human beings as incomplete assumes that creation and evolution is the order of the world. A world that is perfect allows for no interpretation, creation, and evolution. Such a world offers no possibility for either meaning creation or interpretation. We have no ability or opportunity to help shape the world, and such a world limits and subordinates us. Conversely, an incomplete world highlights our ability to help with the completion of the world. It is, again, our narrativity that most uniquely defines us as human beings. Narrativity assumes that we are of the world and the world is of us. To be fully narrative is to recognize and thrive on this understanding. To do good by the world is to do good to our own humanity. Compelling narratives connect us to the world and each other. The natural quantum rhythms of the world are also our rhythms.

We can therefore look at the condition of our humanity by looking at the condition of our narrativity. We can look as to whether our narratives are allowing for rich interpretations of the world, or whether our narratives are making for a world with less misery and suffering, or whether our narratives are speaking to our fears rather than to our hopes. In promoting rich and complex interpretations of the world, compelling narratives give us new and different ways of experiencing the world. We come to understand the fecund nature of the world. The world in no way wishes to limit us. Our subordination is of our own doing. It is born out of our fear of the ambiguity, mystery, and complexity of the world. In our attempt to suppress the ambiguity of the world, we suppress the evolution of our own humanity and lose our connection to the world. The world is seen as outside of us and ultimately in conflict with us.

To be fully narrative is to embrace the world's ambiguity, mystery, and complexity. It is also to embrace the infinite potentiality that is of the world. A world devoid of ambiguity is one devoid of passion. Compelling narratives find passion through ambiguity. The ambiguity of the world liberates us from the excess demands of the past and the future. Life, after all, comes with neither promises nor guarantees. No meaning or interpretation can withstand the ambiguity of the world. Disequilibrium is the order of the world. Our meanings and interpretations have to evolve and change, even die, which means that our narratives have to allow and even promote such evolution and devolution.

It is the lending of rich interpretations that most distinguishes compelling narratives from other kinds of narratives. When we cultivate new and different understandings of the world, the ambiguity of the world stretches and enlarges us. It lessens our fears of the world and each other, as is often found in compelling narratives. As a result, embracing the ambiguity of the world releases us of the need to legitimize practices and institutions that thrive on our distrust and suspicion of each other. We close the separation and fragmentation that this distrust and suspicion foster. This addresses the cause that is arguably responsible for a lot of destruction in the world. Indeed, believing that the rigorous pursuit of truth will bring forth progress and make eventually for the *good* society disconnects our humanity from the world and, in so doing, disconnects the condition of our humanity from the condition of the world. We lose sight of the full consequences of our ways of being in the world. A narrow definition of responsibility emerges. We look at responsibility in terms of autonomy. On the other hand, compelling narratives celebrate our connection to the world and each other. Such narratives bind us by weaving us together. No longer do our differences divide and separate us. The forging of compelling narratives expands our understanding of what being human means, and in so doing, enlarges our definition of responsibility. In the end, the forging of compelling narratives makes for a better world by pushing us to be better human beings with the world. To be fully human is indeed to be fully narrative.

Compelling narratives are ultimately about a way of being in the world. It is about a way of engaging other human beings. Louis Michel, Harriett Tubman, Dorothy Day, Albert Switzer, and Medgar Evers are examples of compelling narratives. To look at life in terms of narrativity is to believe that ultimately what matters is what we do and make of the world, and much less about what we know about the world. Does our life create a narrative that makes for new and different possibilities? Do we bring less misery and suffering on the world? In sum, is our life a compelling narrative?

10

ON METHOD

If no methodology can betray its epistemology, and no epistemology can betray its ontology, what is the project of knowledge? Evidently, what we come to view as knowledge is determined by what we are ready and willing to experience and define as knowledge. Every methodology is merely an instrument that only allows us to know what we ready and willing to know. As such, what are all the quarrels about methodologies about? Does any methodology promise to violate what we are ready to experience and define as knowledge? Can any methodology in the social sciences do such a thing? So again, what is all the quarreling about? What is the project of knowledge?

We should have concerns about how ethnographers treat reflexivity: as a methodological practice to produce more authentic knowledge by presumably pushing us to lay bare how we engage and narrate our ethnographies. Much has been written about the vulnerable ethnographer, and even being reflexive of our own reflexivity. However, reflexivity, as seen in qualitative scholarship, only focuses on the inextricable relationship between methodology and theory. It does nothing to change what we are ready and willing to experience, meaning that reflexivity never rises to the level of ontology. Consequently, the reflexivity that ethnographers promote poses no threat to the order of things. We are still, in the end, only knowing that which we are ready and willing to know.

How therefore do we come to know that which we are unwilling to know? Is this enterprise even possible? Moreover, how would we know that we are really knowing that which we are unready and even unwilling to know? On the other hand, how could we continue to stick with an enterprise where we are only knowing that which we are ready and willing to know? Yet the ability of this enterprise to endure and, in so doing, continue to mask the inextricable relationship between ontology, epistemology, and axiology is compelling. But such is what any hegemony can do.

To the question that asks, "Could we really know anything?" I ask, "Do we really need to know anything?" How did knowing become the project of knowledge, that is, knowing as we commonly define knowing? Where did this project come from? But more importantly, why does it continue to endure? My own thesis is that this project eases our deepest anxieties, insecurities, and paranoia—those that come from facing a world with great ambiguity, mystery, and complexity. It gives us some semblance of order and control in the face of such a world—that is, some way of making sense of ourselves. We should therefore be in no way of surprised, as Thomas Kuhn (1996) observed long ago, that there is no progress to the unfolding of science. The mission of science really has nothing to do with knowledge per se. This is why, as Kuhn also observed, science only pursues those questions it can answer. It is really meant to ease our deepest anxieties, insecurities, and paranoia. Everything else is put in service to this end, which is also to say that everything else is about illusions, such as the illusion of separation between methodology and epistemology, theory and method, and so forth. That this paradigm of knowledge continues to endure is only because it continues to allow us to believe that we are lessening the world's infinite ambiguity, mystery, and complexity, as in the case of news every week of another important new discovery to help us eventually cure some kind of horrible disease. We simply need to believe that such knowledge is within our grasp so as to continue to believe all that we already believe. But the world also seems no less determined to collapse our illusions, and to remind us of its infinite ambiguity, mystery, and complexity. What, therefore, do we do? Do we give up our quest to accumulate and stockpile the most knowledge we can? Do we stop our search for the next great medical breakthrough? Do we give up the search to know the world's secrets?

In our story of the world, knowledge emerges as our only weapon against the world's ambiguity, mystery, and complexity. It is presumably knowledge that makes for our continuing survival and prosperity. Therefore the more we can accumulate and stockpile, the more we presumably enhance our chances of surviving and prospering. We believe great stockpiles of knowledge are the hallmarks of great civilizations and nations. However, as much as our stockpiles of knowledge are great, as seen in our huge libraries, most of this knowledge merely reflects what we already believe about the world. We are merely becoming more proficient in knowing more about what we are ready and willing to know. In fact, as we focus more on methodology and less on epistemology, we are arguably knowing less and less about the world. But how could we possibly believe such a claim when every week brings news of another exciting medical breakthrough? How could we forsake a story of the world that promises us so much—the ability to control our destinies by acquiring the means to order and control the world? In this story knowledge is heroic. It is the spear that slays the beast. If we therefore hope to change this project of knowledge, we have to change this story of the world, and this involves problematizing why this story appeals to us, and what is the impact of this story on the world. On the other hand, this is also where qualitative methodologies (especially ethnographies) that claim to offer a different knowledge have problems. These methodologies all come from the same story of the world. With ethnographies, only the descriptions are thicker.

So the world really has no need for more methodologies, or even more refining of presumably alternative methodologies. What we need are new stories of the world, those that give us new definitions of knowledge. We also need new environs that can help us create new stories. On the other hand, maybe this is where the project of knowledge resides—in the creation of new stories. Maybe this is how we get back to epistemology and ontology. Maybe this is how we got to the cult of methodology—by losing the ability to create really new stories. After all, the very things that make for great stories, such as ambiguity, mystery, and complexity, are the very things that our methodologies try to eliminate. But such is the promise of our current knowledge project—to discover, to find, to verify, to identify, to explain.

A more heuristic way to define knowledge is in terms of being rather than knowing—that is, being as knowing, knowing as about how much we can experience and embody. Being foregrounds ontology. It moves us beyond subjectivity and positionality by encouraging us to examine the larger historical forces that situate us in the world. In this way, being enlarges reflexive practice. Rather than merely reflecting on our ways of observing, interviewing, and narrating, reflexive practice is now about probing how we experience the world and our own willingness to experience and understand that which is new and different. It is an everyday, every moment practice. It gives a whole new meaning to the ethnographic life—the life that is always engaging the world, always trying to write a new story of the world. This is the life that knows nothing about where fieldwork begins and ends, and other such methodological matters that continue to occupy people who do ethnographies. Instead, the focus now is on violating and interrupting the stance from which we frame and experience the world—being ethnographies rather than doing ethnographies.

It is about staring down and engaging our deepest anxieties, insecurities, and paranoia—those that most shape how we experience and narrativise the world. It is also about us trying to find the origins of those forces and other arrangements that give these forces safe harbor. Reflexivity emerges as a moral practice—releasing ourselves from our deepest anxieties, insecurities, and paranoia so we can come to experience and understand the world in new ways. It is about the recognition that what we are is what the world is. In this way, reflexivity becomes a world-making practice.

There is no need to deny that through various modes of inquiry we have come to learn really interesting things about the world and different peoples. Instead, my point is that these common modes of inquiry promote no moral development, that is, no modes of being that can save us from our own worse instincts and impulses. For instance, as our vast libraries overflow with books, journals, reports, and papers, and as our great universities educate and graduate more and more persons, the condition of the world grows increasingly dire. What therefore does it profit us to presumably know so much, but yet be somehow incapable of saving ourselves from ourselves? Understandably, many will contend that the problem has nothing to do with the nature of our knowledge per se. It lies somewhere else, as in our ability, or lack thereof, to cope with our increasing knowledge, or to make the tough decisions that our knowledge advises. The problem is therefore a human one. It is presumably our own fallibilities that damn us. But even so, we are still left with the fact that no knowledge comes out of a moral and historical vacuum. We are also left with the fact that our knowledge assumes that the world is in conflict with us, and that our own prosperity requires that we realize the knowledge to subdue the world's malevolent forces. We are also left with the fact that this knowledge poses a perilous threat to the world. Yet the notion of what constitutes knowledge continues escape scrutiny.

A good place to begin is by asking, *What is knowledge for? What is bringing us to this inquiry? What do I wish to know? Where are my insecurities, anxieties, and fears in this inquiry? Why do I wish to know what I wish to know? Why does it matter?* This is how we dismantle the illusion of our knowledge helping us to control and order the world. For in order to prop up our current knowledge project, we have to lie and deceive, such as making believe that we are really asking important questions, and doing important research. We are all complicit in probably one of greatest lies ever told—the lie of knowledge. One way we can stop perpetuating this lie is by beginning to ask the questions I suggest. This is where our reflexivity should begin as this is where we begin to understand where we are in relation to the world. This is also where we begin to do more interesting ethnographies by removing all of the illusions and deceptions. Now the divide between observer and the observed, insider and outsider, will be no more as we become the ethnography, the site of excavation and discovery. There will therefore be no more ethnographies that begin with "This study investigates…." Nor will there be any more ethnographies that give us abstract reasons for why an inquiry is important. Nor will there be any more of those exotic ethnographies that try to achieve importance by merely being exotic. The goal is to change our relationship to knowledge as only in doing so will what we view as knowledge change, and what we are ready to experience and define as knowledge also change. The ultimate goal is to change our story of the world, as only in doing so do we have any chance of saving the world and ourselves.

11

ON EXISTENCE

Because we are inherently narrative beings, eventually we have to devise narratives that make sense of our existence. As with all other narratives, these narratives will employ all manner of assumptions, fictions, and superstitions to achieve some semblance of coherence. But these narratives will endure because they fulfill a vital existential function—they allow us to make sense of our existence. In a world of infinite ambiguity, this is something we have to do. It is an incomplete activity, meaning that we create these narratives according to our own rhyme and reason. What ultimately matters is that these narratives work for us—they give us a sense of purpose and meaning.

Every narrative therefore has its own coherence, its own way of making sense of our existence. But in a world of infinite ambiguity, any coherence is fragile. Still, every narrative strives to achieve coherence. Such is the enterprise of Charles Darwin's theory of evolution. The purpose of this theory is to convince us that what we already believe and are willing to believe is true. What we are ready and willing to believe is that human beings are by nature beasts and savages, and are of a world that is devoid of any moral algorithm. Darwin's theory of evolution shores up this belief by allowing us to believe that this savagery is actually necessary for our survival and prosperity, as this is presumably a world of ruthless competition, survival of the fittest, and hierarchy.

But there are other narratives. In fact, there are many different narratives. For instance, George Dyson (1997) writes,

Darwin's success at explaining the origin of species may have obscured the workings of evolution in different forms. The Darwinian scenario of a population of individuals competing for finite resources, with natural selection guiding the improvement of a species one increment at a time, tempts us to conclude that where circumstances do not fit this scenario—despite the lengths that Darwinism has been stretched—evolutionary processes are not involved. Large, self-organizing systems challenge these assumptions—perhaps even the assumption that a system must be self-reproducing, competing against similar systems and facing certain death or possible extinction, to be classified as evolving or alive. It is possible to construct self-preserving systems that grow, evolve, and learn but do not reproduce, compete, or face death in any given amount of time. (p. 186)

Whereas Darwin's theory of evolution highlights notions like selfishness, competition, information, survival of the fittest, and hierarchy, this alternative narrative believes in a theory of evolution that highlights notions like adaption, innovation, cooperation, communication, and mutuality. This narrative, of course, is born out of different influences and experiences. It is specifically born out of the belief that this is a world of possibility. Life resides in possibility. To promote, cultivate, and generate possibility is to allow for the becoming of life. On the other hand, when we impede, undermine, and torture possibility, life perishes. Evolution is the affirmation of possibility. Through evolution, through the promotion of possibility, life unfolds. The hallmark of evolution is the rise of possibility, including the rise of practices, conditions, and environs that promote possibility.

This is the problem with Charles Darwin's theory of evolution. Competition, survival of the fittest, and hierarchy actually impede evolution. Competition promotes distrust and suspicion. It impedes the sharing of resources that is necessary for innovation and achieving superior kinds of organization and even the most efficient outcomes. This reality is now seen in the success of open-sourcing. But proponents of Darwin's theory would quarrel with this conclusion and claim that only through competition and the recognition of common interests that cooperation arises and endures. Cooperation is referred to as an evolution stable strategy (ESS). It arises out of evolutionary necessity. When this necessity disappears, competition returns. In this way, cooperation is merely another expression of competition. It is about working with others to achieve our own self interest. The notion of common good is actually an illusion. In fact, proponents contend that trust is even unnecessary for the evolution of cooperation. All that is necessary is the threat of retribution for violating cooperation. As such, is this really cooperation? Still, by impeding cooperation, competition impedes communication. Indeed, competition fosters division, separation, and isolation. This is the antithesis of being human. In fact, this is the antithesis of life. Isolation ravages the human condition. It implodes our humanity. It dismantles our constitution. By promoting division, separation, and isolation, competition impedes life.

Charles Darwin's theory of evolution assumes that communication merely constitutes the exchanging of information. But communication constitutes the negation of division, separation, and isolation. In making cooperation possible, communication makes evolution possible. Communication is the womb of possibility. It is where life emerges and flourishes. To view communication in terms of information is to show no understanding of what isolation does to the human condition. Communication ends isolation by pulling us outward and towards each other. Each ecology may no doubt have a different understanding and experiencing of communication, but no ecology can flourish without communication. For without any kind of communication, evolution would be impossible. Yet what distinguishes our own understanding and experiencing of communication is our capacity for communication. As much as we can experience communication through signs, symbols, and language, we can also experience communication without these practices. We are therefore capable of experiencing communication without sharing a common language. Our capacity for communication is found in our vulnerability—our capability of being vulnerable to the world's ambiguity, each other's ambiguity, and our own ambiguity. We achieve communication by being vulnerable to all of this ambiguity. By locating possibility with communication, what also emerges is that our capacity for communication gives us an enormous capacity to generate possibility. It also means being the custodians of the responsibility that comes with this capacity. But ultimately what emerges is an inextricable relationship between possibility and vulnerability—how vulnerable we are capable of being will determine how much becomes possible. We attend to possibility by attending to our vulnerability.

Each flourishing ecology promotes possibility, which in turn pushes other ecologies to promote possibility. But the world is never devoid of possibility. What matters is how much and what kinds of possibilities is the world generating and encouraging. For human beings, generating possibility is difficult. Vulnerability requires courage, as in the courage to be vulnerable to the world's ambiguity. This is why communication constitutes a mode of being. It is about cultivating the courage to be vulnerable. Possibility comes from within and between us. By enlarging our capacity to be vulnerable, we enlarge the realm of the possible. Life becomes what we become. But because our own capacity to be vulnerable is infinite, life is infinite. Our gods are infinite. There is always the possibility for possibility, meaning that there is always the possibility for evolution and redemption. In a world of ambiguity and possibility, redemption will always be possible. But such redemption is only achievable through vulnerability. Without the capacity and courage to be fully vulnerable, such possibility is beyond our grasp. Indeed, in a world of ambiguity, we will never be able to determine the limits or all of the topography of possibility. Trying to achieve the most vulnerability is about prying the world open for possibility. With each new expression comes new meanings, new understandings, new perspectives, new experiences. As possibility unfolds, everything changes. Diversity is inevitable. In fact, diversity is the hallmark of possibility. As we cultivate possibility, we cultivate diversity. Diversity therefore continues to be a reliable measure of any ecology's health and prosperity. But such is another problem with Charles Darwin's theory of evolution and the narrative that encourages the making of this kind of theory.

Competition, survival of the fittest, and hierarchy work in tandem to destroy diversity. Competition means that the most and best resources will go only to those who are the fittest, strongest, and brightest. Those who are different, as in being of different ambitions, will thereby be deprived of valuable resources. Survival of the fittest really means survival of those who share our ambitions, aspirations, and most of all, our fears. It also means survival of those who are willing to play the same game and by the same rules. In Charles Darwin's theory of evolution, hierarchy means fear of extermination. It supposedly arises from the weak being afraid of being vanquished by the strong. Out of this fear, the weak devises a way of servicing the needs of the strong that will afford the weak access to resources and protection from other competitors and predators. As with cooperation, hierarchy is also a product of evolutionary necessity. It is supposedly a highly evolved form of cooperation. Presumably, hierarchy forces the weak to develop only those capacities that meet the needs, desires, and pleasures of the strong. Those who are unwilling to do so will simply perish. Thus conformity is the hallmark of any efficient and proficient hierarchy. But again, what about those who have no fear of dying, no fear of the strong? Why should such diversity face peril, especially when fear is such an unreliable and inefficient way of achieving motivation?

Proponents of Darwin's theory could plausibly argue that an ethos of survival of the fittest actually promotes diversity by forcing species to develop unique capabilities and capacities. This, again, is how species survive, by finding ways to adapt to the environment, by developing new capabilities and capacities. In evolution, homogeneity is death. For proponents of Darwin's theory, evolution, as in survival of the fittest, is responsible for the world's abundant diversity. This may no doubt be the case. Still, this constitutes a narrow case for diversity. Yes, this theory does give us a reliable understanding of diversity that can make for progressive public policy. It also constitutes an attractive description of diversity. There is also the possibility of a biological dimension to the origin of diversity. It probably does begin under duress. Again, Darwin's theory of evolution suggests that diversity evolves out of necessity. Without stress and duress, diversity would be impossible. But is the purpose of diversity purely for necessity, meaning is the origin of diversity purely biological? According to Darwin's theory, hierarchy promotes diversity, and diversity promotes hierarchy. The pressures that hierarchy induces—from the constant struggle of species seeking to survive—force species to develop unique capacities and capabilities. But in reality hierarchy impedes diversity by suppressing conflict, dissent, and disruption. The goal of hierarchy is to achieve order by any means necessary. This often constitutes the violent suppression of any entity or process that threatens the status quo. In this way, hierarchy impedes possibility.

It is possibility that promotes diversity. Or, possibility is the origin of diversity. Without possibility, diversity is impossible. We promote diversity by cultivating possibility. We do the latter by refusing to limit the world's boundless ambiguity, mystery, and complexity. We also do so by cultivating vulnerability as the promotion of possibility—and by that, diversity—obligates us to promote modes of being that are open to new meanings, new experiences, new narratives. This is how the promotion of communication—which is really the promotion of possibility and diversity—ultimately promotes justice and democracy. This is why diversity is the hallmark of democracy. The cultivation of possibility makes for the origin of justice. In this way, diversity is by no means merely descriptive. It is a process. Diversity constitutes the cultivation of possibility, the generation of possibility, the articulation of possibility. Democracy nurtures diversity. It brings diversity and possibility into the world without duress by promoting practices like empathy and vulnerability.

Darwin's theory of evolution undermines diversity by ascribing to us one set of motives, aspirations, and ambitions—the need to survive and procreate by whatever means necessary. We are merely units of biology—supposedly survival machines doing the bidding of selfish genes. Presumably, what diversity is found in the world is merely as a product of evolutionary necessity and utility—a byproduct of evolution. Its goal is to serve our need to survive and procreate. There is therefore no possibility for diversity outside of this mission. Evolution apparently holds diversity on a short leash. But is this diversity? How could this be diversity when hierarchy requires our submission in order to be efficient and proficient? In reality, Darwin's theory of evolution has no place for diversity as we supposedly survive by conforming and submitting to the needs, desires, and pleasures of others.

Conversely, in a theory of evolution that emphasizes notions like cooperation, innovation, and communication, diversity is an expression of possibility and our own vulnerability. It reflects a changing and evolving world. It also reflects a world that is becoming, unwilling to submit to one meaning, one understanding, one truth, one revelation. In a world of ambiguity, diversity is the order of things. But diversity is always changing. In a world of ambiguity, diversity is a verb. We are always achieving diversity, meaning that we are always adding and layering the world with diversity. Diversity comes from cultivating cooperation, promoting innovation, and fostering communication. So whereas Charles Darwin's theory of evolution seeks to limit diversity, the other seeks to unleash diversity. Herein also resides the fundamental differences between the narratives that give us these different theories of evolution.

Besides giving us a way to make sense of our existence, narratives give us a way of making sense of the world. But because no narrative can escape history, the process of narrative-making is profoundly human. How we make sense of our existence and the world is also about how we are ready and willing to do so. We bring all kinds of experiences and influences to the process. The process also reflects our different existential, emotional, geographical, sensual, spiritual, material, and physical positions and inclinations. Most prominent in the narrative that legitimizes Charles Darwin's theory of evolution is a profound fear of the world. This fear permeates everything, shapes everything, legitimizes everything, organizes everything. Every dimension and interpretation of Charles Darwin's theory of evolution manifests this fear. For instance, the theory assumes that we are of this great struggle with the world. Our fear of the world is therefore legitimate. The theory also assumes that we are always in competition with others for scarce resources. Without being able to acquire the resources we need by being ready to scheme or impose our will on others, we will presumably perish. Thus our suspicion of each other is legitimate. This fear of the world that this dominant narrative promotes is by no means merely conceptual. It shapes everything about our being and how we experience the world. For instance, this fear shapes how we use and relate to language.

We are afraid of language. We insist on using language properly for fear that confusion will arise if we do differently. We assume that there is a correct way to use language. We also insist on keeping our languages pure and stable for fear that foreign languages and dialects will pollute our language. We assume that without such diligence our languages will devolve and make for our own devolution. We also insist on controlling and limiting the proliferation of other languages for fear that the lack of a common language will invite chaos and strife. Our fear of the world also shapes our relation to our bodies. We are afraid of our instincts, impulses, desires, fantasies, and yearnings. We strive to use various discursive devices to organize and discipline our bodies for fear that our bodies will overtake us and make for all kinds of deviancy and promiscuity. Yet such devices fail us again and again. We are in constant anguish with our bodies, and no less afraid of the bodies of others. We are obsessed with devising ways to control the bodies of others. We insist on regulating every dimension of the body. Our fear of the world also shapes our conceptions and uses of knowledge. We believe that without stockpiling and amassing knowledge, ignorance will hold us in bondage. We therefore tend to view knowledge as a kind of weapon that will allow us to successfully wage war on ignorance. Presumably, without being able to vanquish ignorance, we will perish. We therefore tend to discuss education as an investment—giving us the means to move away from the perils of ignorance and escape lack of opportunities and resources. Finally, this fear of the world impedes communication. We are afraid to be honest for fear that others will take advantage of our honesty and transparency. Our proclivity is to avoid and suppress conflict. The result being that our relations to each other are devoid of any passion and conviction. There is no intensity, no challenging of each other to reckon with all our ambiguity and complexity. We reduce each other to caricatures, insisting on dealing with each other on our own terms, on our own impressions and preconceptions. There is no courage to realize and forge new meanings. We experience communication from the past, each other from the past, ourselves from the past. We are afraid of the present for fear that meaning will be impossible. We are always afraid of chaos ensuing. We torture the present and future with this fear. We never experience the power that comes with either, as in the ability to begin anew. In sum, our fear of the world impoverishes us. It robs us of the vitality to live courageously, honestly, and transparently—the vitality that is necessary to embrace the present and plunge us into the future. This fear robs us of the capacity to get beyond past wrongs, past misfortunes, past disappointments, past slights, past disappointments, past failures. It imprisons us to the past. Yet this is a world that is constantly changing. The past is always being forsaken. Death is inevitable. Our fear of the world puts us in conflict with the world's natural rhythms. We will of course never prevail in this conflict as the power of the world will always exceed our own. But nothings good promises to come from our doings. Our misery will be in vain.

We could possibly be of a narrative that promotes courage rather than fear. But this is a fundamentally different narrative, constituting a fundamentally different consciousness. In this narrative we accept the world on our own terms. We are at peace with its infinite ambiguity, mystery, and complexity. Yes, death is inevitable. But this is also a world of relationships. Without death, life is impossible. Without ambiguity, meaning is impossible. Without chaos, order is impossible. In this alternative narrative we are of the world. There is no separation or conflict between us and the world. We strive to be in harmony with the world's quantum rhythms. We understand well that life favors the future as this is where possibility resides. So we have no qualms about letting the dead bury the dead. In being committed to the cultivation of possibility, we strive to promote practices and conditions that generate possibility. We understand well that the process is without end. There is no end to possibility. There is therefore no ambition to discover the world's truths. We believe that our redemption resides in possibility rather than in any Truth. Also, as much as we believe that the world is of an order, we perceive this order is emergent. It is also a generative rather than restrictive order. The workings of such an order can be found in language. It is known as Universal Grammar. It means that all languages are organically bound by a common constitution that allows all languages to be recognizable and accessible to each other. There is no need to be afraid of language or the diversity of our languages.

There is also a generative order in communication. It resides in our striving to mean, to understand, to make sense of things. Though we may engage and arrive at meanings differently, what allows us to recognize ourselves in each other is our striving to mean, to understand, to make sense of. We are therefore at peace with the world because we perceive a world that is laden with possibility. Also, because we perceive the world this way, there are places in our narrative for notions like love, hope, grace, mercy, compassion, tenderness, and forgiveness. These practices promote possibility. Moreover, these practices promote courage. Ultimately, these practices promote life by turning us away from the past and towards the future. These are practices of courage, defiance, and resistance. The absence of these practices is indifference, as indifference means no belief in possibility. We are indifferent because we believe that nothing good is possible, either because the world makes this so or we are simply incapable of doing so. Before we can care, love, hope, and forgive, we have to find the resolve to believe in a world that lends for possibility. This is why these practices can find no place in our dominant narrative. This is also why these notions are absent in Charles Darwin's theory of evolution and other popular theories that definitively claim to describe what being human means.

But in a world that is laden with possibility, these practices actually play a vital role in cultivating possibility. For instance, hope allows us to find the possible in the impossible. Without hope, the impossible will remain outside of our grasp. Our realm of possibilities would be less. Just as well, love gives us the resolve to believe in the impossible. This is why love is an act of defiance, an act of resistance. Love emancipates possibility. Through love we defy the realm of possibilities that are given to us as legitimate, as well as the worldviews and institutions that present us with these possibilities. Love is an act of sedition, an act of revolution. Through love we declare our belief in possibilities that defy the imagination and will of the status quo. Those who choose to love, choose to die. Love requires of us the most courage, and without such courage, or a willingness to realize such courage, possibility—and life—ends. We therefore choose to love because we believe that the world is deserving of love. Through love we help realize and complete the world. This is how our alternative narrative makes sense of our existence. It no doubt constitutes a fundamentally different way of making sense of our existence. But it comes down to which narrative seems the most heuristic? That is, which narrative serves us best? Which narrative makes for a world with less misery and suffering? Which narrative makes for the least destruction? Which narrative promises the least harm, the least peril? On the other hand, which narrative seems to give us the most compelling description of what being human means? But ultimately what really matters is which narrative we are willing to believe.

12

ON PERCEPTION

We continue to believe in the promise of modernity. Through our sciences, technologies, and institutions we will prevail in our conflict with the world. Such is the way we are perceiving and aiming to fix our environmental problems. We believe that through our science and technology we can solve these problems. We also believe that capitalism can offer the necessary incentives and rewards to encourage the rise of the necessary science and technology that will save us from ecological armageddon. Supposedly, our environmental problems are challenging us to begin another phase in our evolution that will further enable our survival and prosperity by allowing us to gain more control over the world. Through the coming of a zero carbon emission economy we will presumably become more efficient in our use of the world's natural resources. Our focus is on investing in alternative energy resources, making lifestyle changes that decrease our carbon footprint, incentivizing science and industry to develop alternative materials, instituting new regulations that disincentivise a carbon-based economy, and establishing treaties and international agreements that promote the sharing of technology, curtailing carbon emissions, and helping developing and low-lying nations deal with the ravages of a changing planet.

But of course how we frame and perceive a problem will determine how we engage and resolve the problem. Every problem is discursive—born out of a certain set of beliefs, values, fears, assumptions, biases, and prejudices. In the case of our supposed environmental problems, we assume a divide between us and the planet, thus the ubiquitous images of snow caps melting and sea levels rising. Such images reinforce our belief that our environmental problems are about the environment, therefore requiring environmental solutions. But what happens when the divide between the environment and us becomes undone? That is, what happens when we realize that our proposed solutions will do nothing to limit our supposed environmental problems? Also, what happens after we realize that our science, technology, and institutions were never capable of solving these problems or ultimately saving us from our destructive ways? In sum, what happens when our illusions become undone and the world decides to bring to an end to the way we perceive ourselves in relation to the world? What becomes of us?

Our supposed environmental problem is exposing the illusion of there being a divide between us and the world. What is happening to the planet is really about what is happening to us. Our degradation of the planet is about our degradation of each other and ourselves. Our reckless plundering of the planet's resources is about our exploitation of each other. Our indifference to the condition of the planet is about our indifference to each other. It is we who are in crisis and in peril. What is happening to the planet is merely a reflection of what is happening to us. Saving ourselves will only come from the evolution of a worldview that ends our degradation and exploitation of each other.

But no worldview will enable its own undoing. Worldviews must implode before new worldviews arise. This is why most of us continue to believe that what is happening to the planet has nothing to do with our doing. We are even suspicious of claims about the perils the environment is facing. We continue to insist that our welfare should come before that of the environment. In the face of these harsh realities, the rise of a new worldview seems all but impossible. But we have been here before. As Jared Diamond shows well in *Collapse: How Societies Choose to Fail or Succeed*, all great civilizations knew well the perils they faced, but were simply incapable of changing course, the reason, again, being that every worldview is self-perpetuating. We perceive what we believe, and what we perceive and believe shape what we experience and value. Modernity is born out of our most primal instincts and impulses. It is a worldview that, in most cases, requires barely anything from us. What emerges is a moral vision that appeals to our most primal instincts and impulses. There is no moral, relational, or ecological obligation to each other. Greed is good. Selfishness is good. Competition is good. Aggression is good.

But such are the illusions of modernity. Regardless of what may become of us as our crisis deepens, what is also becoming evident is that our path could have been fundamentally different. By simply being of a worldview that makes no division between us and the world, we could have saved ourselves all of the misery that we continue to bring upon the world and each other. But for some reason we seem incapable of resisting our most primal instincts and impulses. We were never capable of realizing our best ecological, existential, spiritual, and relational virtues. We therefore never achieved what we were fully capable of achieving. We never even were willing to imagine the possibility of us being of a capacity and potentiality to create worlds devoid of any kind of degradation and exploitation. Instead, misery and death were all we were willing to accept as truth. It could have all been so different. But we continue to miss every opportunity to change course. This is what is so frustrating about our deepening ecological crisis. It is as if the world is begging us to change course. Yet once again we seem incapable of doing so. So now peril awaits us.

13

ON BEING AND TIME

What does it mean to be of a knowledge enterprise that believes in human inequality? What also does it mean to be of a knowledge enterprise that believes that human beings are by nature beasts and savages? I am referring to a knowledge enterprise where Plato, Aristotle, Socrates, and Pythagoras are the founding fathers. I am referring to a knowledge enterprise where Husserl, Heidegger, Kant, Hegel, Nietzsche, Hume, and company are perceived as saints. I am referring to the many apostles and disciples in academe who propagate this enterprise of knowledge as gospel. I am referring to the rest of us who come to this enterprise—on the belief of acquiring knowledge—ready to believe completely and absolutely. When a knowledge enterprise has the power to shape and dominate every discourse about knowledge, what is the possibility of knowledge diversity? In fact, what is the value of any diversity that has no origin in knowledge diversity?

But all of this is why we are yet to come to terms with our own complicity in the making of the Holocaust and other such cruelties found in our history. How can we oppose these cruelties when we believe in human inequality and all manner of dualities that separate and divide us? How much a gap is there between persecuting, vilifying, and demonizing a group of human beings, and enslaving, brutalizing, and exterminating those human beings? Our knowledge enterprise, in assuming human inequality, has no way of proposing or imagining elegant theories of human diversity. This is why our diversity discourses are fraught with all kinds of contradictions and confusions. To believe in human inequality is to believe that those who are presumably superior have the ability to create a superior knowledge, and ultimately a superior culture. This, of course, is exactly what we believe. This is why there can be no knowledge diversity. How can we justify cultivating inferior knowledges or making believe that our different knowledges are of comparable value? But is our own knowledge morally superior? How can a knowledge that is responsible for so much death and destruction assume to be superior? How can the people who are responsible for creating this knowledge assume to be superior?

But what is knowledge? Presumably, knowledge is the search for truth, and, according to Plato, by acquiring knowledge we will become closer to God. For Heidegger, who is considered one of the "greatest" philosophers of the twentieth century, knowledge means "to master in clarity the essence of things, and by the force of this power to be resolved to act." Knowledge is supposedly a process of discovery. It supposedly reflects the truths that we find in the world, as well as the methodologies and theories we use to acquire these truths. But what exactly are these truths? Presumably, truths are descriptions and observations of things found in the world. For instance, gravity is a description of something found in the world. We believe that our knowledge contains the most truths, and the most effective means of deriving, stockpiling, and integrating these truths. No doubt, this world does contain truths. It probably contains as many truths as beaches contain sand pebbles. But how did the pursuit of knowledge become the goal of knowledge? Why does it matter that we know that all objects fall to the ground, or that the earth revolves around the sun, or that atoms are the building blocks of nature? These truths are no doubt important, but are they ultimately important? As Jesus Christ asks, "What good is it for a man to gain the whole world, yet forfeit his soul?" In other words, is our supposedly superior knowledge saving our soul? As we continue to acquire and stockpile the world's truths, is our survival in less peril? Is the world devoid of less misery and suffering? Is our reckless plundering of the planet's natural resources abating? Does our knowledge enrich our lives with meaning and value?

There is no correlation between our acquisition of truths and our moral development. What then is the value of this knowledge enterprise? Most likely the enterprise has nothing to do with knowledge or truth. Maybe it is all about us wanting to find a way to cope with the world's infinite ambiguity. Maybe it merely constitutes a dysfunctional way of doing so. But how else do we explain the irrelevance of so much of the enterprise and knowledge? How else to make sense of the seeming inability of the enterprise to save us from ourselves and each other? Yet our faith in the enterprise is without doubt. We continue to believe that through this enterprise we will achieve progress and civilization. In the case of Heidegger, what was merely missing is our knowledge about the truth of being. However, as Heidegger was articulating this knowledge about the truth of being, he was putting "Heil Hitler" at the end of his personal letters. What then is really the truth of being? What also is the value of this knowledge that philosophy was missing? According to Heidegger, knowing the truth of being will make for a more complete knowledge. It will enable our quest to find the essence of things. But Heidegger never assumes or mentions how this knowledge will save us from ourselves and each other. Nor is there any mention how this knowledge will make for a more humane world. For Heidegger, the problem with being concerns methodology. He is trying to build a better mousetrap—to improve our ability to know the essence of things. But this is why Heidegger was able to continue to sign letters with "Heil Hitler."

Even though Heidegger believes that our inattention to being compromises philosophy, being for him never rises to the level of ontology. He comes to being with a narrow conception of being. Thus in Heidegger's elaborate discussion about being and the supposed truth about being, there is no mention of love, grace, mercy, empathy, compassion, forgiveness, and tenderness. Presumably, the truth of being has nothing to do with these notions. Nor is there any mention of the potentiality and beauty of being. Being is merely about being in the world. To understand being merely involves understanding the discursive environs that shape being and in turn are shaped by being. Thus, as much as Heidegger's discussion of being is interesting, and understanding the truth of being is heuristic, nothing about Heidegger's truth of being poses any threat to the order of things. This, again, is why Heidegger could continue to end letters with "Heil Hitler." Even the best mousetrap is meant to catch only mouse. Heidegger is by no means interested in the soul of being, or the spirit of being, or the beauty and potentiality of being. Heidegger's truth of being still falls within a knowledge enterprise that assumes that through knowledge we will achieve prosperity and civilization. We merely have to commit to building better mousetraps. But as we continue to do so the condition of the world is only becoming more perilous. How long can we therefore continue to believe that what the world needs is better mousetraps?

The reality is that our knowledge enterprise poses no threat to us and demands nothing much from us. To be really interested in being as ontology rather than methodology requires us to openly reckon with all the forces and performances that shape our own being. There are always historical forces that shape what we believe and value. To be committed to understanding being is to be committed to understanding our own humanity or lack thereof. It is also to be committed to questioning the legitimacy of the forces and performances that shape our being. In this case of Heidegger, this would have involved, amongst other things, looking at the origins of his own definition of knowledge. Why is knowing the essence of things important? Where did this motive come from? This is by no means an exercise in self-discovery. This is a matter of recognizing the forces that locate and situate us in the world, and how these forces define what we experience and value. In short, this is a process of discovering how our own humanity is shaped by the humanity of others. We are never outside of history. Yet there is always the possibility of being outside of history by merely finding the courage and resolve to be so.

There is value in knowing the world's truths. But how did we come to this knowledge enterprise? What about how we came to this enterprise shapes the doing and valuing of the enterprise? What about our ways of being in the world make us amenable to this enterprise? On the other hand, what other enterprises are our current ways of being impeding that could potentially be much more heuristic? Which of our beliefs, fears, assumptions, and norms are obstructing our capacity to be vulnerable to other enterprises? What about our ways of being impede our ability to imagine new enterprises? What is most striking about the enterprise of knowledge is the lack of imagination. It is all about repetition and regurgitation. The enterprise discourages imagination. We are always looking to the past for direction and legitimacy. Do our processes align with those set down by Plato, Aristotle, and Socrates, and follow the tradition of Kant, Hegel, Hume, Heidegger, Wittgenstein, Foucault, and company? Subordination is status quo. But what is the value of any enterprise that encourages subordination and discourages imagination? What is the value of any enterprise that encourages conformity, predictability, and ultimately, mediocrity? How could any knowledge that emerges from such an enterprise be valuable? Where would the audacity and diversity come from that would be necessary to challenge our knowledge claims and even the integrity of the enterprise? Conversely, what is the value of any enterprise that undermines such scrutiny, and what enterprise can evolve and mature without diversity? Put differently, what is the value of any enterprise that undermines our capacity to look at the world anew? What kind of human beings does such an enterprise produce, and ultimately, what kind of society does such an enterprise cultivate? Evidently, a society that is hostile to diversity and persons who lack the audacity to ask bold questions. In sum, what results is a society that reduces us to cowards by reducing education to instruction—a set of curriculum processes that promise to equip us with knowledge and expertise that will make us productive citizens.

There are various ways we measure progress. We measure progress by how much knowledge we are acquiring and stockpiling. We therefore assume that our superior stockpiles of knowledge reflect a superior culture. We also measure progress by our investment and commitment to produce this vast stockpile of knowledge. No other civilization can boast a comparable amount of colleges, universities, and research institutions. We also measure progress by our commitment to propagate and disseminate our vast stockpiles of knowledge. We believe that it is important that people go to college and acquire all manner of education. This process will supposedly make for a civilized society as education will civilize the savage and crude mind. We therefore believe that an elaborate education system is the hallmark of a superior culture. But at the core of our elaborate education infrastructure is a knowledge enterprise that is hostile to diversity. Such an infrastructure is born out of a deep hostility to diversity and all that is necessary to cultivate diversity. In fact, there is no institution that is more vital to sustaining the status quo than the modern university. Although the modern university is assumed to be a place of learning, hardly any occurs. The modern university encourages subordination by requiring students to submit obediently to a complex set of arbitrary curriculum processes that mistake instruction for education. Only for the cowardly sake of graduating and acquiring a diploma that promises financial security and upward mobility will most obediently submit. But there is no learning that can occur through such cowardly submission.

How instruction came to displace education can be found in how we define and experience. We experience knowledge as a commodity, something we can accumulate, manipulate, and exchange. We believe that through reading and studying we will acquire knowledge and cultivate our minds. For us, knowledge is a cognitive activity. We process knowledge the way a bank processes currency. But only the coward succeeds in our education system. For only the coward is willing to submit to arbitrary processes that require no courage, no risking of life, no responsibility. Only the coward is willing to sacrifice liberty for security, and only the coward is gullible enough to believe that knowledge involves no courage, no fortitude, no resolve. Thus, as unsurpassed numbers of us commit to producing and acquiring knowledge, and colleges and universities increasingly offer all kinds of arbitrary and unnecessary specializations and programs, the world faces increasing peril. With all our vast stockpiles of knowledge and elaborate knowledge infrastructure, there is no compelling case to be made that we are morally superior or becoming so. Our claims of progress are also much in doubt as our supposed progress is responsible for unsurpassed ecological destruction. There is also no case to be made that our knowledge enterprise will eventually solve these coming catastrophes and bring prosperity. Yet this enterprise continues to proliferate as developing nations aspire to achieve progress and prosperity by adopting it. There is no pause about how this enterprise will obliterate indigenous epistemologies and thereby lessen the world's knowledge diversity. But, again, this is only the beginning of the story. What about the cowardice and mediocrity this knowledge enterprise promotes? What about its inability to promote knowledge diversity? What about its neocolonizing proclivity by having us look to Plato, Aristotle, Socrates, Kant, Hegel, Hume, Foucault, Wittgenstein, Derrida, Heidegger, Popper, and company for scholarly direction and legitimacy? What about the enormous cost and investment this knowledge enterprise requires and places on developing nations? What about how this enterprise corrupts what education means and involves?

DEFINING EDUCATION

Education is a moral and spiritual undertaking. Education involves fostering the courage and resolve and fortitude to examine openly and honestly the origins of all the forces and performances that constitute our humanity and identity. It is a process of becoming and unfolding. We will never identify all of the forces that constitute our humanity as our complexity, mystery, and ambiguity is infinite. What matters is how much courage and fortitude and resolve we are capable of bringing to the activity. The courage and resolve and fortitude will fundamentally enlarge how we define, perceive, and experience the world, each other, and even ourselves. This is the inherent threat that education poses to the status quo. It is always insurgent. As we acquire the courage and fortitude and resolve to be vulnerable, our relation to the world changes. We will perceive no divide between us and the world. We will recognize our separation from the world and each other as an illusion. To look at our own humanity openly and honestly is to look at the world truthfully and courageously. So yes, truth is important. But truth cannot be imposed on us as there are always forces that shape and determine what we perceive and are willing to perceive. What we perceive is also inseparable from what we believe. Education recognizes this inseparable and inviolable relationship. But what we believe or choose to believe comes from somewhere or some experience. Education is about trying to find where and why. Why do we believe what we believe? Why do certain beliefs seduce us rather than others? How does what we believe shape what we perceive? How does what we believe impede other ways of perceiving the world? The goal of education is illumination, but illumination always fosters action.

We engage the world by finding the courage and resolve and fortitude to engage how we shape and perceive each other.

When we look at education in terms of courage, fortitude, and resolve, our definition of knowledge changes. We no longer believe that our redemption resides in our capacity to acquire and stockpile knowledge. We also no longer believe that we can separate what we believe from what we perceive. Knowledge becomes politicized and historicized. We also no longer believe that we can consume and manipulate knowledge like a commodity, nor assume that we have no responsibility for what consequences come from our knowledge. In other words, we no longer assume that the enterprise of knowledge is outside of history and culture. We can value all kinds of knowledges. We can even value the supposed absence of knowledges, and things other than knowledge. For instance, as much as we can value knowing the essence of things, we can also value the capacity to love, to hope, to be compassionate, to be merciful, to be patient. We in no way believe that our perception primordially resides in only knowing the essence of things. We believe that there is knowledge that comes from loving, forgiving, empathizing, and sharing. There is nothing deficient about this knowledge. It is merely a different knowledge. The world lends for all kinds of knowledges as no ecological frame is the same. Every frame requires a different knowledge. The knowledge that Eskimos need to survive and flourish is different to what Aborigines need. It would be in every way wrong to try to impose the knowledge of one on the other.

This in no way means that one cannot learn anything from the other. It merely means that frames matter. Without frames, knowledge diversity would be impossible. Frames reflect our interpretive facility. We can shape and determine what things mean. The challenge of education is to understand what forces and experiences shape and determine what things mean to us. Thus, as much as education begins with us, education never ends with us. Through education we eventually come to realize that our humanity is intertwined with the humanity of others, and the environs we share and co-create with others. This recognition, and the coming to this recognition, does something to us. It alters our view of ourselves, each other, and the world. But most importantly, education enlarges our responsibility to the world and each other by exposing our connection to the world and each other. In this way, education is always morally enlarging and morally demanding. In changing our perception of things, education changes our responsibility to things. Indeed, education assumes that our lack of responsibility for the affairs of the world and each other is what is ultimately responsible for our increasing peril.

But we continue to believe that the crisis of humanity is a crisis of knowledge. By acquiring and disseminating knowledge we will supposedly save ourselves from ourselves. In this narrative, the primary function of education is to help us effectively acquire and disseminate as much knowledge as is humanly possible. We assume that by acquiring knowledge we will act rationally and consequently, less impulsively. Education cultivates order. It presumably saves us from chaos. This is supposedly the moral function of education. We point to our own supposed high levels of civilization as proof that our focus on acquiring and stockpiling knowledge works. But when did the world ever suffer from a lack of knowledge, and who amongst would have us assume that the world only lends for only one kind of knowledge, and this is the knowledge the world now needs?

Every knowledge enterprise contains a moral vision—a vision of how the world is and could be. To acquire the theories, methodologies, and pedagogies of a knowledge enterprise is also to acquire the moral vision that the knowledge enterprise contains. For instance, the theories, methodologies, and pedagogies of fishing also mean that there is value in fishing. On the other hand, the value of fishing relegitimizes the knowledge enterprise that makes for our knowledge of fishing. This is how epistemologies perpetuate themselves. What this reality also means is that different epistemologies tend to value different things. This is why the epistemologies of the Eskimos are different to that of the Aborigines. Both epistemologies have different moral visions. But this in no way means that both epistemologies are morally comparable or that there is no basis to critique a knowledge enterprise. What this means is that the business of learning theories and methodologies is also about acquiring a moral vision. What this also means is that for natives and indigenous peoples, the business of learning the theories and methodologies of other peoples is always potentially colonizing.

To take on a moral vision is to acquire a set of ambitions and expectations. By shaping how we define, acquire, and experience knowledge, every knowledge enterprise confines us to only that knowledge which serves its moral vision. We will therefore value and aspire for only that knowledge which serves the moral vision. The success of our knowledge enterprise results from our ability to make believe that our theories and methodologies are devoid of ideology, and thereby our knowledge is also devoid of ideology and bias. This in turn allows us to believe that our knowledge is objectively describing the world. But of course our knowledge enterprise does nothing of the sort. Our theories and methodologies are actually perpetuating a certain moral vision. Still, the illusion persists that our knowledge is objectively and accurately describing the world. What explains the success of this illusion? What does this illusion do for us? In fact, how did this illusion come to be? Arguably, the illusion begins in our separation from the world, the primordial illusion. This separation allows us to assume or believe that we are capable of describing a world that is outside of us. It also allows us to shift the focus away from us, or to assume such is the case. But as there is no real separation between the world and us, our knowledge and lack thereof is always speaking to us. Every description of the world is about us and our relation to the world. When we believe we are describing the world we are actually describing how we perceive the world, and the many forces and experiences that shape how we perceive the world. Just as much as we can perceive the world as outside and separate from us, just as much we are capable of perceiving no divide between the world and us. But to do so requires a different moral constitution. We must be ready to be responsible for all the world, meaning that to perceive the world as inside of us and us inside the world is to perceive the world with care and love. However, to perceive the world as separate and outside from us requires a constitution that reflects an obsession and fixation with selfhood. There is only concern for self. As much as this constitutes a distorted view of being human, what really hurts us is the lack of concern and care that comes with our way of perceiving the world. What emerges is a knowledge that is devoid of any concern and care for the world—a knowledge that naturally makes for all kind of death and destruction. Yet we continue to believe that nothing is inherently wrong with our knowledge enterprise. We are merely describing what the world is. The problem is presumably with how we use this knowledge, as science is supposedly devoid of any bias or prejudice. We are presumably devoid of any responsibility for how the world is. But our knowledge is at fault. This knowledge is by no means inevitable. After all, this knowledge begins on an illusion—that the world is outside and separate from us. This will always be an illusion. What is real is that the knowledge that is born of this illusion will continue to make for all manner of misery, and ultimately, for our demise.

What will determine our prosperity is our courage to love. Yes, to love. Love requires the most courage, the most resolve, the most fortitude. This is the challenge of education, and what education inevitably does by exposing our responsibility for the world and each other. Love constitutes the highest obligation. It demands the most from us, including the most risk, the most vulnerability. But this is also how love enlarges our humanity and fundamentally alters our perception of the world and each other. No amount of reading and studying can do either. This is also why our knowledge enterprise poses no threat to the status quo. Education involves doing, and ultimately trying to do the impossible, such as loving those who seem most different to us. Only such doing promises the most understanding and knowing. As such, the measure of knowledge is the ability to love.

Besides the mediocrity and apathy, what is also striking is the lack of imagination in our knowledge enterprise. There is no asking of bold questions. There is no desire to reimagine the world. But this is what happens in a closed system. This is what happens when a system is determined to keep us beholden to the past for fear of fermenting chaos and anarchy. This is what happens when we lack the courage and resolve to engage the world openly and honestly. Education becomes merely another means of sustaining the status quo. Regurgitation and repetition make for curriculums that allow for no brilliance and excellence. What can being human mean without the courage and resolve to imagine the world anew? But such is the order of things. The traditions that guide and legitimize our knowledge enterprise undermine imagination. The focus is on consumption rather than imagination. Ultimately, our aim is to produce a knowledge that is reliable and capable of creating and sustaining order—a knowledge that will appease what we believe. But what is the value of any enterprise or knowledge that is only capable of serving what we already believe? How could any such enterprise claim to be serving the cause of knowledge? What is the promise of a society that values and propagates this enterprise? What also is the promise of an enterprise that is always turning us inward and towards the past? It can be found in what is increasingly unfolding before us—unparalleled ecological destruction, the increasing threat of nuclear armageddon, and escalating misery and social isolation. Of course many challenge this description. But what seems without much doubt is that no other civilization has brought the world to the brink of destruction. How did such a possibility now become a reality? It is by no means inevitable. The holocaust is of our own doing. We are in no way close to recognizing, much less owning the ecological axiom that all life is intertwined, and as such, what harms one life harms all life.

It is the most obvious of axioms, but also the most profound. What about this observation is so difficult to make? Why does it continue to elude us? The answer can be found in that inseparable relation between what we perceive and believe. We are either unready or unwilling to believe that all of life is intertwined. This belief requires courage, for to be of this belief forces us, besides changing how we perceive the world, to change how we behave and relate to each other and the world. It fundamentally changes our ethics, politics, and economics. It in every way enlarges our being, pushing us to own responsibility for the condition of the world and the well-being of each other. Thus, though the axiom is obvious, the implications and consequences are profound. It speaks to the fact that the crisis of humanity is by no means a crisis of knowledge. It is a crisis of imagination.

14

ON LAW

How did we come to believe that human beings need to make law and impose law on each other in order to achieve civility and prosperity? How did we come to this moral vision? It is by no means obvious that our obsession with making and imposing laws makes us increasingly civil and decent. Slavery, Jim Crow, apartheid, and the Holocaust were all legal. In fact, hardly is there a case of evil that had no legal cover. Of course proponents of the status quo will claim that these legal abominations are merely examples of bad laws. Eventually, the system self-corrected. But what of all the good laws, such as those that protect person and property, or those that protect our liberty and rights? What also about those international laws that control the conduct of war and relations between nations of unequal power and resources?

But are our laws really achieving all of those things? Do laws protect our person, property, and liberty? That is, are our laws affording progress and civilization by taming our supposed savage instincts and impulses?

Would anarchy ensue if there were no laws? What about law enforcement? How would law enforcement be possible without laws? Who would ensure law and order, and how? What about the courts? Who would dispense justice, and how? How would civilization be possible without laws? No doubt, the idea of a community being civil, decent, and prosperous without laws seems unfathomable. But why is such the case when again, there is no obvious correlation between the rise of laws and our achieving civility and prosperity? Why does this belief in the civilizing nature of law have such a hold on us? From where did this belief arise that we are devoid of any natural capacity to live peacefully and productively without laws and the threat of retribution?

So let us fathom the unfathomable. Actually, laws impede our social evolution by undermining our responsibility for each other's well-being. Yes, laws make us less human by diminishing our responsibility and obligation to each other. Our redemption resides within this responsibility and obligation. But achieving this responsibility and obligation is our most difficult challenge. It requires the most courage, the most resolve, the most fortitude. Laws release us of this challenge, and in the process ultimately do us no favors. However, laws fundamentally distort our notions of decency and civility.

Civility is generally defined in terms of being law-abiding. But what is decent about upholding laws that support slavery, Jim Crow, and other such evils? What is also decent about upholding laws that criminalize the use of natural herbs and plants? In fact, when one is determined to be law-abiding, how does one distinguish just laws from unjust laws, and thereby which ones to obey and disobey? What calculus must one use? Also, how could any person be decent while being unwilling to oppose or undermine any law that is unjust? Yet to be willing to do so is most often considered indecent. This is what Washington, Adams, Jefferson, Madison, and others did. This is also what John Brown and Sojourner Truth did. This is what Martin Luther King, Jr. did. In fact, this is what Jesus Christ did. So on one hand, we encourage people to be law-abiding for the sake of achieving order, but on the other, we have no way of reliably determining which laws to obey and disobey. How then can being law-abiding be inherently a good thing? It would seem that there is more virtue in doing otherwise.

But always looming is that fear of anarchy. How can we possibly encourage people to do as Jesus Christ did, or Sojourner Truth did, or Martin Luther King, Jr. did, without fermenting anarchy? We can do so by enlarging our capacity and constitution for empathy, compassion, forgiveness, and mercy. Only by enlarging our obligation and responsibility for each other will justice emerge. Thus, laws have nothing to do with justice. The purpose of laws is merely to achieve order, meaning that order is assumed to absent without laws. But this is a false order, for how can forcing persons to submit to unjust laws be just? How can punishing persons for violating unjust laws be just? That is, how can punishing persons for being like Jesus Christ be just? To be law-abiding requires no resolve, no fortitude, no courage. It is the domain of the coward. But this is also why laws create a false order. Only cowards can be law-abiding. Only those without empathy and compassion can be law-abiding. Only those who have no deep obligation and responsibility for each other can be law-abiding. Only those who lack the courage to dissent can be law-abiding. Indeed, only those who are unwilling to die can be law-abiding. This again is why laws create a false order. To be law-abiding requires us to be willing and ready to squash dissent. We too must be ready to put Jesus Christ on the cross. We must be adverse to different ways of being, different ways of understanding, and different ways of interpreting what is just from what is unjust. To be law-abiding requires an aversion to diversity. We must assume that conformity, besides being good, is necessary. It supposedly saves us from the ravages of anarchy and disunity. This again is why the order that laws create is false and contrary to the rhythms of the natural world.

The natural world, as seen in any forest, river, ocean, and so forth, achieves order by promoting diversity. Through diversity the natural world evolves and flourishes. There is no order without diversity. Diversity pushes naturally occurring ecologies to look at the world anew. It also challenges every ecology to develop new abilities and capacities. This is also how diversity makes an ecology resilient and sturdy. It allows an ecology to adapt and even exploit changing conditions and environs. It even allows an ecology to neutralize emerging threats and challenges. Without diversity, an ecology perishes. But this is also why the natural world is devoid of our kinds of laws. The natural world achieves order by cultivating mutuality, symbiocity, and community. These processes allow order to emerge organically from within an ecology, meaning that within every ecology there is always a potentiality and capacity for order. But this order is fundamentally different to our order. This is an unfolding and changing order that lends for flexibility, spontaneity, and diversity. Its mission is ultimately to promote life. That there is always a proclivity for order means that there is no contest between order and chaos. Order is achieved by promoting diversity rather than ending chaos. There is always chaos, always randomness. Order in no way means the end of chaos, or seeks to end chaos. Instead, order is always fluid, always in motion. There is no final order—that is, no order that seeks or promises to end chaos. Order is always open to new expressions, new interpretations. It is never finished, or pretending to be so. It is also never trying to end confusions and disruptions. Sometimes revolutions are necessary to attain order. The natural world achieves order by increasing the intensity and density of mutuality, symbiocity, and community. There is neither isolation nor separation. Every life form becomes increasingly dependent and obligated to each other's well-being.

Yet we remain determined to use laws to end chaos. Besides our obsession with laws, there is our obsession with rules, regulations, and requirements. Chaos will find no protection from us. But what does it mean to be of this obsession to find laws, regulations, rules, and requirements that will end chaos? What does it mean to be of a humanity that is shaped by this war against chaos? It means a dependency on bureaucracy and hierarchy. We are increasingly devoid of any capacity to function independently, courageously, creatively, and imaginatively. We cannot find our way without bureaucracy and hierarchy. We have neither the will nor the imagination to do so. We are in every way paralyzed. We are laden with fear and tortured by all kinds of psychoses and neuroses. Such is what happens when human beings have no capacity to function deliberately and courageously. We are at the mercy of life's rapids and currents. There is only reaction and desperation, misery and despair. Our only recourse is to look cowardly to laws, rules, and regulations for security and direction. We are too afraid to look to each other, as doing so requires resolve and fortitude because human beings are enormously complex and no less difficult and ambiguous. Laws, rules, and regulations save us from this complexity, ambiguity, and most of all, our actions and lack thereof. We merely have to follow, submit, obey. The result is always misery and death. But of course such misery and death is never our fault, never our doing. We were merely, as always, following and obeying orders, enforcing the rules, abiding and upholding the laws.

Human beings need complexity, difficulty, ambiguity, and accountability. We have to be constantly challenged to look and experience the world anew. This is how we acquire the resolve and fortitude that is vital to engage the world deliberately and imaginatively. This is also how we develop the constitution to deal with life's confusions, frustrations, and tribulations. But most of all, this is how we enlarge how we perceive, experience, and define the world. There is an integral relation between being and perceiving. As much as our bodies shape our minds, our ways of being shape our ways of perceiving the world. Before we can change how we perceive the world, we have to be ready to change our ways of being in the world. But this, again, is where laws harm what being human means.

Laws limit our modes of being to that which involves no risk, no audacity, no imagination. As with any bureaucracy, laws restrict us to only those modes of being that pose no threat to the order of things. There shall be no exploration, no disruption, and definitely no innovation. However, in severely limiting our modes of being, laws ultimately retard our experiences of being. As with any bureaucracy, laws strip us of everything that makes us human. All that remains is a way of being that can only follow, submit, and obey—that is, one that is paralyzed by fear and laden with all manner of anxiety. What remains is us, and our increasing isolation.

This is what happens when being becomes a closed system. Such a system is destined to become self-destructive. When human beings are constantly challenged to look and experience the world anew, being becomes an open system. It is open to new experiences, new interpretations, new observations. Bureaucracy reduces us to beasts by denying us the environs and practices that are vital to making us human. Such is the threat that bureaucracy poses to what being human means. But such is also why bureaucracy will continue to seduce us. Devoid of any capacity to live courageously, passionately, and creatively, all that remains is for us to follow, submit, and obey. In sum, all that remains is our perception that bureaucracy and hierarchy are necessary and even natural. Such is how our ways of being affect our ways of perceiving. But such is also the challenge that comes with ending our obsession with rules, laws, and regulations. We have to discover how to promote methods of being that make for new ways of perceiving the world. Without being able to do so, we will continue to assume that this is a world where rules, regulations, and laws are necessary.

15

ON MIND & BODY

As seen in Shaun Gallagher's *How The Mind Shapes The Body* and George Lakoff and Mark Johnson's *Philosophy In The Flesh*, academe now seems ready to admit that one of the central tenets of western philosophy is false. There is no separation between mind and body. Of course most indigenous and native peoples have long known this. For sure, Black folks always knew this. Indeed, every oral culture knows this. Only for us in the west does this constitute a ground-breaking observation. But what does this reality now mean for the way we have long defined, experienced, acquired, shared, valued, and appraised knowledge? What now becomes the purchase of any knowledge that was born of the belief that there is a divide between mind and body? What also is the value of any knowledge that deliberately sought to have nothing do with the body? Yet such is the knowledge that now rules the world. Such also is the knowledge that is increasingly displacing indigenous knowledge systems, and shaping how emerging nations define and achieve prosperity. But as always, let us begin at the beginning.

How did we ever come to believe that there was a divide between mind and body? What made us seducible to this belief? Or, how did this belief come to seduce us? On the other hand, what does it mean to engage the world in ways that try to erase the body or simply assume an absence of the body? What kind of knowledge emerges from this experience? Arguably, what emerges is a knowledge devoid of any imagination and all else that makes us human. It is within the body that the soul resides, the heart beats, the spirit dwells. To assume a divide between mind and body is to cultivate a notion of mind that is devoid of all the forces that dwell within the body, and also averse to these notions. What emerges is a shallow conception of mind. Such a mind lacks the elasticity and complexity to appreciate the world's infinite ambiguity, mystery, and complexity. In fact, what emerges is a mind that produces a knowledge that assumes no such ambiguity, mystery, and complexity. What emerges is a knowledge that is no less shallow than the mind from which it comes. But again, such is the knowledge that is increasingly ruling the world. Such is also the knowledge that is increasingly displacing all of the world's different knowledges. Moreover, such is the knowledge that continues to shape our understanding of us, each other, and the world.

What is the nature or promise of any mind or knowledge that assumes a mind/body divide? How could any knowledge born of this mind escape being perverse? But now such perversity pervades everything. After all, how could any knowledge that continues to make for so much misery, death, and peril be anything other than perverse? How could any mind that is responsible for creating this kind of knowledge be anything other than perverse? We will need a new mind before we can have a new knowledge. More than merely assuming no divide between mind and body, we need a mind that actually embraces the body, including all the complexity, mystery, and ambiguity that comes with the body. Only such a mind will finally end the suspicion and perversion that continues to surround the body. That is, only such a mind will finally get us beyond the torment of being ashamed of the body, being repulsed by the body, being tortured by the body.

We have long been determined to construct a better body—one that is less corruptible and susceptible to life's ravages. But without this divide between mind and body, racism, heterosexism, ethnocentrism, and sexism would be impossible. These things come from the perversion that comes from this divide. This is why these things are inherently perverse. The perversions that make for so much misery, death, and peril begin in the divide between mind and body.

For us, the body is hell. It is the source of all our temptations, seductions, confusions, and perversions. For us, the body is always conspiring against the mind. It is always trying to have us act impulsively and promiscuously rather than rationally and responsibly. For us, there can be no reasoning with the body. The body must be regulated, controlled, monitored, and disciplined. This is supposedly the only way to achieve progress and prosperity. We must have a hegemony of the mind, which means creating institutions, structures, and arrangements that will mentor and develop a rational mind—that is, institutions that will allow us to develop a mind that will rule authoritatively and completely over the body. This, as history seems to make plain, continues to be our quest. This conflict between mind and body is found in many different cultures, religions, and peoples. It seems to be a defining human struggle, and why a knowledge that comes out of this divide is capable of seducing so many different peoples. But the supposed conflict also hardens and reinforces the belief that the body threatens our prosperity. Increasing our regulation and suppression of the body becomes necessary. As this belief hardens, our regulation of the body expands. The result is a distorted, mutilated, and tortured body—one that is devoid of any imagination, conviction, and passion. This body is devoid of any capacity to act deliberately, courageously, and imaginatively. It is constantly afraid and laden with all manner of fear, anxiety, and paranoia. It can only act by being coerced, manipulated, and threatened. Without hierarchy, this body can supposedly do nothing. It can sustain no kind of bold moral action.

But the mind also suffers when the body is suppressed. As the separation between mind and body hardens, the mind narrows. It loses the ability to grasp the world in all its complexity and totality. It reduces the world to abstractions, models, and diagrams. This mind feels nothing, or at least feels nothing intensely. It perceives the world in terms of input, output, and throughput. The world is a problem to be solved. It is reducible, manipulable, and quantifiable. For this mind, numbers are preferred as mathematics supposedly allows us to speak decisively to a world that is inherently quantifiable, and thereby seemingly devoid of any profound ambiguity, mystery, and complexity. This is a mind that wants to be shaped by mathematical forces and concepts. It is constantly striving to impose a mathematical and seemingly rational order on the world.

Eventually the illusion becomes reality. We begin to assume that the world actually lends for a mathematical order. Such is what has long been going on with this mind. This mind can only process and absorb. It can neither imagine nor innovate. This is a subservient mind. This is the mind that treats education as a process of acquiring and learning information. This is also the mind that believes that the expansion of mind happens by exposing persons to increasing volumes of information. Suffice to say, this mind believes that the process capacity of mind can be reduced to a number. It is quantifiable. It is presumably like the rest of the world, merely waiting on us to attach a number and thereby a value. Yes, for this mind, numbers describe and evaluate. This is how this mind makes sense of what being human means. For this mind, mathematics is value-free. It is presumably devoid of any bias or prejudice. Mathematics is objective, beyond human subjectivity. The reality of addition, subtraction, division, and multiplication is presumably true for all peoples, all cultures, all civilizations. Thus mathematics must be capturing a world that is outside of human forces. What emerges is a belief that any culture that commands mathematics is inherently superior to those without mathematics. That our mind is supposedly responsible for the most advanced system of mathematics is therefore seen by us as the defining measure of our cultural and civilizational superiority. Through mathematics we have presumably found the natural order of the world, thereby achieving a pure and pristine knowledge. Now all that is left for us to do is to submit to the will of this knowledge. Paul Dirac, a Nobel Laureate for physics, once said (echoing Galileo), "that mathematics is the language that nature speaks. When expressed in mathematical equations, the laws of quantum mechanics are clear and unambiguous. Confusion arises from misguided attempts to translate the laws from mathematics to human language. Human language describes the world of everyday life, and lacks the concepts that could describe quantum processes accurately."

But mathematics is merely another interpretive system, laden with all manner of human subjectivity. As much as our version of mathematics in the west is born out of the belief that there is a divide between mind and body, the body is always present. It is always intruding and shaping the affairs of mind. Mind and body are always bound up with each other. There is always interpretation, always imagination, or lack thereof. Mathematics merely gives us the illusion that there is no body. But every description is an act of interpretation. Or, as Lakoff and Johnson would claim, mind is metaphorical. Every description comes out of a metaphor. So yes, multiplication, addition, subtraction, and division do seem to stand outside of space and time, but such processes are merely another interpretation of the world. There is always the possibility of other interpretations as the body possesses a boundless capacity for interpretation and imagination. That mathematics is true in no way means that everything else is false. Behind every epistemology is a moral vision—a vision of how the world is and should be. Mathematics is also bound to this reality.

Mathematics is of an epistemology that believes that the world is quantifiable, and that this is a good thing. However, even if this is true, it in no way means that other moral visions are false. But this is what happens when the body is suppressed. Hegemonism, racism, and ethnocentrism become inevitable. We lose sight of our own biases, prejudices, and all else that shape our view of the world. Through our moral visions the body is most present, which again reminds us that the body is always bound up with the mind. It also reminds us that moral visions matter. What we can imagine will shape what we perceive, experience, and value. Before we can change what we perceive as knowledge, we have to be ready to change what we are capable of imagining as knowledge, and experiencing and embodying as knowledge. So the expansion of mind is really about the expansion of the body. Such again is the problem that comes with the hegemonism that surrounds our epistemology. In suppressing the body, our current dominant epistemology—and by that our current methodologies, pedagogies, and theories—encourages no imagination. After all, if our epistemology is already revealing the world's natural order, what can imagination do?

In being determined to separate mind from body, our epistemology discourages imagination. This is most evident in educational systems that stress regurgitation, repetition, and consumption. It all reflects our determination to suppress and control the body. But this is also how our epistemology becomes self-fulfilling. Our own lack of imagination has us believing that our vision of the world is the only viable vision. Without imagination, what other visions are possible? So again, racism, hegemonism, and ethnocentrism become inevitable. The suppression of the body eventually makes for our own oppression as our own epistemology binds us to one way of understanding the world, and ultimately one reality of the world. Moreover, the fact that this epistemology shapes the organization of our society, including our systems of politics, economics, and justice, means that this epistemology shapes everything. It also means that our own lack of imagination and innovation pervades everything.

Our own racism, hegemonisn, and ethnocentrism runs deep. We have no qualms about imposing our vision of the world on others, for behind our determination to do so is our belief that our intentions are good and noble. We are merely bringing prosperity to the backward by sharing our epistemology and institutions. We take offense of being seen as imperialists as we supposedly have no ambitions of acquiring lands and resources and conquering peoples. We are, again, merely interested in sharing our knowledge and resources. But this is still colonization. This is still a process of lessening the world's diversity. This is still a process of coercion, manipulation, and domination, for no indigenous or native peoples possess the means to resist our epistemology. Our epistemology arrives in all kinds of forms, all kinds of forces, all kinds of conditions, all kinds of justifications, all kinds of institutions. It never awaits an invitation.

16

ON DISPOSABILITY

It was inevitable. With goods and services becoming increasingly disposable, with the planet becoming disposable, with nations becoming disposable as manufacturers pick up and leave at a moment's notice, with labor becoming disposable as machines replace human beings, with relationships becoming disposable, the disposability of human beings was all but certain. It was also necessary, presumably. After all, in a disposable world, what else is there to do with us? But what becomes of a world where human beings are disposable? What does it mean to experience ourselves as disposable? What does it mean to experience each other as disposable?

Disposability means many different things. It means apathy. We have no concern for each other's well-being. We are either unwilling to care for each other's well-being or simply afraid to do so. Either way, your well-being means nothing to us, as does anything that demands much from us. Disposability also means that we lack the resiliency and muscularity to care for each other's well-being. We lack the courage and resolve to do so. We are therefore incapable of being committed to each other. We are disposable. Disposability also means distrust, suspicion, and fear. We are afraid to find out what being human means. That our own humanity could be bound up with the humanity of others is terrifying. So we choose to believe and need to believe that we have no deep commitment to each other.

Disposability is a matter of survival, of calculation, of weighing risks and rewards. I need to perceive you as disposable, as being committed to you presents too many risks and comes with too much obligation. That is, too many risks to be hurt, to be taken advantage of, to be duped, to be betrayed. Disposability is about self-preservation. I need to believe that my humanity is separate from yours. In this way, disposability is about alienation. It is about being incapable of recognizing our humanity in each other. Disposability is also about believing that I am disposable. I am undeserving or devoid of any need for love, compassion, and generosity. I merely need to have my desires pleased and my urges relieved. It then becomes a matter of figuring out the costs to do so. In a disposable world, everything is purchasable, everything has a price. It becomes merely a matter of determining the price. Thus in a disposable world, markets are vital. Through markets desires are pleased and urges relieved. In a disposable world, nothing is sacred. Everything has a price and everyone is for sale.

In a disposable society being human means nothing. We are merely bundles of needs, desires, and urges. Our well-being means nothing to each other. Indeed, disposability is about trash. It is about us treating each other as trash, as garbage. But of course it is really about us treating ourselves as trash, as garbage. Disposability is about us sanitizing and legitimizing this reality. What else to make of our moral acceptance of the incarceration of so many persons for non-violent offenses? How did so many human beings become so disposable? How did we come to have no qualms of disposing of so many human beings? But in a disposable society, this is what happens. We develop all kinds of means to justify our disposing of each other. We become, to use Pink Floyd's words, comfortably numb. We feel nothing, or at least nothing deeply that could encumber our need to move on. There is no ambition to live honestly, transparently, and courageously. We desire merely to purchase, consume, and dispose. Nothing means anything, and everything means nothing. Yes, this is what happens in a disposable society. This is what happens when human beings become disposable. Living is reduced to existing. There is no compassion in a disposable world. Compassion requires us to feel something. We must be willing to become attached and involved. But a disposable society cannot afford such attachments and involvements. These things make disposability difficult. In other words, these things make life difficult. These things bring complexity, and the promise of a disposable society is the absence of complexity, including relational complexity. In fact, the hallmark of a disposable society is simplicity and the ability to quickly and efficiently satisfy our desires, needs, and urges. What emerges is a promiscuous society. In a world of disposability, promiscuity is the order of things. We hook-up rather than have relationships. Promiscuity is what evolves when human beings are disposable, or when the goal is to use each other as means to satisfy our desires, needs, and urges, or when selfless attachments are seen as annoyances and hindrances.

But what of the other ways we legitimize this disposability and promiscuity? Apparently, being promiscuous is merely being true to our animality. Promiscuity allows us to keep our mating options open. It allows us to escape being weighed down by all kinds of arbitrary obligations. It also allows us to escape all kinds of unnecessary complexities and ambiguities. Simply put, promiscuity is supposedly rational. It constitutes evolutionary necessity. This, again, is our way of rationalizing promiscuity and convincing ourselves that disposability is natural and even necessary.

17

ON DIVERSITY

The fact that nearly every opportunity, reward, or privilege is determined by our score on a ubiquitous standardized test means this is still a society that believes deeply in human inequality. However, we also claim to value diversity, embrace diversity, celebrate diversity. But these positions are irreconcilable. How and why should we value peoples who are supposedly inherently inferior to us? Yet we have been able to convince ourselves that there is no contradiction between these beliefs and values. So, as these standardized tests continue to play an integral role in ordering and structuring our society, we continue to profess how much we value diversity and aspire to achieve a society that celebrates our differences. We seem to experience no schism over this conflict. How is this possible?

It begins with our depoliticizing of diversity, reducing diversity to a noun, an object. This means reducing diversity to race, ethnicity, sexuality, gender, nationality, disability, and so on. It also involves separating diversity from justice. We do this by defining diversity in terms of inclusion, accommodation, assimilation, and toleration. This kind of inclusion also depoliticizes diversity. It requires that diversity pose no threat to the order of things. It must already be assimilable, accommodable, tolerable. For instance, there can be no challenge to our belief in human inequality. In fact, there can be no challenges to any of our core beliefs and values, and neither will any opportunity be given for this to occur. In other words, there can be no challenge to the integrity of the institutions, structures, and arrangements that constitute the status quo. There must be no threat of revolution. But we still profess to value diversity, embrace diversity, celebrate diversity. Why even bother? Why the need to pretend? Deception, dishonesty, and deceit play an integral role in allowing us to avoid the tension and conflict between diversity and inequality.

The status quo reflects our own lack of courage to be honest. Lack of authenticity is the order of our lives. Nothing is really what it seems or pretends to be. Words mean nothing. Language means nothing. In fact, even the truth means nothing. It is all about illusions, fabrications, and distortions—refusing or simply lacking the courage to be honest with ourselves and each other. Deception shapes everything. What kind of world could come from so much dishonesty and lack of authenticity? What becomes of truth, integrity, and character in such a world?

What constitutes our valuing of diversity, embracing of diversity, celebrating of diversity, is merely an expression of us trying to limit, control, and bring order to a world that is assumed to be without any. Such a world, in demanding nothing from us, poses no threat to us. Indeed, such a world undermines authenticity. It requires no courage, no resolve, no fortitude. Yet without these things, the ability to experience the world in new and imaginative ways become impossible. That is, without these things, diversity becomes impossible. So authenticity is vital to diversity. But this is also why diversity always poses a threat to the order of things. Diversity, in being a hallmark of authenticity, should always be a threat to the illusions, fabrications, and deceptions that mask our complicity in perpetuating systems that safeguard our privileges and views of things. If anything, diversity should challenge us to be honest and open. It should also challenge us to look honestly and openly at our fears, beliefs, values, and all the other forces that shape how we perceive and situate ourselves and each other. Besides awakening us, diversity should always torment us. It should heighten our experiencing of ourselves and each other by at least pushing us to reckon with all of each other. Moreover, diversity should promote vulnerability. It should challenge us to be vulnerable, thereby pushing us to reveal all of our frustrations, confusions, and tribulations. Through diversity we should come to recognize our common humanity and all the struggles we share by simply being first and foremost human beings. In this way, through diversity equity should emerge. Equity begins with us recognizing our humanity in each other. It also comes from us recognizing the implications and consequences of our actions and lack thereof on each other. But most of all, equity comes from us being less afraid of each other. Indeed, diversity should make us less afraid of each other. It should lessen the threat of our differences, and heal us from the ravages of our own mystification and alienation by pushing us to live honestly, courageously, and openly.

The fact that what now constitutes diversity is achieving none of these things, and even conspiring against these things, reflects how fundamentally corrupt is our supposed valuing, embracing, and celebrating of diversity. Lack of authenticity is status quo. But what else to make of the rise of speech codes and other punitive efforts to restrict language? How is authenticity possible without the capacity to share ourselves openly and honestly, and with conviction and passion? What is the possibility of democracy and diversity without the ability to express ourselves without fear of retribution? Of course we are to believe from those who profess to value to diversity that speech codes are necessary to end offensive speech and hate speech. But there is no such thing as hate speech. Meaning resides within us. Human beings shape and determine what words, language, and symbols mean. What is offensive speech to one person can be something entirely different to another person. This is what diversity means. We experience the world differently. To deny this reality is to promote stereotyping. But why should the interpretation of a few apply to the rest of us? Yes, race, gender, ethnicity, sexuality, nationality, and disability should matter in any discussion of diversity as there are laws, codes, and customs that punitively target certain orientations. But diversity also resides in our different rationalities, sensibilities, spiritualities, modalities, and histories, all of which shape and influence how we engage and relate to language.

We need to note the increasing lack of authenticity as we value, embrace, and celebrate diversity. We are increasingly isolated and shut off from each other, and tortured by all kinds of neuroses and psychoses. Our increasing fear of each other is really about our increasing fear of ourselves. But this is what the end of diversity means. Our inability to be honest with each other is about our inability to be honest with ourselves. The crisis of diversity will always be a crisis of authenticity. But note that I am in no way defining authenticity in terms of expressing our true self. There is no such self. There is therefore no kind of identity that completely separates us from each other. Identity is something that happens between us. It is relational rather than individual. Our obsession with identity is most interesting, as identity means nothing. It constitutes a distorted understanding of what being human means. Our obsession with identity is merely another way we try to lessen the world's ambiguity, complexity, and mystery. Identity will always be synonymous with boxes. Yet any attempt to box us distorts our complexity, masks our relationality, and, ultimately, diminishes our diversity. Our diversity is always unfolding, evolving, and changing. It is always in motion. Even those who fanatically try to hold onto identity as something fixed and constant must eventually come to terms with this reality.

But to whom does identity matter most? What is the purchase of reifying diversity? How did identity become integral in our valuing, embracing, and celebrating of diversity? There is a claim that diversity advocates use identity to steer us away from inequality. Again, my own position is that identity is merely another way we try to lessen the world's ambiguity, complexity, and mystery. It is also another way of trying to bring order to a world is assumed to be devoid of any. Identity is what happens when we are incapable of recognizing our humanity in each other. Of course we are to believe that diversity is about valuing, embracing, and celebrating our different identities. But this is how our multicultural project reminds us that it really wants nothing to do with diversity. For what does it mean to value, embrace, and celebrate something that actually diminishes our diversity by masking of all the complexity, ambiguity, and mystery that make us different?

This world will always be laden with diversity, and the world will go as diversity goes. Those who struggle to limit the world's diversity only put themselves in peril. In other words, our diversity problem has nothing to do with identity. It even has nothing to do with diversity. Yes, there is a determination to devalue the contributions and even the humanity of Other peoples and cultures. This hostility and determination to lessen our diversity reflects a worldview that is committed to ending the world's complexity and ambiguity. Without bringing an end to this worldview, all of the world's diversity will remain in peril. But ultimately, all of the world will remain in peril. We will only realize a world that is abundant with diversity when we arrive at a worldview that, besides allowing us to recognize ourselves in each other, allows us to recognize ourselves in the world.

18

ON BLASPHEMY

What is this business of blasphemy, this business of maiming and murdering in the name of God, this business of using violence to keep us beholden to a God of vengeance, this business of using God to justify hate, this business of using God to justify our own willingness to maim and murder? What kind of God would have us believe that violence and vengeance have a righteous place in the world or in serving any God? How could any God that claims to be of love and mercy speak of the righteousness of violence and vengeance?

What about those of us who find blasphemy to be an abomination to God? What about those of us who actually believe in a God of love, compassion, mercy, and forgiveness? In our God there is no place for violence and vengeance, no justification to hurt, maim, and kill. Our God is beyond blasphemy. There is no fear in our relation to God, especially no fear of retribution in the name of God. Our relation is born purely out of love. We choose to love God because love is the highest expression of being human. Through love we realize that creation is an act of love. We are born out of love, and our redemption resides in love. We therefore believe in a God that is beyond human comprehension. A God of love is always evolving, changing, and unfolding. Submission has no place in such a God. Human beings have no capacity to offend such a God, and neither does any such God need mortals to protect what is inherently sacred. What is sacred will always be eternal. We are by no means the be-all and end-all of God's love. All of the world, all of the planets, all of the stars are born out of God's love. Behind charges of blasphemy is always a petty and petulant God. This is a God that is born out of small minds, small hearts, small souls. This God will always be devoid of beauty and imagination. This is what blasphemy means, a lack of moral imagination. No mortal can ever offend a magnificent God, a God that is born out of large minds, large hearts, large souls. This will always be a God that will push the limits of our imagination. This will always be a God that demands the best from us. Any coward, any fool can main and kill. Submission requires nothing from us. It is the refuge of the coward. But love, compassion, mercy, selflessness, and forgiveness require everything from us. These practices push us to the limits. Only the extraordinary person can love in the face of hate, be selfless in the face of selfishness, and believe in peace in the face of war. Only an extraordinary person will know God's love and mercy. Submission will never allow us to know such a God. But submission, in requiring nothing from us, will always seduce and threaten us.

There are those warn about a coming religious conflict between peoples of different religions. Many also point to the fact that religion seems to be increasingly fueling many of the world's wars and conflicts. We are supposedly on the brink of religious armageddon. To avoid such peril, there is a call to rid the world of religion, or at least get religion out of the public sphere. Presumably, religion encourages hate and ignorance, and in so doing, will always be a threat to reason, science, and civility. But there is no coming religious armageddon. What continues to torture us and probably make for our demise is the increasing influence of peoples who lack the courage and resolve to love. Yes, many religions are culpable in this state of affairs. But many religions also nurture our capacity to love. It was religion that gave us John Brown, Martin Luther King, and Harriett Tubman. We therefore cannot blame religion for the entire state of affairs, and neither will ridding the world of religion save us from ourselves. To believe this illusion is to have no regard for history. It involves no less ignorance than what many religions require.

History vividly shows that our cruelties and miseries come from our inability to love completely. We never had a problem of knowledge, that is, a lack of knowledge about the value of love. All of the world's great scriptures lend for interpretations that promote the need to love. Yet to believe that knowledge will save us from the ravages of ignorance also shows no regard for history. It was never a lack of knowledge that was responsible for the Holocaust, or slavery, or Jim Crow, or apartheid, or the gulags, or the rape of Nanking, or our plundering of the planet's natural resources. No amount of knowledge will save us now. The peril that the world faces is by no means a problem of knowledge. Yes, knowledge matters, but what matters most is that we find the courage and resolve to love completely. Our redemption resides in us realizing a world that was conceived in love. If we are incapable of finding our way to this love, our demise is all but certain. But this would be merely our doing, our responsibility. No God of love wants this for us. In being born out of love, this love is already with us. By realizing this love we help with the world's completion. Therefore through love we come to union and communion with God. So love is an action, an orientation, a way of praying, and worshipping.

We only come to union and communion with God by loving each other completely and absolutely. By coming to union and communion with each other we come to union and communion with God. Love is merely the means we realize this communion and union. But the crisis of humanity is the crisis of union and communion. It is separation and fragmentation that threaten us and put us in peril. When I claim that the Bible or the Koran states that the wages of blasphemy is death, this is an expression of separation and fragmentation. It says that God is outside and separate from us. It says that our understanding and relation to God is determined by an object (a book) that is separate and outside of us. It says that our understanding of God is dependent on us having access to the object. No Bible, no God. No Koran, no God. But what kind of magnificent God would choose to reside in an object rather than in our minds, our hearts, our souls, or even in the oceans and forests? What to make of those peoples who never had access to a Bible or a Koran or a Gita? Did God forsake these peoples? But what kind of God would do so, and especially so many peoples? How could any God that is willing to forsake so many peoples for simply never possessing a book be worthy of our love?

But what does it mean to say that a certain book is a book of God? Why would any God want to be in the book business? In fact, why does God, like any ordinary device, need a manual? Any God that is supposed to be magnificent must surely know that language is promiscuous. Meanings are always changing. No language can hold meaning constant. This is why religious diversity is inevitable. Of course every denomination claims to know exactly what the language means, and is even ready to maim and kill to defend these meanings. This is the origin of blasphemy. Blasphemy requires us to believe that our religion or denomination knows exactly and precisely the meaning of the language in these books. That is, blasphemy requires us to dismiss the harsh reality that human beings are fundamentally interpretive beings. In this way, blasphemy requires us to be fools, to have no regards for theory or reality. Blasphemy also requires us to suppress—or at least try to suppress—an integral component of our humanity, and even a blessing from God. Our interpretive capacity makes diversity possible. There would also be no possibility of love without this capacity. It is because of this capacity we have the ability to use language as a paint brush rather than allow language to use us as a canvas.

Without this capacity, agency would be impossible. But what is the value of any love without agency? How could any great God deny us agency, or even threaten to punish us for exercising agency? Such is the problem that confounds blasphemy. Blasphemy wants us to submit obediently to God. But this God is a product of interpretation, an act of imagination, or lack thereof. There is simply no conception of God that is outside and separate of us. Blasphemy is really about us wanting others to submit obediently to our—and only our—interpretation of God. It is about our determination to even maim and kill to achieve this goal. So what is blasphemy? It is about us wanting to end the world's diversity, ambiguity, and mystery out of the belief that diversity invites chaos. It is about homogenizing the world. It is also about believing that domination, coercion, and the threat of retribution are necessary to achieve order that is presumably without any. The goal of blasphemy is to stop chaos. This is why hierarchy is presumably necessary. Blasphemy is merely another way of trying to limit the world's diversity. It is another way of perpetuating the belief that this is a world devoid of order. Apparently, our purpose is to bring order to the world. But how could any world born out of love have no order? What also about us being made in the image and likeness of God? If order requires coercion, submission, and even the threat of retribution, what does this reveal about God? Is God too without order? Does God too need coercion?

There is much beauty in the fact that God resides in our interpretation and imagination. It means that our conception of God comes from within us. It comes from our minds, our hearts, our souls. No institution can deny us our conception of God. It also means that no conception of God is complete and absolute. Our conception of God can change, evolve, and mature. It also means that every conception of God is an act of imagination, or lack thereof. We are obligated to look honestly and seriously at every conception of God. To profess to have an absolute and complete conception of God is really about us reducing God to our image and likeness. It is about us pretending to be gods of our own. For how great would be any God that could be completely reduced to human understanding? Can an ant comprehend what being human means? What also of language? Blasphemy would have us believe that through language we can acquire an absolute and complete understanding of God. But again, how great would be any God that could be fully captured by language? This is the kind of hubris that blasphemy requires. There is no humility, no doubt, no faith. There is only fanaticism, dogmatism, and absolutism—everything that comes with the religious fundamentalism that is always threatening retribution for blasphemy, and also the fundamentalism that continues to be responsible for so much misery in the world. What kind of God would sanction any kind of behavior that puts us at each other's throats? That our conception of God will never be complete or absolute in no ways means that every conception of God is morally equal, or that every conception of God should be encouraged. It merely means that every conception deserves compassion.

19

ON REDEMPTION

We are of a world where the unknown will always exceed the known. This is what being human means. We are always in the presence of the unknown. We are always in the presence of God. To be human is to be God. We are never separate or outside of God, and neither is God ever separate and outside of us. God is always in our presence. So again, what is God? God dwells within the unknown, and is the sum of all the possibilities that reside within the unknown. Although we will always be in the presence of God, and will never be forsaken by God, we will never know all of God. The unknown will always exceed the known, meaning that we will never command the world's ambiguity and mystery. This also means that we will never realize all that is possible.

We will never have a conception of God that is devoid of doubt, and therefore require no faith. Doubt is inevitable. But doubt is also heuristic. Without doubt, faith would be impossible. We would have no choice but to submit and obey. Without doubt, diversity would be impossible. There would be no possibility to look and experience the world anew. Without doubt, meaning would be impossible. We would have no way to shape the world. On the other hand, to look at God in terms of the unknown is to recognize the need for humility. To appreciate being in the presence of the unknown involves being humble to the unknown. It also involves grace, as in our need to be generous in our understanding of each other. To be in the presence of the unknown also means releasing ourselves of the need for certainty and absolutes. Our knowledge of events and each other will always be incomplete. To be in the presence of God is about learning how to be in the presence of God.

However, to say that God resides in the unknown is by no means to suggest that the realm of the unknown is separate from the realm of the known. There is no such divide. There is only tension. Each defines the other. Each enriches the other. What we perceive as the realm of the known is always laden with ambiguity. Even our most famous and rigorous calculations are laden with ambiguity. There are always assumptions, omissions, and distortions. On the other hand, without the realm of the unknown, meaning would be impossible. We would, again, have no way of shaping the world. So both realms complement each other. The fact that ambiguity is infinite means that meaning is also infinite. God lends for understanding, but no understanding will be complete or absolute. However, pursuing such understandings only cultivates various illusions and perversions. That the unknown is unconquerable means that God will always be with us, of us, and beyond us.

Faith is about being between the realm of the known and unknown. It is about releasing ourselves from the supposed conflict between meaning and ambiguity, ending our obsession to rid meaning of ambiguity. These things pull us away from God. But to do so is really to pull us away from each other. For what is the origin of the conflict between ambiguity and meaning, faith and reason, flesh and mind, order and chaos? It is about being of a world that comes with an unrelenting ambiguity. It is about being thrown into this world. But regardless of our determination to end ambiguity, God will always be with us as the world's ambiguity will always be beyond our full grasp. There is always the possibility for a new relation to God. This is what makes us spiritual beings. We are compelled to have a relation to the unknown, and thereby must always exercise faith and belief.

It becomes a matter of what will be the nature of this relationship. Will this relationship be of fear, suspicion, and distrust? That is, what conception of God awaits us and will nurture us and shape our view of the world? No culture is devoid of a conception of God. But every conception serves us differently. Many serve us ill by promoting separation, division, and fragmentation. But there is always a conception of God that is bearing down on us. It becomes a matter of determining which conception is the most heuristic. It is of course nearly impossible to rid ourselves of a conception of God that our community gives us, as these conceptions tend to shape everything. There is also the difficulty of openly accessing and exploring other conceptions. But this current moment in history is different. We can now look at the consequences and implications that attend to different conceptions. We can also compare the value of different conceptions, and even propose new ones without fear of retribution.

What is uniquely heuristic about viewing God in terms of the unknown is the fostering of an ethos that keeps our hands off each other's throats. It undermines the possibility of war and violent conflict. In a world that remains tortured by war, this is no doubt important. But there is also the need to make sense of the world and even our own existence. We all have our tribulations, confusions, and desperations. Every conception of God will so often abandon us. Such is simply the reality of being of a world that lends for no certainty. Every conception of God has stitches and patches. To abandon any conception of God is difficult, even when a lot of stitching and patching is necessary. After all, many of us simply cannot fathom an entirely different conception of God. But as our world unfolds, many of our conceptions are buckling. The world now seems to be demanding much more expansive conceptions of God. Without such conceptions, there is hardly a chance of all this ending well.

We have always had compelling conceptions of God. The notion of God being of the unknown can be found in many religious interpretations. It is by no means a new revelation. But this is the conception of God that now seems the most expansive and constructive. That both the unknown and the known reside within each other means that there is no set conception of God. We can never completely define God. Any conception of God will be laden with ambiguity. There is always the possibility for even a completely new understanding of God. It also means that no institution has any moral authority to limit the possibility of new conceptions of God. To do so is to limit our evolution and also our imagination of God. That our conception of God will change and evolve as we change and evolve means that God resides in our evolution and that of the world. As life unfolds, God unfolds. So to be in the presence of God means to be always in the presence of possibility, such as the possibility of a new meaning, a new revelation, a new relationship, a new understanding. It is within possibility resides the boundless power of God. That the world's unknown is infinite means that possibility is infinite. To appreciate being in the presence of God requires us to be of discursive, communicative, and performative practices that promote rather than limit possibility. This is what being holy means. That which is sacred is that which promotes possibility and thereby enlarges our experiencing, understanding, and realizing of God. Indeed, to be committed to possibility is to be committed to life. As possibility emerges, life evolves, and as life blossoms, possibility flourishes. Possibility is the antithesis of death. So determining whether an action or position is holy and sacred merely requires us asking whether the action or position emancipates possibility. This is what makes blasphemy unholy. This is also what makes retribution unholy. These actions undermine possibility, and in so doing impede our experiencing of God.

But this is also why love, mercy, compassion, and forgiveness are holy. These actions promote possibility. These actions assume that through possibility redemption is always possible. Redemption can only be taken seriously by believing that an infinite God is ultimately a God of infinite possibility. Any action or position that impedes possibility is therefore an affront to any God that is of infinite ambiguity.

A God of the unknown also gives us a life politics. It gives us a calculus to determine what kinds of actions and positions we should be encouraging and pursuing. A life politics opposes any kind of coercion and retribution that purely aims to limit possibility. Yes, sometimes coercion is necessary to stop certain human beings from harming other human beings, but this will often be necessary to promote life and possibility. So as regards to determining which position or decision is most productive, the matter comes down to determining which action or decision promotes the possibility within the given context. In other words, which action or decision enlarges our experiencing of God? The crisis the world faces is actually a crisis of God, specifically our continuing inability to enlarge our conception of God. To enlarge our experiencing of God requires us to realize a new way of being human.

We are no doubt capable of realizing this possibility. But this is going to require enormous courage and resolve. However, what of the misery and peril that await us by perpetuating the status quo? All of our misery and death is purely of our own doing. No God wants this for us, especially any conception of God that wishes to be taken seriously. Our increasing perilous condition is the result of no heavenly retribution. That death now consumes us is about our doing. But how did we become so averse to life? How did we become so estranged from God? How could any religion sanction maiming and killing in the name of God? But again, how did we become so estranged from God when God is always in our presence? How did violence and vengeance become morally acceptable? What matters now is how do we embrace God's presence? It begins with us dismantling structures and ending practices that impede possibility, such as those that impede our ability to imagine and experience the world anew. It also begins in fostering discursive, communicative, and performative practices that enlarge our experiencing of God in our lives, each other, and in the world. The goal is to maintain a robust tension between meaning and ambiguity so that our meanings never remain bound to the past, and accordingly, keep us bound to the past. To look at God in terms of the unknown is to recognize the need to maintain a communication gesture that allows God to unfold before us and through us.

Communication is fundamentally of God as meaning is always laden with ambiguity. Ambiguity catalyzes meaning. Without ambiguity, meaning is impossible, even our meaning of God. So without ambiguity, without meaning, any conception of God is impossible. Communication is always speaking and reflecting a relation to God. Thus definitions of communication that view ambiguity as a threat to communication diminish our experiencing and understanding of God. To say such definitions are status quo means that such definitions have us assuming that communication has nothing to do with God. It is merely a tool of evolutionary necessity that makes for superior kinds of coordination. But communication has absolutely everything to do with God. Only through communication we can imagine God, relate to God, experience God.

20

ON ACADEME

What happens when you realize that academe has nothing to do with knowledge and your own pursuit of knowledge is all about your own cowardice? What also happens when you realize that academe is against knowledge and you also really want nothing to do with knowledge? What also happens when you realize that academe is merely another apparatus to maintain order and social control? Further, what happens you realize that academe is the most insidious and dangerous of all these disciplinary apparatuses? There are the arbitrary curriculums that dictate to us what is a discipline, and what constitutes the knowledge and expertise that define that discipline. Then there are the gods, the saints, and the disciples that define the discipline and shape the discourses, that is, those who define and legitimize the knowledge that shapes the discipline. Then there are always the theories and methodologies that define a discipline and influence what knowledge adherents to that discipline will pursue and validate as knowledge. But of all of this, including taking the compulsory courses that define a discipline, is only a miniscule way academe serves the status quo. It all begins with the elaborate infrastructure we use to define, value, and acquire knowledge.

Theories and methodologies are the sine qua non of academe. These are presumably the devices that allow us to generate and accumulate knowledge. We are to believe that theories illuminate, thereby allowing us to make sense of things, such as revealing the relationships that constitute things. We compare theories by how much illumination each theory provides. We use the language of power to compare theories. With methodologies we use the language of reliability and validity. Our methodologies must be able to reliably acquire what we define as knowledge. We then bring our theories to bear on what our methodologies have found. Our goal is to make sense of the knowledge and also to determine the value of the knowledge. On the other hand, theories will determine what methodologies we use to acquire knowledge, where we use these methodologies, and upon whom. There is really no divide between theories and methodologies. But either way, academe is about achieving proficiency in the ways we pursue, accumulate, and validate knowledge. Such proficiency supposedly reflects our ability to add to our knowledge of the world. This is what academics do, and is the mission of academe—to proficiently produce people who can generate knowledge, evaluate knowledge, and determine what knowledge our society needs.

But what happens when we begin to ask who gets to determine what knowledge our society needs? What, again, happens when we begin to realize that academe has nothing to do with knowledge? As Kuhn once said, "No part of the aim of normal science is to call forth new sorts of phenomena; indeed those that will not fit the box are often not seen at all. Nor do scientists normally aim to invent new theories, and they are often intolerant of those invented by others. Instead, normal-scientific research is directed to the articulation of those phenomena and theories that the paradigm already supplies" (p. 24). How is this hostility to knowledge possible when academe makes so much of being committed to pursuing knowledge, regardless of what any knowledge means? What also of the value of any enterprise that is hostile to the asking of new questions? Why do we continue to promote and encourage such enterprises?

The reality is that we are of a worldview that fears the world's ambiguity, mystery, and complexity. We therefore value stability, safety, security, predictability, and homogeneity. We desire order, or at least an order that is derived by suppressing the world's proclivity for chaos. Ultimately the goal of our worldview is to impose order on the world. Thus every institution values and promotes conformity. For instance, Wilhelm Reich, who many view as one of the most important psychologists of the last century, claims that the only goal of marriage is to promote conformity by ending sexual curiosity and exploration. However, suppressing such exploration retards our intellectual imagination and ability to rebel. Indeed, the ability to pursue new questions does require courage, such as the courage to face the world alone, and also a vibrant moral imagination. But nowhere is our lack of imagination more evident than how we use theories and methodologies to acquire knowledge.

We define theory as a device that allows us to make sense of things. But theories also define the world we will make sense of. For instance, symbolic interaction theory allows us to make sense of how human beings use symbols to navigate the world. The theory assumes that human beings are inherently a symbol-using, symbol-consuming, and symbol-misusing species. Theories are only capable of describing what is already being assumed. The ability to derive any knowledge that is contrary to the status quo is all but impossible. Our theories therefore pose no threat to the order of things. But this is only because of how we continue to define and engage theory, and our own lack of courage to define theory in more expansive ways. We no doubt have the capacity to define and engage theories in ways that allow us to imagine new worlds. But such theories can only come from a place of courage, and academe conspires in every way against such a place. The reality is that academe constitutes the most dangerous and insidious apparatus that serves the aims of our worldview. By being given the authority and responsibility for the generation of knowledge, the evaluation of knowledge, and the dissemination of knowledge, academe preserves the social, political, and cultural order. Most importantly, by discouraging and even blocking the rise of new knowledge, academe saves us from the courage that is vital to fully engage the world's ambiguity. Herein resides our own complicity in perpetuating the status quo in academe. Academe masks our own lack of courage. It allows us to make believe that this world requires no courage, no resolve, no fortitude. We can instead allow ourselves to believe that we are achieving progress and pushing back the forces of ambiguity and chaos. It is this illusion, or the propping up of this illusion, that ultimately matters. This is also what the university does better than any other institution. Our increasing volumes of books and papers would have us believe that our knowledge of the world is expanding, and in so doing, our ability to control our fates. We are, again, supposedly achieving progress. We are snatching meaning from ambiguity and conquering the world's proclivity for chaos. But what happens when all of these illusions begin to implode? What must academics do? In fact, what can academics do when our illusions begin to collapse before us?

21

ON COMMUNICATION

The story of communication begins in evolution. Supposedly, communication evolved out of evolutionary necessity. It supposedly grew out of our evolutionary need to achieve complex levels of organization and coordination, so as to accomplish various complex tasks that were necessary for our survival. Thus communication is commonly cast as a tool of necessity. Without communication, organization is impossible, and without organization, evolution ends. But this story underestimates the inseparable relation between communication and being human. No doubt, communication facilitates organization and coordination. However, communication also saves us from isolation. For human beings and probably all life forms, isolation is death. It implodes our humanity. It dehumanizes us. Without communication, being human would be impossible. So as much as the origin of communication is probably biological, there is also a moral, existential, and spiritual dimension to this story. That communication allows us to be human means that communication shapes our world and situates us in relation to this world. Communication is a world-making, human-making activity. Through communication we become human.

In fact, communication has nothing much to do with communication. Yes, through communication human beings exchange messages and even create and share messages. But this constitutes a narrow understanding of communication, and a no less shallow way of experiencing communication. Again, such an understanding begins on the belief that communication is a tool of necessity and that human beings are fundamentally survival machines. How could isolation be possibly a concern or threat to survival machines who are purely concerned with surviving, and are biologically obligated to do any kind of scheming to do so? Moreover, to look at communication in terms of a process that is fundamentally about the exchanging and sharing of messages is to assume a divide between humans. This is how we arrive at the distinction between sender and receiver, encoder and decoder. Communication supposedly bridges the divide by allowing us to move messages between sender and receiver.

Of course, the goal is to move messages effectively and efficiently from one point to the next. This involves conquering confusion or ridding communication of confusion. This is why slide presentation technology was born. It is another example of us trying to bring order and meaning on the world and ourselves. But as always, what emerges is a war upon ourselves as confusion is seen as arising from within us. Our understanding of communication by no means merely puts meaning in conflict with ambiguity. It also puts us in conflict with ourselves by assuming that our own supposed confusion is a threat to communication, and a threat to everything that springs from communication. Thus our endless anxiety about never being able to command our thoughts and emotions, and never being able to express ourselves clearly, concisely, and coherently. We are always apologizing for our confusion, for failing to find the supposedly correct words and phrases to express our thoughts and emotions. After all, the goal is clarity. We expect persons to express themselves clearly and effectively. This is a measure of character and strength. But this is an impossible task as no language is capable of capturing or commanding our complexity, or even that of the world.

We are asking language to do something that is simply impossible. Languages are open systems. This is why languages are always changing and evolving. Languages are inherently promiscuous. To force language to capture and command our complexity is to disfigure language. We rob language of its elasticity, spontaneity, plurality, and promiscuity. We also rob language of its natural proclivity to explore and take on new meanings, meaning that we block language from evolving and maturing. By treating language as a closed system, we deprive language of its vitality. We destroy language. We reduce language to a set of signs, symbols, and rules that merely allow us to convey our meanings to each other. Yet when we do this we also destroy the democratic and pluralistic impulse that is at the core of language. In being inherently promiscuous, language is always taking on different meanings. We can never know exactly what language means. Meanings are always in flux. There is always the possibility for a new meaning. We should therefore never assume to know what language means. We must probe, explore, investigate, and even doing this promises no resolution. For again, meaning is always shifting, moving, and changing.

This is where the democratic and pluralistic impulse of language originates. This is also how the promiscuous nature of language promotes a democratic and pluralistic sensibility. This is also how language vitalizes us. To endeavor to suppress this promiscuity, for fear that this promiscuity will impede the possibility of communication and the rise of a civil society, is to make for the beginnings of autocracy, bureaucracy, and totalitarianism. This promiscuity poses no threat to communication. In fact, this promiscuity enlivens and catalyzes communication. A democratic and pluralistic sensibility pushes us to be vulnerable to each other's meanings, including what we are trying to mean, hoping to mean, and even incapable of meaning. Language has nothing much to do with communication. What really matters is our capacity to be vulnerable to each other, and to each other's confusions, frustrations, and tribulations. Out of this vulnerability we recognize our humanity in each other. Thus, communication has nothing much to do with communication. Communication is about our ability to recognize our humanity in each other, and how deeply and completely we can do so. Even language diversity poses no threat to communication. Communication problems are fundamentally problems of vulnerability, specifically the lack thereof, and such problems are ideological, epistemological, and moral in nature.

The promotion of vulnerability involves releasing ourselves of the fear that this is a world devoid of order, and that human beings have no natural capacity to peacefully coexist. It also involves believing that the negation of communication is chaos. But this is by no means true. The negation of communication is separation, fragmentation, and ultimately, aggression. There is no divide between human beings. We become what others allow us to become. However, the fact that my humanity is bound up with your humanity means that there is always something that is shared. There is always something that we can recognize in each other that lessens the threat of our differences. Empathy is always possible. But how much we recognize in each other is about how much we are capable and willing to recognize in ourselves. Also, how much we are willing to recognize in each other will shape how much we are willing to recognize in ourselves. Therefore how much we come to recognize in ourselves is inseparable from much we recognize in others. The fact that we continue to be of an ethics and politics that assume that we can recognize nothing in each other as a result of us being of different worlds is merely about our own unwillingness to recognize ourselves in each other. Regardless of our differences, our humanity will always reside in each other, and thereby there is always something that we can recognize in each other. To believe otherwise is an illusion. But to continue to believe so also means increasingly divorcing and estranging ourselves from each other. It rips us from each other, tearing us into pieces. To recognize ourselves in each other requires us to enlarge our humanity so as to draw the humanity of others into our humanity. It is never simply a process of recognizing or sharing. It is about opening ourselves to each other, which involves releasing ourselves of the beliefs, fears, and suspicions that separate us. It is also about finding the courage, resolve, and fortitude to be completely vulnerable to each other.

But our obsession with lessening and suppressing language's promiscuity and elasticity and plurality also disfigures us. In addition to undermining our own coming to a democratic and pluralistic sensibility, such suppression distorts our own conception of personhood. We are simply too magnificent to be bound by any language. Identity is impossible. Indeed, any attempt to use language to produce any kind of coherent identity only fosters illusions.

Every language reflects a way of perceiving and experiencing the world. As Alphonso Lingis reminds us, languages contain images. Languages are by no means merely a collection of signs, symbols, and rules. Languages come with ideologies and epistemologies. To be of a language is to be of the ideology and epistemology that come with that language. Language is much more than merely a process of speaking and writing. It constitutes a way of being. This means that language cuts both ways. Language gives us a way to describe the world, and also a vision of that world. This is why languages have power. But this in no way means that the limit of language is the limit of our world. As much power as language possesses, it can never match our power as any power that language possesses is ultimately our power. That language now possesses enormous power is purely of our doing. Language possesses this power because we believe that the world is devoid of order. We have put language in the service of our struggle to bring order to this world. We expect language to help push back the forces of chaos and impose order on the world and ourselves. This task involved first and foremost bringing order to language, which meant developing an elaborate system of grammar, syntax, and rules. The task also involved developing institutions to disseminate and institutionalize all of these rules so that language use—either in writing or speaking—would be orderly. In the process of doing all of this we also propagate the belief—and fear—that without these rules communication would be impossible and anarchy would reign. As such, the proliferation of these institutions engenders the belief that this is a world devoid of order and that to use language competently constitutes an effective means of combating chaos, including, of course, the supposed chaos within us. But this is only one story of colonialism.

The most insidious way we use language to achieve order is by making believe that language can capture and convey the complexity of our realities. This allows us to view language as a reliable means of conveying our experiences. For instance, to announce that I am heterosexual is also to announce my belief that we can organize our sexuality, such as separating our spirituality from our sexuality, and that doing so is important. The announcement constitutes a way of bringing order to my personhood and also describing my world. Again, every language comes with an ideology and epistemology. But the language of sexuality, as well as the language of ethnicity, nationality, and so forth is purely arbitrary. Such language is born purely of the need to bring a certain conception of order to ourselves and the world. Yet to invoke the language of sexuality, or ethnicity, or nationality, or any such language, is to impose a certain sensibility, rationality, and performativity on ourselves. Of course, all languages order the world in different ways. But to believe that any language can capture and convey the complexity of our humanity requires us to deny this complexity. We are to believe we are categorizable, and thereby truly capable of distinguishing friend from foe. Therefore any attempt to use language to capture our boundless complexity reduces and disfigures our humanity, which in turn divides us and puts us at each other's throats.

A world laden with intractable conflict is by no means inevitable. We can save ourselves from such a world. Theoretically, at least, a different world is within our capacity. But the possibility of such a world begins in us fundamentally changing our relation to language, which of course involves changing our relation to the world and ourselves. The challenge is to emancipate language from ideologies and epistemologies that disfigure it and ultimately disfigure us. We must also emancipate language from communication. Language is merely a dimension of communication, by no means the sine qua non of communication. However, to release language from communication is the only way to explore the limits of communication. If all life forms are of the same well of life, why is communication seemingly impossible between us and plants, us and other animals, us and the oceans? Why is communication also seemingly impossible between peoples of different time and space? Theoretically, at least, such communication should be in no way impossible. But besides being completely open to even a different conception of communication, such communication is going to involve surrendering ourselves to the world's rhythms. We will have to allow communication and language to just flow, and flow, and flow. But this will involve achieving deep levels of vulnerability and allowing life to unfold on its own terms and rhythms. We will have to achieve a newfound faith in the world and ourselves. Without such faith, vulnerability is impossible. Also, without faith, trust is impossible. But for now the possibility of communication between us and other life forms is secondary. What matters is that vulnerability saves us from ourselves. It naturally changes our relation to language, as in releasing us of the fear that suppressing language's promiscuity is good and even necessary for communication. Deep levels of vulnerability impede the disfiguring of language, and our own disfiguring. Thus the value of vulnerability cannot be overstated in understanding the human experience.

22

ON COLONIALISM

The *post* in postcolonialism and postcolonial theory is misleading. The *post* is supposed to mean that this is a period after colonialism or is different to colonialism. We are now supposed to be studying and theorizing about the impact of colonialism on locals and indigenous peoples. The *post* in postcolonialism is about the literatures, practices, and institutions that are emerging after colonialism. It is also about the struggles that come with cultivating these literatures, practices, and institutions. The *neo* in neocolonialism is also misleading. The neo is supposed to mean new kinds of colonialisms. These kinds of colonialisms are supposed to be much more discursive and invasive. The *neo* in neocolonialism is therefore supposed to be about the rise of a much more dangerous and insidious kind of colonialisms.

But this was always the goal of colonialism. It always sought to be fully discursive and invasive. The goal was to achieve a social and ideological order that was complete and absolute. Any threat of rebellion would be impossible. This is also how society would be most efficient. By being fully discursive and invasive, there would be no need for the elites of wealth and power to expend resources to manage tensions and frictions. The locals would discipline and police each other.

But there is neither postcolonialism nor neocolonialism. There is only colonialism, and will only ever be colonialism. Colonialism is merely changing, adapting, and morphing. What colonialism needs most is our complicity, and in most cases, colonialism has always had this. It was our own beliefs in human separation that made colonialism possible. This in no way discounts the fact that colonialism often came at the end of a gun, or the brutality involved in achieving colonialism. But many natives and indigenous peoples have long been enslaving, brutalizing, and pillaging other peoples. For what would have been the possibility of slavery in the new world without slavery in Africa? The history of colonialism is old. It predates and exceeds the European world. This was merely one expression of colonialism. Nearly every civilization has a version of colonialism, each as bloody as the other.

Colonialism is about coercively imposing our worldview on others, and the employment of all manner of devices and practices to do so. It is inherently monologic, undemocratic, ethnocentric, and narcissistic. This is what makes colonialism so dangerous. Its goal is to homogenize and eradicate difference, which means removing or neutralizing anything that can challenge us to look and experience the world anew. At the core of colonialism is something that is fundamentally human, our aversion of difference. This is in no way the sum of colonialism. But colonialism heightens, legitimizes, and institutionalizes our aversion to that which is different. Colonialism aims to keep us bound to the past by blocking the evolution of new truths, new meanings, and new experiences that exceed our vision of the world. This can be amply seen in what is now commonly referred to in academe as development economics, which aims to identify economic policies and programs that can help developing nations achieve prosperity. Development economists use a variety of methodologies to measure the effectiveness of different programs and policies. The goal is to use these results to help policymakers and donors effectively allocate and distribute resources. Naturally, this field of economics is a product of scholars who believe that our modern methodologies and technologies can be used to bring prosperity to the world's poor. These economists also tend to have monetary backing of donor organizations that also have the most noble of intentions, helping the world's poor escape poverty and despair.

But development economics is colonialism. It also constitutes the most insidious kind of colonialism. In development economics, the focus is on the world's poor, specifically the economics of the world's poor. Its most famous adherents run "field experiments that measure different ways to save the world." But the world in question is really the world's poor, especially those found in supposedly developing nations. How did the world's poor from supposedly developed nations become deserving of this kind of scholarly attention by economists? That is, how did the world's poor become to be seen as being devoid of the capabilities and epistemologies to lift themselves out of poverty and despair? The problem with development economics is theory. According to Esther Duflo, the Abdul Latif Jameel Professor of Poverty Alleviation and Development Economics in the Department of Economics at MIT, and a founder and director of the Jameel Poverty Action Lab (J-PAL), a center "devoted to fighting poverty by ensuring that poverty policy is based on scientific evidence," economics "is about behavior, rational and less rational. And about how behavior responds to the environment, and how we can shape the environment to get people to act differently, and whether it's good for them. Very quickly, when you start evaluating programs, you get into these kinds of issues." But who determines what behaviors are rational, and which ones are less so? In other words, within development economics resides a vision of the world that includes a definition of development, and how that development should be achieved. The goal is to bring this model of development to the world's poor. In the case of development economics, development is fundamentally about economics, and prosperity is fundamentally about economic prosperity. Development is supposedly observable, measurable, and quantifiable. It constitutes another triumph of science. As Duflo asserts, development economics "takes the guess-work out of policy-making."

The goal of development economics is to help poor peoples in developing nations become rational, to make and support only those programs that have been statistically proven to work. Thus development economics is committed to improving the efficiency of markets. On the other hand, development economics assumes that what plagues the world's poor is a lack of rationality—the making of poor decisions that often compound other less rational decisions. According Rachel Glennerster, executive director of the Abdul Latif Jameel Poverty Action Lab, "You're not just learning about what this particular program does in this particular place but understanding human behavior better. For example: Why do people not do the things that are good for them? Why do people not invest in preventative health? That's an incredibly important conundrum for saving the world." Development economics assumes that developed nations have no such rational behavior problems. After all, the object of study is the world's poor. But besides markets, rationality also resides in the methodologies that form development economics. For Esther Duflo, there must be data: "There is a lot of noise in the world. And there is a lot of idiosyncrasy. But there are also regularities and phenomena. And what the data is going to be able to do—if there's enough of it—is uncover, in the mess and the noise of the world, some lines of music that actually have harmony. It's there, somewhere." In short, with enough data, science will eventually identify what is rational. Thus without markets, without science, finding that which is rational is presumably impossible. This is supposedly the curse that faces the world's poor. In presumably lacking our markets and science, such peoples are supposedly destined to make only less rational decisions. If so, however, what explains the lack of rationality in the developed world? Was either World War I or II rational? Was the Holocaust rational? Was slavery rational? Was Jim Crow rational? Was the Iraq war rational? Is our reckless plundering of the planet's natural resources rational? In fact, is much rational in the supposedly developed world? The point being that our science reflects a conception of rationality that is by no means demonstratively or inherently superior to that found amongst indigenous peoples. Thus any attempt, regardless of however noble the intention, to impose our rationality on others impedes the rise of other kinds of rational systems that could possibly be superior to our own, or simply be better suited for a given context.

Witnessing millions die of poverty and disease is a revolting reality. For the best amongst us, nothing is too much to end this reality. But what exactly we must and can do to save others from the misery of poverty and disease requires a tremendous amount of caution. It also involves accepting a set of harsh truths. Our moral evolution comes from reckoning with the full consequences and implications of our actions and lack thereof. We should never be spared the anguish and misery that come from our actions and lack thereof. To attempt to do so undermines our ability to learn and morally evolve, which usually involves forming new ways of perceiving and making sense of the world. Also, reckoning with the full implications and consequences of our actions and lack thereof forces us to be resilient and exposes our complicity. It forces us to own our responsibility for alleviating our misery. Most importantly, misery and death lend for wisdom as every action and decision forces us to consider and weigh all the implications and consequences. Caution replaces recklessness. So yes, there is no doubt a yearning to release us of our anguish and misery, but intervening the way development economics does threatens our prosperity by undermining our ability to create our own worlds, on our own terms, with our own expertise and knowledge. Simply put, such interventions impede the making of an evolved humanity. Without such a humanity, prosperity is impossible. Intervention in the affairs and conditions of different peoples through foreign aid and supplying foreign expertise needs to be discouraged as such charity only serves to further paralyze, colonize, and dehumanize these peoples. If emancipation must mean anything, it should at least mean the ability to create our own worlds on our own terms by our own hands. How did we also come to know what programs and what kinds of aid are best for other peoples? Indeed, how did we come to believe that other peoples were seemingly incapable of creating and identifying the programs and policies that were best for them? In sum, how did we come to believe that our own programs and expertise are inherently superior, and thereby worthy of emulation? This is the mentality that constitutes colonialism and imperialism. We must believe, or be ready to believe, that our vision of the world can supply all our solutions. This is why Duflo wants development economics to act as a vetting process for policy-makers—engaging "decision-makers not just as experimental partners but as adopters of programs that have already been vetted." But in most cases, the programs being evaluated and vetted by development economists are funded by foreign aid. Also, the vetting process is inherently ideological. We determine, by our values, beliefs, assumptions, biases, and so forth, what constitutes an effective program. What are the options for locals and indigenous peoples? Whose vision of the world is dictating the rules of the game, and whose expertise and knowledge is doing the vetting? But colonialism damns those who are being colonized and those who are doing the colonizing. Where is the diversity going to come from to challenge our vision of the world, to force us to understand the world anew, to experience the world anew? That is, where is the catalyst going to come from to inspire us? How also would our knowledge and expertise evolve without diversity? Our diversity poses no threat to the world. It is instead our own unwillingness to look genuinely at the world from the perspective of others. It is also, of course, our unwillingness to allow others to form different visions of the world by us being determined to impose ours on them. In this regard, colonialism ultimately colonizes the colonizer—seeking to impose our worldview on others imprisons and shackles us to that worldview.

So what are the limits of our obligations to each other, such as those that are mired in poverty? What are the limits of us being of a common humanity? How can our generosity and compassion be separated from the making of a new colonialism? There is no easy formulation to resolving these challenges. Human beings are complex beings, and as a result, our issues are no less so. But there are questions that can guide us, such as: Do our expertise and knowledge coercively impede the rise of other expertise and knowledge? Do our politics and ethics show concern for the integrity and humanity of others, meaning that do our politics and ethics acknowledge our diversity? To assume that we share a common humanity in no way means that diversity threatens our arriving at a common destiny. In fact, without diversity, such a destiny is impossible. Diversity is about coming to new ways of understanding and experiencing the world, ourselves, and each other. It emerges between us rather than something that is possessed by us. As diversity flourishes, our humanity evolves. We become less myopic, narcissistic, and militaristic. Our vision of the world becomes more expansive and inclusive. We become less inclined to impose our worldview on others. We thereby become less colonialistic and more democratic. We are open to that which is new and different. There is therefore a psychology that constitutes colonialism, and which colonialism propagates. Understanding this psychology is vital to understanding how colonialism behaves, and also the dangers that colonialism poses to all of humanity. Its fallout exceeds the political and social realms. To understand the psychology of colonialism is also to understand what makes colonialism so seductive. It gives us the illusion of lessening the world's complexity, ambiguity, and mystery. In development economics, this complexity, ambiguity, and mystery is referred to as noise. But this is the appeal of development economics—the promise to remove this complexity and thereby the unpredictability from the development process. This is what supposedly constitutes removing the guesswork from the process.

So the promise of colonialism is an order that is characterized by clarity, predictability, and certainty. This is supposedly the highest order that is humanly attainable. It is also the hallmark of colonialism. We have many instances of this order. Yet when this order arises, nothing but misery and death follow, and the order is illusory. Even development economists admit that, for various reasons, many questions cannot be reduced to measurable results. Also, Duflo acknowledges that as much as there must be data, "It can't only be data. Even to understand what data means, and what data I need, I need to form an intuition about things. And that process is as ad hoc and impressionistic as anybody's." In the end, what get us are the illusions, and the struggle to sustain the illusions. In development economics, the illusion is that development is quantifiable and measurable. It can be reduced to equations and calculations. But human beings are too complex for such a thesis. We are, besides material and physical beings, also emotional, sensual, existential, relational, historical, and even spiritual beings. We respond to our environments, but also make our environments. Thus what determines which actions are rational and which ones are less so is laden with ambiguity, complexity, and mystery. We will only have the illusion of rationality.

There is also the matter of embeddedness, where every ecology is embedded within other ecologies. No ecology is outside the influence of other ecologies, or can survive by ignoring the influence of other ecologies. That we will always be of different histories means that we will always be of different ecologies. We will always have to deal with different influences. So again, what will be rational for one ecology will be different for another ecology. As regards determining what decision or action is rational, context matters, and every context will be different, and should be different. This of course also means that identifying programs or solutions that work best across contexts will be nearly impossible to achieve. It also means that knowing what is best for each ecology must be determined locally, organically, and hopefully, democratically. Yet this in no way means that locals will make the best decisions for all. There is always the reality of power, privilege, and greed. Parachuting programs and solutions into ecologies only compounds corrupt practices by deepening our dependency on the status quo for permission to set up these foreign aid-sponsored programs. This is why foreign aid has such a horrid history of encouraging local corruption. However, we serve the interest of the marginalized, downtrodden, and forsaken in any ecology by actually embracing the fact that every ecology is embedded within other ecologies. We can challenge and pressure other ecologies to adopt new practices. We can also build coalitions that increase our influence on other ecologies. These coalitions can also disincentivize certain practices and encourage others. That ecologies are embedded within other ecologies means that there is always a tremendous amount of leverage and influence that they can bring to bear upon each other to force change.

Colonialism narrows our vision of the world, and in so doing narrows our ways of understanding what ails the world. In the case of development economics, this can be seen in how problems are conceptualized. It is supposedly poverty, disease, and lack of resources that impede prosperity and development in developing nations. Presumably, by creating a set of vetted programs, these nations can achieve prosperity and eventually become a developed nation, that is, a nation that is supposedly like ours. Behind development economics is the mission of making other nations into our likeness. In this way, development economics aims to lessen the world's diversity. It perceives diversity as a problem that threatens the world. Of course development economists would contend that this assertion is false. It is poverty, disease, and famine that threaten the world. The goal is to end the practices that give rise to these problems. But are these really the problems that threaten the world, or merely symptoms of problems? Accordingly, do the origins and thereby solutions to these problems begin in these developing nations, and will simply identifying and implementing the programs that development economists vet end these problems? We in supposedly developed nations seem to be fundamentally separated from these problems. Our goal is charity—to offer aid and expertise to help these developing nations conquer these problems. Thus a lot of our debates are about how much to increase our foreign aid. Presumably, a generous nation gives a lot of aid. The amount of our aid becomes a measure of our decency, and those who call for increased aid appeal to our sense of decency and charity. But charity constitutes no binding moral obligation. In a world where ecologies are embedded within other ecologies, and where all ecologies are inseparable from each other, our problems and solutions to these problems are also inseparable. Every problem is a system problem, implicating how an ecology is configured and related to every other ecology.

How an ecology happens upon a problem is largely controlled by what is happenings with other ecologies, including what resources (material and ideological) an ecology is acquiring from other ecologies, and also what practices embedding ecologies are either encouraging or discouraging. Poverty, disease, and misery in no way just happen to an ecology. These problems have origins in how each ecology is related to every other ecology, as every ecology can only exist by drawing upon the resources and influences that come from other ecologies. As such, problems of poverty are inseparable from issues of plenty, and problems of famine are inseparable from issues of abundance, and problems of scarcity are inseparable from issues of greed. For instance, although the US only constitutes five percent the world population, we consume about twenty percent of the world's energy, which means that our consumption has consequences for other nations, especially developing nations. As an analyst notes, "The point is that the population problem isn't just something "over there" in "those poor countries," where they may be having more children. From a consumption perspective, the developed countries have a bigger population growth problem than the developing countries!"

Being ecologically inseparable means that our actions (and lack thereof) have consequences and implications for others. This in no way exonerates locals of any culpability for acting cruelly. It merely means that understanding the problems that torment a community or nation requires a much more expansive understanding of the world. But what comes with such a view is our complicity in the making of the problems that torment others. What also becomes apparent is our responsibility and obligation to do what is necessary to end these problems. Colonialism releases us of this task by encouraging us to believe that the condition of our humanity is separate from the condition of others. Charity, as in foreign aid, is supposedly our highest obligation to each other. Development economics further legitimizes this colonial mentality by advocating for increased aid to developing nations. Development succeeds by supposedly offering us another means to do good in the world. It allows us to do scholarship in a way that seems important, a scholarship that aspires to "save the world." Again, a primary mission of development economics is to help decision-makers use foreign aid resources more efficiently and effectively.

Development economics succeeds by releasing us of any culpability—and thereby any responsibility—in the making of the problems that torment peoples in developing nations. There is no studying, no testing, no randomizing of how our own practices and programs contribute to the misery of others. The notion of trying to understand how we interact with our environment and make less rational decisions is for others. The object of study is always others. The vetted programs are for others. Other than charity, development economics asks nothing from us, and thereby poses no threat to the status quo. The viability of development economics is dependent on preserving the status quo as without foreign aid, development economics all but collapses. This is why development economics will always have a problem with theory, and will also remain obsessed with methodologies and technologies that can supposedly supply us with the most reliable data. Theory is inherently political. It illuminates the forces and experiences that make for the construction of our social worlds. Thus with development economics, there is no indictment of our worldview, or of the institutions and structures that are born of this worldview. Neither is there any indictment of the practices that encourage our apathy and gluttony. Neither are there any calls for a new ethics, politics, and economics. We are never the objects of study. There are no programs that are being tested and vetted for us. The problem is elsewhere, supposedly.

23

ON CRIME & PUNISHMENT

SUPREME COURT OF THE UNITED STATES
GRAHAM V. FLORIDA
NO. 08-7412. ARGUED NOVEMBER 9,
2009—DECIDED MAY 17, 2010

*T*he issue before the Court is whether the Constitution permits a juvenile offender to be sentenced to life in prison without parole for a nonhomicide crime. The sentence was imposed by the State of Florida. Petitioner challenges the sentence under the Eighth Amendment's Cruel and Unusual Punishments Clause, made applicable to the States by the Due Process Clause of the Fourteenth Amendment. Robinson v. California, 370 U. S. 660 (1962).[1]

Petitioner is Terrance Jamar Graham. He was born on January 6, 1987. Graham's parents were addicted to crack cocaine, and their drug use persisted in his early years. Graham was diagnosed with attention deficit hyperactivity

---

1 All excerpts taken verbatim from *Graham v. Florida*.

disorder in elementary school. He began drinking alcohol and using tobacco at age 9 and smoked marijuana at age 13. In July 2003, when Graham was age 16, he and three other school-age youths attempted to rob a barbeque restaurant in Jacksonville, Florida. One youth, who worked at the restaurant, left the back door unlocked just before closing time. Graham and another youth, wearing masks, entered through the unlocked door. Graham's masked accomplice twice struck the restaurant manager in the back of the head with a metal bar. When the manager started yelling at the assailant and Graham, the two youths ran out and escaped in a car driven by the third accomplice. The restaurant manager required stitches for his head injury. No money was taken.

Graham was arrested for the robbery attempt. Under Florida law, it is within a prosecutor's discretion whether to charge 16- and 17-year-olds as adults or juveniles for most felony crimes. Graham's prosecutor elected to charge Graham as an adult. The charges against Graham were armed burglary with assault or battery, a first-degree felony carrying a maximum penalty of life imprisonment without the possibility of parole; and attempted armed-robbery, a second-degree felony carrying a maximum penalty of 15 years' imprisonment.

On December 18, 2003, Graham pleaded guilty to both charges under a plea agreement. Graham wrote a letter to the trial court. After reciting "this is my first and last time getting in trouble," he continued "I've decided to turn my life around." App. 379–380. Graham said "I made a promise to God and myself that if I get a second chance, I'm going to do whatever it takes to get to the [National Football League]."

The trial court accepted the plea agreement. The court withheld adjudication of guilt as to both charges and sentenced Graham to concurrent 3-year terms of probation. Graham was required to spend the first 12 months of his probation in the county jail, but he received credit for the time he had served awaiting trial, and was released on June 25, 2004.

Less than 6 months later, on the night of December 2, 2004, Graham again was arrested. The State's case was as follows: Earlier that evening, Graham participated in a home invasion robbery. His two accomplices were

Meigo Bailey and Kirkland Lawrence, both 20-year-old men. According to the State, at 7 p.m. that night, Graham, Bailey, and Lawrence knocked on the door of the home where Carlos Rodriguez lived. Graham, followed by Bailey and Lawrence, forcibly entered the home and held a pistol to Rodriguez's chest. For the next 30 minutes, the three held Rodriguez and another man, a friend of Rodriguez, at gunpoint while they ransacked the home searching for money. Before leaving, Graham and his accomplices barricaded Rodriguez and his friend inside a closet.

The State further alleged that Graham, Bailey, and Lawrence, later the same evening, attempted a second robbery, during which Bailey was shot. Graham, who had borrowed his father's car, drove Bailey and Lawrence to the hospital and left them there. As Graham drove away, a police sergeant signaled him to stop. Graham continued at a high speed but crashed into a telephone pole. He tried to flee on foot but was apprehended. Three handguns were found in his car.

When detectives interviewed Graham, he denied involvement in the crimes. He said he encountered Bailey and Lawrence only after Bailey had been shot. One of the detectives told Graham that the victims of the home invasion had identified him. He asked Graham, "Aside from the two robberies tonight how many more were you involved in?" Graham responded, "Two to three before tonight." The night that Graham allegedly committed the robbery, he was 34 days short of his 18th birthday.

On December 13, 2004, Graham's probation officer filed with the trial court an affidavit asserting that Graham had violated the conditions of his probation by possessing a firearm, committing crimes, and associating with persons engaged in criminal activity. The trial court held hearings on Graham's violations about a year later, in December 2005 and January 2006. The judge who presided was not the same judge who had accepted Graham's guilty plea to the earlier offenses.

Graham maintained that he had no involvement in the home invasion robbery; but, even after the court underscored that the admission could expose him to a life sentence on the earlier charges, he admitted violating probation conditions by fleeing. The State presented evidence related to the home invasion, including testimony from the victims. The trial court noted that Graham, in admitting his attempt to avoid arrest, had acknowledged violating his probation. The court further found that Graham had violated his probation by committing a home invasion robbery, by possessing a firearm, and by associating with persons engaged in criminal activity.

The trial court held a sentencing hearing. Under Florida law the minimum sentence Graham could receive absent a downward departure by the judge was 5 years' imprisonment. The maximum was life imprisonment. Graham's attorney requested the minimum non-departure sentence of 5 years. A presentence report prepared by the Florida Department of Corrections recommended that Graham receive an even lower sentence—at most 4 years' imprisonment. The State recommended that Graham receive 30 years on the armed burglary count and 15 years on the attempted armed robbery count.

After hearing Graham's testimony, the trial court explained the sentence it was about to pronounce:

"Mr. Graham, as I look back on your case, yours is really candidly a sad situation. You had, as far as I can tell, you have quite a family structure. You had a lot of people who wanted to try and help you get your life turned around including the court system, and you had a judge who took the step to try and give you direction through his probation order to give you a chance to get back onto track. And at the time you seemed through your letters that that is exactly what you wanted to do. And I don't know why it is that you threw your life away. I don't know why. But you did, and that is what is so sad about this today is that you have actually been given a chance to get through this, the original charge, which were very serious charges to begin with... The attempted robbery with a weapon was a very serious charge.

". . .[I]n a very short period of time you were back before the Court on a violation of this probation, and then here you are two years later standing before me, literally the—facing a life sentence as to—up to life as to count 1 and up to 15 years as to count 2. And I don't understand why you would be given such a great opportunity to do something with your life and why you would throw it away. The only thing that I can rationalize is that you decided that this is how you were going to lead your life and that there is nothing that we can do for you. And as the state pointed out, that this is an escalating pattern of criminal conduct on your part and that we can't help your life, and I don't know why you are going to. You've made that decision. I have no idea. But, evidently, that is what you decided to do. So then it becomes a focus, if I can't do anything to help you, if I can't do anything to get you back on the right path, then I have to start focusing on the community and trying to protect the community from your actions. And, unfortunately, that is where we are today is I don't see where I can do anything to help you any further. You've evidently decided this is the direction you're going to take in life, and it's unfortunate that you made that choice.

"I have reviewed the statute. I don't see where any further juvenile sanctions would be appropriate. I don't see where any youthful offender sanctions would be appropriate. Given your escalating pattern of criminal conduct, it is apparent to the Court that you have decided that this is the way you are going to live your life and that the only thing I can do now is to try and protect the community from your actions."

The trial court found Graham guilty of the earlier armed burglary and attempted armed robbery charges. It sentenced him to the maximum sentence authorized by law on each charge: life imprisonment for the armed burglary and 15 years for the attempted armed robbery. Because Florida has abolished its parole system, a life sentence gives a defendant no possibility of release unless he is granted executive clemency.

Graham filed a motion in the trial court challenging his sentence under the Eighth Amendment. The motion was deemed denied after the trial court failed to rule on it within 60 days. The First District Court of Appeal of Florida affirmed, concluding that Graham's sentence was not grossly disproportionate to his crimes. The court took note of the seriousness of Graham's *offenses and their violent nature, as well as the fact that they "were not committed by a pre-teen, but a seventeen year-old who was ultimately sentenced at the age of nineteen." The court concluded further that Graham was incapable of rehabilitation. Although Graham "was given an unheard of probationary sentence for a life felony, ... wrote a letter expressing his remorse and promising to refrain from the commission of further crime, and ... had a strong family structure to support him," the court noted, he "rejected his second chance and chose to continue committing crimes at an escalating pace." The Florida Supreme Court denied review.*

RULING OF THE COURT

The Supreme Court reversed the ruling by the Florida Supreme Court. The court ruled that the Eighth Amendment's Cruel and Unusual Punishments Clause does not permit a juvenile offender to be sentenced to life in prison without parole for a nonhomicide crime. The following is a summary of the court ruling:

(a) Embodied in the cruel and unusual punishments ban is the "precept ... that punishment for crime should be graduated and proportioned to [the] offense." Weems v. United States, 217 U. S. 349, 367. The Court's cases implementing the proportionality standard fall within two general classifications. In cases of the first type, the Court has considered all the circumstances to determine whether the length of a term-of-years sentence is unconstitutionally excessive for a particular defendant's crime. The second classification comprises cases in which the Court has applied certain categorical rules against the death penalty. In a subset of such cases considering the nature of the offense, the Court has concluded that capital punishment is impermissible for nonhomicide crimes against individuals. In a second subset, cases turning on the offender's characteristics, the Court has prohibited death for defendants who committed their crimes before age 18, Roper v. Simmons, 543 U. S. 551, or whose intellectual functioning is in a low range, Atkins v.

Virginia, 536 U. S. 304. *In cases involving categorical rules, the Court first considers "objective indicia of society's standards, as expressed in legislative enactments and state practice" to determine whether there is a national consensus against the sentencing practice at issue. Next, looking to "the standards elaborated by controlling precedents and by the Court's own understanding and interpretation of the Eighth Amendment's text, history, meaning, and purpose," Kennedy, supra, at ___, the Court determines in the exercise of its own independent judgment whether the punishment in question violates the Constitution, Roper, supra, at 564. Because this case implicates a particular type of sentence as it applies to an entire class of offenders who have committed a range of crimes, the appropriate analysis is the categorical approach used in Atkins, Roper, and Kennedy.*

(b) Application of the foregoing approach convinces the Court that the sentencing practice at issue is unconstitutional.

(1) Six jurisdictions do not allow life without parole sentences for any juvenile offenders. Seven jurisdictions permit life without parole for juvenile offenders, but only for homicide crimes. Thirty-seven States, the District of Columbia, and the Federal Government permit sentences of life without parole for a juvenile nonhomicide offender in some circumstances. The State relies on these data to argue that no national consensus against the sentencing practice in question exists. An examination of actual sentencing practices in those jurisdictions that permit life without parole for juvenile nonhomicide offenders, however, discloses a consensus against the sentence. Nationwide, there are only 129 juvenile offenders serving life without parole sentences for nonhomicide crimes. Because 77 of those offenders are serving sentences imposed in Florida and the other 52 are imprisoned in just 10 States and in the federal system, it appears that only 12 jurisdictions nationwide in fact impose life without parole sentences on juvenile nonhomicide offenders, while 26 States and the District of Columbia do not impose them despite apparent statutory authorization. Given that the statistics reflect nearly all

juvenile nonhomicide offenders who have received a life without parole sentence stretching back many years, moreover, it is clear how rare these sentences are, even within the States that do sometimes impose them. While more common in terms of absolute numbers than the sentencing practices in, e.g., Atkins and Enmund v. Florida, 458 U. S. 782, the type of sentence at issue is actually as rare as those other sentencing practices when viewed in proportion to the opportunities for its imposition. The fact that many jurisdictions do not expressly prohibit the sentencing practice at issue is not dispositive because it does not necessarily follow that the legislatures in those jurisdictions have deliberately concluded that such sentences would be appropriate.

(2) The inadequacy of penological theory to justify life without parole sentences for juvenile nonhomicide offenders, the limited culpability of such offenders, and the severity of these sentences all lead the Court to conclude that the sentencing practice at issue is cruel and unusual. No recent data provide reason to reconsider Roper's holding that because juveniles have lessened culpability they are less deserving of the most serious forms of punishment. 543 U. S., at 551. Moreover, defendants who do not kill, intend to kill, or foresee that life will be taken are categorically less deserving of such punishments than are murderers. Serious nonhomicide crimes "may be devastating in their harm . . . but 'in terms of moral depravity and of the injury to the person and to the public,' . . . they cannot be compared to murder in their 'severity and irrevocability.'" Thus, when compared to an adult murderer, a juvenile offender who did not kill or intend to kill has a twice diminished moral culpability. Age and the nature of the crime each bear on the analysis. As for the punishment, life without parole is "the second most severe penalty permitted by law," Harmelin v. Michigan, 501 U. S. 957, 1001, and is especially harsh for a juvenile offender, who will on average serve more years and a greater percentage of his life in prison than an adult offender, see, e.g., Roper, supra, at 572. And none of the legitimate goals of

penal sanctions—retribution, deterrence, incapacitation, and rehabilitation is adequate to justify life without parole for juvenile nonhomicide offenders. Because age "18 is the point where society draws the line for many purposes between childhood and adulthood," it is the age below which a defendant may not be sentenced to life without parole for a nonhomicide crime. A State is not required to guarantee eventual freedom to such an offender, but must impose a sentence that provides some meaningful opportunity for release based on demonstrated maturity and rehabilitation. It is for the State, in the first instance, to explore the means and mechanisms for compliance.

(3) A categorical rule is necessary, given the inadequacy of two alternative approaches to address the relevant constitutional concerns. First, although Florida and other States have made substantial efforts to enact comprehensive rules governing the treatment of youthful offenders, such laws allow the imposition of the type of sentence at issue based only on a discretionary, subjective judgment by a judge or jury that the juvenile offender is irredeemably depraved, and are therefore insufficient to prevent the possibility that the offender will receive such a sentence despite a lack of moral culpability. Second, a case-by-case approach requiring that the particular offender's age be weighed against the seriousness of the crime as part of a gross disproportionality inquiry would not allow courts to distinguish with sufficient accuracy the few juvenile offenders having sufficient psychological maturity and depravity to merit a life without parole sentence from the many that have the capacity for change. Nor does such an approach take account of special difficulties encountered by counsel in juvenile representation, given juveniles' impulsiveness, difficulty thinking in terms of long term benefits, and reluctance to trust adults. A categorical rule avoids the risk that, as a result of these difficulties, a court or jury will erroneously conclude that a particular juvenile is sufficiently culpable to deserve life without parole for a nonhomicide. It also gives the juvenile offender a chance to demonstrate maturity and reform.

(4) Additional support for the Court's conclusion lies in the fact that the sentencing practice at issue has been rejected the world over: The United States is the only Nation that imposes this type of sentence. While the judgments of other nations and the international community are not dispositive as to the meaning of the Eighth Amendment, the Court has looked abroad to support its independent conclusion that a particular punishment is cruel and unusual.

CHIEF JUSTICE ROBERTS, *concurring in the judgment.*

I agree with the Court that Terrance Graham's sentence of life without parole violates the Eighth Amendment's prohibition on "cruel and unusual punishments." Unlike the majority, however, I see no need to invent a new constitutional rule of dubious provenance in reaching that conclusion....

Today, the Court views Roper as providing the basis for a new categorical rule that juveniles may never receive a sentence of life without parole for nonhomicide crimes. I disagree. In Roper, the Court tailored its analysis of juvenile characteristics to the specific question whether juvenile offenders could constitutionally be subject to capital punishment. Our answer that they could not be sentenced to death was based on the explicit conclusion that they "cannot with reliability be classified among the worst offenders."

This conclusion does not establish that juveniles can never be eligible for life without parole. A life sentence is of course far less severe than a death sentence, and we have never required that it be imposed only on the very worst offenders, as we have with capital punishment. Treating juvenile life sentences as analogous to capital punishment is at odds with our longstanding view that "the death penalty is different from other punishments in kind rather than degree." It is also at odds with Roper itself, which drew the line at capital punishment by blessing juvenile sentences that are "less severe than death" despite involving "forfeiture of some of the most basic liberties." Indeed, Roper explicitly relied on the possible imposition of life without parole on some juvenile offenders.

But the fact that Roper does not support a categorical rule barring life sentences for all juveniles does not mean that a criminal defendant's age is irrelevant to those sentences. On the contrary, our cases establish that the "narrow proportionality" review applicable to noncapital cases itself takes the personal "culpability of the offender" into account in examining whether a given punishment is proportionate to the crime. There is no reason why an offender's juvenile status should be excluded from the analysis. Indeed, given Roper's conclusion that juveniles are typically less blameworthy than adults, 543 U. S., at 571, an offender's juvenile status can play a central role in the inquiry. . . .

I begin with the threshold inquiry comparing the gravity of Graham's conduct to the harshness of his penalty. There is no question that the crime for which Graham received his life sentence—armed burglary of a nondomicil with an assault or battery—is "a serious crime deserving serious punishment." So too is the home invasion robbery that was the basis of Graham's probation violation. But these crimes are certainly less serious than other crimes, such as murder or rape. . . .

The fact that Graham committed the crimes that he did proves that he was dangerous and deserved to be punished. But it does not establish that he was particularly dangerous—at least relative to the murderers and rapists for whom the sentence of life without parole is typically reserved. On the contrary, his lack of prior criminal convictions, his youth and immaturity, and the difficult circumstances of his upbringing noted by the majority, ante, at 1, all suggest that he was markedly less culpable than atypical adult who commits the same offenses. . . .

The Court uses Graham's case as a vehicle to proclaim a new constitutional rule—applicable well beyond the particular facts of Graham's case—that a sentence of life without parole imposed on any juvenile for any nonhomicide offense is unconstitutional. This categorical conclusion is as unnecessary as it is unwise.

A holding this broad is unnecessary because the particular conduct and circumstances at issue in the case before us are not serious enough to justify

Graham's sentence. In reaching this conclusion, there is no need for the Court to decide whether that same sentence would be constitutional if imposed for other more heinous nonhomicide crimes.

A more restrained approach is especially appropriate in light of the Court's apparent recognition that it is perfectly legitimate for a juvenile to receive a sentence of life without parole for committing murder. This means that there is nothing inherently unconstitutional about imposing sentences of life without parole on juvenile offenders; rather, the constitutionality of such sentences depends on the particular crimes for which they are imposed. But if the constitutionality of the sentence turns on the particular crime being punished, then the Court should limit its holding to the particular offenses that Graham committed here, and should decline to consider other hypothetical crimes not presented by this case.

In any event, the Court's categorical conclusion is also unwise. Most importantly, it ignores the fact that some nonhomicide crimes . . . are especially heinous or grotesque, and thus may be deserving of more severe punishment. Those under 18 years old may as a general matter have "diminished" culpability relative to adults who commit the same crimes, Roper, 543 U. S., at 571, but that does not mean that their culpability is always insufficient to justify a life sentence. . . .

Terrance Graham committed serious offenses, for which he deserves serious punishment. But he was only 16 years old, and under our Court's precedents, his youth is one factor, among others, that should be considered in deciding whether his punishment was unconstitutionally excessive. In my view, Graham's age—together with the nature of his criminal activity and the unusual severity of his sentence—tips the constitutional balance. I thus concur in the Court's judgment that Graham's sentence of life without parole violated the Eighth Amendment. I would not, however, reach the same conclusion in every case involving a juvenile offender. Some crimes are so heinous, and some juvenile offenders so highly culpable, that a sentence of life without parole may be entirely justified under the Constitution. As we have said, "successful challenges" to noncapital sentences under the Eighth Amendment have been—and, in my view, should continue to be—"exceedingly rare." But Graham's sentence presents the exceptional case that our precedents have recognized will come along. We should grant Graham the relief to which he is entitled under the Eighth Amendment. The Court errs, however, in using this case as a vehicle for unsettling our established jurisprudence and fashioning a categorical rule applicable to far different cases.

JUSTICE THOMAS, with whom JUSTICE SCALIA and JUSTICE ALITO join, dissenting.

The Court holds today that it is "grossly disproportionate" and hence unconstitutional for any judge or jury to impose a sentence of life without parole on an offender less than 18 years old, unless he has committed a homicide. Although the text of the Constitution is silent regarding the permissibility of this sentencing practice, and although it would not have offended the standards that prevailed at the founding, the Court insists that the standards of American society have evolved such that the Constitution now requires its prohibition.

The news of this evolution will, I think, come as a surprise to the American people. Congress, the District of Columbia, and 37 States allow judges and juries to consider this sentencing practice in juvenile nonhomicide cases, and those judges and juries have decided to use it in the very worst cases they have encountered.

The Court does not conclude that life without parole itself is a cruel and unusual punishment. It instead rejects the judgments of those legislatures, judges, and juries regarding what the Court describes as the "moral" question of whether this sentence can ever be "proportionat[e]" when applied to the category of offenders at issue here.

I am unwilling to assume that we, as members of this Court, are any more capable of making such moral judgments than our fellow citizens. Nothing in *our training as judges qualifies us for that task, and nothing in Article III gives us that authority.*

I respectfully dissent.

The Court has nonetheless invoked proportionality to declare that capital punishment—though not unconstitutional per se—is categorically too harsh a penalty to apply to certain types of crimes and certain classes of offenders. See Coker v. Georgia, 433 U. S. 584 (1977) (plurality opinion) (rape of an adult woman); Kennedy v. Louisiana, 554 U. S. ____ (2008) (rape of a child); Enmund v. Florida, 458 U. S. 782 (1982) (felony murder in which the defendant participated in the felony but did not kill or intend to kill); Thompson v. Oklahoma, 487 U. S. 815 (1988) (plurality opinion) (juveniles under 16); Roper v. Simmons, 543 U. S. 551 (2005) (juveniles under 18); Atkins v. Virginia, 536 U. S. 304 (2002) (mentally retarded offenders). In adopting these categorical proportionality rules, the Court intrudes upon areas that the Constitution reserves to other (state and federal) organs of government. The Eighth Amendment prohibits the government from inflicting a cruel and unusual method of punishment upon a defendant. Other constitutional provisions ensure the defendant's right to fair process before any punishment is imposed. But, as members of today's majority note, "[s]ociety changes," and the Eighth Amendment leaves the unavoidably moral question of who "deserves" a particular nonprohibited method of punishment to the judgment of the legislatures that authorize the penalty, the prosecutors who seek it, and the judges and juries that impose it under circumstances they deem appropriate.

The Court has nonetheless adopted categorical rules that shield entire classes of offenses and offenders from the death penalty on the theory that "evolving standards of decency" require this result. The Court has offered assurances that these standards can be reliably measured by "'objective indicia'" of "national consensus," such as state and federal legislation, jury behavior, and (surprisingly, given that we are talking about "national" consensus) international opinion. Yet even assuming that is true, the Framers did not provide for the constitutionality of a particular type of punishment to turn on a "snapshot of American public opinion" taken at the moment a case is decided. By holding otherwise, the Court pretermits in all but one direction the evolution of the standards it describes, thus "calling a constitutional halt to what may well be a pendulum swing in social attitudes," and "stunt[ing] legislative consideration" of new questions of penal policy as they emerge....

The categorical proportionality review the Court employs in capital cases thus lacks a principled foundation. The Court's decision today is significant because it does not merely apply this standard—it remarkably expands its reach. For the first time in its history, the Court declares an entire class of offenders immune from a noncapital sentence using the categorical approach it previously reserved for death penalty cases alone....

According to the Court, proper Eighth Amendment analysis "begins with objective indicia of national consensus," and "[t]he clearest and most reliable objective evidence of contemporary values is the legislation enacted by the country's legislatures," at 10–11 (internal quota quickly, because a national "consensus" in favor of the Court's result simply does not exist. The laws of all 50 States, the Federal Government, and the District of Columbia provide that juveniles over a certain age may be tried in adult court if charged with certain crimes. Forty-five States, the Federal Government, and the District of Columbia expose juvenile offenders charged in adult court to the very same range of punishments faced by adults charged with the same crimes. Eight of those States do not make life-without-parole sentences available for any nonhomicide offender, regardless of age. All remaining jurisdictions—the Federal Government, the other 37 States, and the District—authorize life-without-parole sentences for certain nonhomicide offenses, and authorize the imposition of such sentences on persons under 18. Only five States prohibit juvenile offenders from receiving a life-without parole sentence that could be imposed on an adult convicted of the same crime.

No plausible claim of a consensus against this sentencing practice can be made in light of this overwhelming legislative evidence. The sole fact that federal law authorizes this practice singlehandedly refutes the claim that our

Nation finds it morally repugnant. The additional reality that 37 out of 50 States (a supermajority of 74%) permit the practice makes the claim utterly implausible. Not only is there no consensus against this penalty, there is a clear legislative consensus in favor of its availability....

In my view, the Court cannot point to a national consensus in favor of its rule without assuming a consensus in favor of the two penological points it later discusses: (1) Juveniles are always less culpable than similarly-situated adults, and (2) juveniles who commit nonhomicide crimes should always receive an opportunity to demonstrate rehabilitation through parole. But legislative trends make that assumption untenable.

First, States over the past 20 years have consistently increased the severity of punishments for juvenile offenders. See 1999 DOJ National Report 89 (referring to the 1990's as "a time of unprecedented change as State legislatures crack[ed] down on juvenile crime"); (noting that, during that period, "legislatures in 47 States and the District of Columbia enacted laws that made their juvenile justice systems more punitive," principally by "ma[king] it easier to transfer juvenile offenders from the juvenile justice system to the [adult] criminal justice system"). This, in my view, reveals the States' widespread agreement that juveniles can sometimes act with the same culpability as adults and that the law should permit judges and juries to consider adult sentences—including life without parole—in those rare and unfortunate cases. See Feld, Unmitigated Punishment: Adolescent Criminal Responsibility and LWOP Sentences, 10 J. Law & Family Studies 11, 69–70 (2007) (noting that life-without-parole sentences for juveniles have increased since the 1980's); Amnesty International & Human Rights Watch, The Rest of Their Lives: Life Without Parole for Child Offenders in the United States 2, 31 (2005) (same).

Second, legislatures have moved away from parole over the same period. Congress abolished parole for federal offenders in 1984 amid criticism that it was subject to "gamesmanship and cynicism," Breyer, Federal Sentencing Guidelines Revisited, 11 Fed. Sentencing Rep. 180(1999) (discussing the Sentencing Reform Act of 1984, 98Stat. 1987), and several States have followed suit, see T. Hughes, D. Wilson, & A. Beck, Dept. of Justice, Bureau of Justice Statistics, Trends in State Parole, 1990–2000, p. 1(2001) (noting that, by the end of 2000, 16 States had abolished parole for all offenses, while another 4 States had abolished it for certain ones). In light of these developments, the argument that there is nationwide consensus that parole must be available to offenders less than 18 years old in every nonhomicide case simply fails. . . .

The fact that the laws of a jurisdiction permit this sentencing practice demonstrates, at a minimum, that the citizens of that jurisdiction find tolerable the possibility that a jury of their peers could impose a life-without parole sentence on a juvenile whose nonhomicide crime is sufficiently depraved. . . .

In sum, the Court's calculation that 129 juvenile nonhomicide life-without-parole sentences have been imposed nationwide in recent memory, even if accepted, hardly amounts to strong evidence that the sentencing practice offends our common sense of decency. . . .

The Court responds that a categorical rule is nonetheless necessary to prevent the "'unacceptable likelihood'" that a judge or jury, unduly swayed by "'the brutality or cold-blooded nature'" of a juvenile's nonhomicide crime, will sentence him to a life-without-parole sentence for which he possesses "'insufficient culpability,'" ante, at 27 (quoting Roper, supra, at 572–573). I find that justification entirely insufficient. The integrity of our criminal justice system depends on the ability of citizens to stand between the defendant and an outraged public and dispassionately determine his guilt and the proper amount of punishment based on the evidence presented. That process necessarily admits of human error. But so does the process of judging in which we engage. As between the two, I find far more "unacceptable" that this Court, swayed by studies reflecting the general tendencies of youth, decree that the people of this country are not fit to decide for themselves when the rare case requires different treatment. . . .

The fact that the Court categorically prohibits life-without-parole sentences for juvenile nonhomicide offenders in the face of an overwhelming legislative majority in favor of leaving that sentencing option available under certain cases simply illustrates how far beyond any cognizable constitutional principle the Court has reached to ensure that its own sense of morality and retributive justice pre-empts that of the people and their representatives....

I respectfully dissent.

ON DECENCY AND CIVILITY

What does decency and civility mean when only recently the U.S. Supreme Court, by only a narrow majority, prohibited persons who are mentally disabled from receiving death sentences?

What does decency and civility mean when only recently the U.S. Supreme Court, by only a narrow majority, prohibited juveniles below the age of 16 from receiving death sentences?

What does decency and civility mean when only recently the U.S. Supreme Court, by only a narrow majority, prohibited juveniles from receiving death sentences that allow for no possibility of parole for nonhomicide offenses?

What does decency and civility mean when, as Justice Thomas points out, the same justices who ruled in favor of these prohibitions, also "upheld the application of the death penalty against a 16-year-old, despite the fact that no such punishment had been carried out on a person of that age in this country in nearly 30 years."

What does decency and civility mean when all the justices on the Supreme Court, including those who are cast as liberal and progressive justices, believe that "retribution is a legitimate reason to punish ... Society is entitled to impose severe sanctions on a juvenile nonhomicide offender to express its condemnation of the crime and to seek restoration of the moral imbalance caused by the offense"?

What does decency and civility mean when the United States, which is always professing to be a Christian nation, "is the only Nation that imposes this type of sentence" (sentences without the possibility of parole for juveniles for nonhomicide offenses)?

What does decency and civility mean when "The State acknowledged at oral argument that even a 5-year-old, theoretically, could receive such a sentence under the letter of the law"?

What does decency and civility mean when, as Justice Stevens observes, "Justice Thomas would apparently not rule out a death sentence for a $50 theft by a 7-year-old"?

What does decency and civility mean when, as Chief Justice Roberts observes, the Supreme Court recognizes "that it is perfectly legitimate for a juvenile to receive a sentence of life without parole for committing murder"? In fact, according to Chief Justice Roberts, "there is nothing inherently unconstitutional about imposing sentences of life without parole on juvenile offenders; rather, the constitutionality of such sentences depends on the particular crimes for which they are imposed."

What does decency and civility mean when Justice Thomas believes that sentencing juveniles to life sentences without the possibility for parole for nonhomicide offenses "hardly . . . offends our common sense of decency"?

24

ON BELIEF

To believe is really, really hard. For instance, how does one continue to believe that we are made in the image and likeness of God in the face of our sordid history of savagery, cruelty, and destruction? Of course many would have us believe that the fault lies with our Original sin. But for us to have Original sin also means that God also has to be of Original sin. For where else could our Original sin come from? But again, maybe to believe is supposed to be really, really hard.

To believe means that I have doubts. I even have frustrations and confusions. For if God only made Adam and Eve, who in turn made Cain and Abel, where did humanity come from? Or, if the world came from some other source, what made for that source, where did that source come from? To believe means that I will never have closure. There will always be doubt. But the glory comes from learning to live with the doubt, learning to even embrace doubt. To live with doubt requires humility. We have to be capable of recognizing, acknowledging, and even encouraging the beliefs of others.

It means that my being is hostile to any manner of dogmatism, hegemonism, and ethnocentrism. It means that I am willing to grapple with beliefs that are in every way alien to mine, even those that seek to erase mine. To believe therefore means that I believe in an infinite God, one that is simply too great to submit completely to human understanding. In other words, to believe means that I believe in a God of love and mercy. Only such a God is beyond my imagination. This is the God that makes for doubt. This is the God that pushes us to believe. But most of all, this is the God that inspires us to forgive, to love. To believe means that I have no way of knowing the limits of God, which means that I also have no way of knowing my own limits and the limits of others. In this way, to believe means that I must always believe in the possibility of redemption. This is why to believe is hard. It means that I will never fully know the mind of God. I must allow always for the possibility of God's will, God's grace. To believe means that I oppose vengeance, even when perpetrated by the state in the name of justice. Vengeance only makes for cycles of retribution. It impedes the possibility of a new reality. It undermines doubt. It therefore impedes our ability to believe, as in believing in the power of God's grace. With vengeance, as in the case of capital punishment, the matter is final. There is no allowance for error, much less for doubt. To murder in the name of vengeance, for supposedly the sake of justice, requires absolute certainty, as in being absolutely certain that the person is beyond the reach of God's grace and mercy, or that our own processes of committing a person to death are certain. With capital punishment, our decision cannot be undone. We must be without doubt, without belief. We must be gods, nothing but gods. Vengeance can only be the business of God. But what does it mean when we pretend to be gods? What does it mean when we pretend to know for certain (without any doubt) the mind of God, or the limits of God's grace, love, and mercy? What does being of faith then mean?

To believe means that we will never aid nor abet the creation of false gods. We will refrain from any activity or matter that promises to end doubt, or end the world's ambiguity and mystery. To believe means that we find virtue in doubt. We can only believe because we are of an infinite God. Yet to believe in no way means that all beliefs are morally equal. It is about what our beliefs do for us. Does believing enlarge what we perceive and experience? Does it tame our savage instincts and impulses? Does it save us from ourselves and each other? In sum, does our believing show us to be made in the image and likeness of a God?

It is really a question of in what God's image and likeness are we made. If we are made in the image and likeness of a finite and vengeful God, believing is impossible. If, however, we are made in the image and likeness of a God of love and mercy, then believing is possible. Our image and likeness of God is about our image and likeness of ourselves. To be capable of imagining a God of infinite love and mercy is about being capable of imagining ourselves of being capable of such love and mercy. But the problem of imagining this God are the obligations that come with this God. This God requires mercy rather than vengeance from us. This God also requires us to nurture doubt, even embrace doubt. To believe in a finite God is easy. Such a God requires no courage. There is no obligation to engage different beliefs. There is no need to even believe, much less examine, scrutinize, and explore. But as history reminds us again and again, there is a price that comes with such gods. So, yes, what we choose to believe is important, but more importantly is our willingness to believe. By choosing to believe in God, we are choosing to believe in ourselves and our own capacity to create more just and humane worlds. Only a God of love and mercy would bless us with such a capacity. Only such a God would invite us to help with the world's creation.

But all of this is merely what I believe. It is my story of God. I could always be wrong. But at least what I believe will make for no misery and cruelty. No blood will be shed in my name or that of my God. If only our neighbors could say as much, how good would be the world?

25

ON VIOLENCE

Our redemption will depend on whether we can arrive at a way of being that is beyond violence. This means arriving at a way of being that is resolved to love selflessly. I am of course by no means simply referring to the violence that comes with guns and bombs. Neither am I only referring to the violence that we inflict upon each other. I am referring to the violence that is intricately woven into our rhetorical, social, ideological, communicational, epistemological, spiritual, and cultural practices. I am referring to both the material and discursive ways we inflict misery and despair upon each other, and in so doing, upon ourselves. I am also referring to the actions and decisions we set in motion to insidiously and coercively limit and even destroy possibility.

I am also referring to the violence we inflict on the planet. These are by no means different kinds of violence. Neither are these supposedly different kinds of violence of a different origin. There is no love for others that can be separate from a love for the planet. Any love that professes to be so or acts accordingly is merely infatuation. It is still shaped by violence, and thereby merely another way of exercising violence, achieving violence, or submitting to the seduction of violence. The deception eventually comes out as the manipulation, coercion, and domination become too apparent to miss. But in a world of violence, there are supposedly no alternatives. There is only infatuation and the practices necessary to sustain the illusion of love. As always, the goal is to neutralize and even humanize violence. Love supposedly requires this of us. It is supposedly what love makes us do. The violence is because we supposedly care too much to do otherwise. It is an expression of our love and devotion. Violence is presumably good. But in reality violence is about our determination to impose order on the world, on each other, on ourselves. Or at least violence gives us the illusion of doing so. But violence does more than merely distort our vision of the world. It also disfigures and mutilates our vision of the world and ourselves. As there is no separation between the world and us, and us and each other, violence always falls back on us. To subject others to violence is to subject ourselves to violence. Violence is therefore only possible when we experience the world as separate and outside of us. This is how we come to never fully recognize what violence does to us. This is also how we sustain the illusion of violence, as in, violence is necessary, violence works, and violence is good. But even the best illusions are still illusions.

Violence is as much about what we do to ourselves as we do to the world and others. It is born out of fear, as in our fear of ourselves, our fear of the world, our fear of each other. But such fears are by no means the cause of violence or what gives life to violence. Violence needs an episteme, a community that provides a rationale, a language, a purpose. This is why crucifixion was necessary to stop a threat. Without violence, the world will presumably devolve into chaos. Violence saves us from ourselves. This is the promise of violence. This is the belief that sustains violence. This is the hope. Without this belief, this hope, violence would be impossible. Therefore behind violence dwells a certain conception of the human condition. We presumably need violence to function morally. Also behind violence is a vision of the world. Without violence, chaos will ensue. This, again, was the rationale for the crucifixion of Jesus Christ. Violence is necessary. Violence is good. All that remains to be determined is degree and kind. Should the penalty for adultery be death by stoning or life without the possibility of parole? Should children who commit murder be put to death or given life without the possibility of parole? Should a person who possesses a certain amount of illicit substances be subject to one or two decades in prison? Should a person found guilty of theft be subject to incarceration or amputation? It is, after all, through violence that God supposedly achieves our devotion. But what does such a reality really mean? What is the value of any God that must use violence to achieve our love and devotion? How did we come to believe that we are deserving of such an infantile God? How did we come to create and imagine such a God? Why and how do we continue to believe that such an abominable and despicable conception of God is viable, reasonable, and plausible?

This is how violence disfigures us. Only a humanity that is born of violence could come to imagine and value such a horrible conception of God. Besides encouraging and legitimizing violence, what is the value of this God? Where is the beauty and wonder in this God? How could such a God be perceived as great? In the end, violence creates fear, anxiety, and despair. It impedes our ability to act deliberately and courageously. It cripples us, distorting our view of ourselves, as well as our view of others. Why would any supposedly great God wish to do this to us? How did this become a great conception of God? But such is the case with violence. Violence disfigures everything, mutilates everything, ravages everything. Nothing good, nothing just, nothing decent, nothing great comes from violence. It diminishes our understanding of the sacred. After all, how could anything be good that needs violence to be so? What would our being made in the image and likeness of God mean when such a God needs violence in order to make anything good, just, and beautiful? How could any God only be capable of using violence to do so, and what does believing that our own image and likeness can be found in such a God mean? It is means that violence is good, necessary, and just. It means that we are deserving of violence. If God uses violence to shape us, then surely our use of violence to shape others and ourselves is no less just. But in this regard how is slavery, apartheid, or the Holocaust abominable? How is the Holocaust fundamentally different from our modern incarceration system that is filled with persons who did nothing to harm others? Behind both systems is the belief that violence is good and also necessary to achieve the good society. Without violence, chaos will ensue. Of course the quantity and quality of violence is different, but the rationale is the same. Thus how could the distinction between good and evil be merely matter of degree and kind? What becomes of the divide between the sacred and profane? Is such a divide possible when both sides share the same view of God? How do we begin to distinguish the sacred from the profane? In a world of violence, the distinction is always arbitrary. This is why as much as we can find slavery, Jim Crow, and the Holocaust morally abominable, we can simultaneously find the execution of persons who are mentally disabled, the mass incarceration of persons for nonviolent offenses, and the execution of children morally tolerable. We simply have no way of reliably determining which kinds of violence are morally objectionable. What then are we to do? What then can we do? We can of course continue to do as we do now, that is, continue to believe that our standards of decency change and evolve. But this belief presents obvious problems. How could a just God be of a changing and evolving morality? What would be just and sacred mean? Would this mean that every abomination needs to be judged according to prevailing contexts, and thereby nothing is inherently evil? But all of this also supposes that our own morality is also evolving, and our humanity is improving and our conception of God is enlarging. Yet history challenges this reality. The world is increasingly tortured by violence and the threat of violence that promises to bring unimaginable death and destruction. But of course nothing less promises to come from a world that believes in violence. That violence begets violence means any world that is of violence will end in violence.

The problem with any view of violence that begins with violence is the lack imagination. There is, in fact, no imagination. Such a God will never make sense. It will always be a God of fools. But such a vision of God continues to rule the world. This is the God that continues to encourage and legitimize violence, and accordingly, continues to be the cause of so much misery and death. Without a different conception of God, the violence that this God brings into the world will soon make for our demise.

Love saves us from the ravages of violence. Love exposes our connection to each other, enlarges our obligation to each other, illuminates our connection to the oceans, the forests, the rivers, the lakes, lessens our distrust and suspicion of each other, and exercises our moral imagination. But this love constitutes a way of viewing of the world, perceiving the world, relating to the world, understanding the world, and experiencing the world. To love is to pull upon the world and pull ourselves towards the world. To love is to struggle for union, integration, and communion in the face of division, separation, and even fragmentation. Love is always up against dread and despair. It is never completely achieved. But one loves in spite of and in the face of the dread and despair. For love is the only path to redemption. To love is also to develop a new consciousness of the world. In pulling us towards the world, love merges our consciousness with the world. This is how love enlarges our consciousness. It dissolves our separation from the world. But this dissolve will never be complete or absolute. There will always be separation, division, and even fragmentation. We will therefore most likely never arrive at a consciousness that will allow us to fly like eagles or glide like dolphins. But nothing is inherently debilitative about such separation. To love is to struggle to remove—within ourselves and social worlds—the forces and practices that engender and heighten our separation and division, and in so doing, distort our conception of ourselves and each other. It is about putting the forces of division and separation in harmony with the forces of union and communion. To love is to recognize that the world's beauty, potentiality, and fecundity reside in the tensions between the forces of separation and division and those of union and communion. There is no meaning without ambiguity, no order without chaos, no unity with diversity, no communication without confusion, no knowledge without ignorance. To love is to embrace all these tensions. Thus to love is to recognize that ultimately our redemption resides in our relation to each other. Regardless of our diversity, our fates are always bound.

26

ON POLITICS

What happens at the end of politics? What happens when we come to realize that we are probably incapable of saving ourselves from each other? What becomes of truth, reason, and knowledge in such a case? It becomes plain that these things are nothing but illusions, born out of our desire and desperation to avoid the unrelenting reality that dealing with ourselves and each other is impossible. These things allow us to look away from each other, to look outside of ourselves for redemption. That is, these things allow us to avoid our own complicity in what becomes of the world. This is why we have made believe that truth, reason, and knowledge are such magnificent things. If only we could have more truth, more reason, more knowledge, the world would be a better place. This mindset absolves us of any responsibility for the condition of the world.

But this is why politics is now dead. As the illusions implode what becomes plain is our own complicity in the state of affairs. No amount of truth, reason, or knowledge can spare us of this reality. All that will save us now is action. By action I mean our capacity to lay bare all the consequences and implications that come with our actions and lack thereof. It means owning our complicity and responsibility for all our actions and lack thereof. Moreover, action means removing all the illusions, devices, and institutions that mask our responsibility for our actions and lack thereof, as well as those that seek to excuse and even release us of such responsibility. In other words, the goal is to end politics, and thereby the illusion that we are devoid of responsibility for the condition of the world. Action is about disabusing us of all the deception, deceit, and duplicity that come with propping up this illusion. It is about instilling honesty, accountability, and responsibility. It is also about reminding us what being made in the image and likeness of God means—possessing the power to create and destroy worlds, and of course being responsible for such power. Action is about affirming and stretching and tapping our boundless capacity to create, imagine, and innovate. Eventually, action will bring us to love. It is inevitable.

Love is an admission that we are responsible for each other and the condition of the world. Politics allows us to deny this reality, or gives us the illusion of denying. Action implicates others. There is no action—or lack thereof—that is devoid of consequences for ourselves and others. There are always consequences and implications. Action is about coming to terms with what are the consequences and for whom. Action exposes the reality that politics allows us to deny—that we are our brother's and sister's keepers. This is why politics seduces us again and again. It absolves us of any responsibility for the condition of others. Blame our scheming representatives. But who made these persons our representatives? Who did the voting? Who never went to the polls? Who never sought to know the issues and challenges? Of course the absolution is illusory. Politics dehumanizes us. This is what happens when we are made to believe that our actions—especially our lack thereof—are devoid of consequences and implications. This is the origin of genocide and all manner of human savagery. It is also why politics infantilizes us. Nothing is as destructive as trying to absolve us of responsibility for the condition of the world.

But now the end of politics is upon us. The chickens are coming home to roost. All the consequences and implications of our actions and lack thereof are now bearing down on us. We, naturally, remain determined to be blameless. We demand the heads of our representatives for making this mess. We profess to be angry, and of course the status quo never calls us on our complicity. To the end, politics will never forsake us. It has no choice. To do otherwise is to finally admit it was always an illusion. So now all that is left for us to do is to throw tantrums like children, and to assume that such behavior is appropriate, especially when the world faces such serious problems. Politics will always appeal to the worst in us. It will always conspire against our potentiality, creativity, and beauty. It will do any and everything to make love impossible. Indeed, the mission of all prophets is to end politics. This is why the kingdom of God is of another world, a world devoid of politics, and thereby a world devoid of all the laws, institutions, and discursive formations that are of politics. This is also why the prophets put nothing in writing. The focus is always on action—loving, forgiving, empathizing, sharing, caring, and doing what is good and just and fair. Every prophet teaches that our redemption resides in action. Only through action we will realize that other kingdom where our redemption resides.

27

ON MEDIOCRITY

Academe makes believe that our redemption resides outside of ourselves. Through academe we will supposedly acquire the knowledge, truth, and temperament we need in order to save ourselves from the world and each other. We therefore view academe as this indispensible institution, even the crowning achievement of civilized peoples. But what could be more perverse than believing that others can do for us what we are unwilling to do for ourselves? Academe can do nothing to change what we are willing to believe or imagine. Only we can do these things because only we can choose to do these things. These are also the things that matter and will determine what becomes of us. What are we willing to believe? What do we have the courage to believe? What are we willing to imagine? How much are we ready and willing to love, to care, to forgive?

But this is why academe is perverse. It divorces being from knowing, and in so doing makes us believe, or allows us to believe, that knowing has nothing to do with being. What emerges is a way of knowing that wants nothing to do with being, and a knowledge that can neither make sense of anything nor do anything. No one can do anything to change what a person is ready and willing to believe, or what a person is ready to imagine, or how much a person is ready to love. We can no doubt torment and harass, and probably inspire and influence. But that is all. We can only be of use to those who are willing to believe something new. But academe is always conspiring against us, busying us with doing all manner of nonsense that has nothing to do with anything. What is so insidious about academe is that we are to believe that academe has nothing to do with politics. It is simply an institution that is devoted to acquiring, processing, and distributing knowledge. Its fidelity is only to knowledge. In fact, we are to believe that academe is committed to keeping politics away from these processes. Yet academe is as much about politics as any other institution. Without politics, academe would be impossible. It is the mission of academe to engender, as well as reify the belief that our redemption resides outside of us. If the world is therefore in peril, the fault supposedly resides in our lack of knowledge. Academe absolves us of any responsibility for the condition of the world. Once again the fault lies elsewhere, as in our lack of knowledge. This is why we continue to invest so greatly in academe so we can supposedly have the knowledge we need to make the world better. This is also why we defer to academe as regards what constitutes a proper course of study.

There are many ways to define mediocrity. But for sure, mediocrity is the inability to act decisively, courageously, and imaginatively. It is pure cowardice, which academe cultivates through and through. With its elaborate disciplines, curriculums, and departments, academe impedes our ability to view the world on our own terms. It becomes impossible to create our own knowledge of the world. We must always rely on the ideas and structures of others. We supposedly lack the capacity to create, define, and organize our own knowledge. We must defer to academe, which means taking the courses and following the arbitrary curriculums that academe sets out before us. Academe releases us of any responsibility for forming our own knowledge of the world.

Academe impoverishes our conception of enlightenment. In academe, the goal is to acquire expertise, or to pry the mind open so stuff can pour in and enlarge our thinking. Thus the adage of minds being like parachutes, they only work when they are open. So the mission of academe is to use elaborate curriculums to pry open our closed minds. Enlightenment is supposedly about being of an open mind. Who wants, after all, to be close-minded, and like a person with a closed parachute, fall and perish? But there is no curriculum that can pry open our minds. For there is no separation between mind and soul, mind and heart, mind and spirit, and mind and body. The mind is the totality of our being. A closed mind is really about a closed soul, a closed heart, a closed body. We will only perceive what we are willing to believe. Therefore achieving enlightenment is really about achieving a certain manner of being. It is about enlarging what we are ready and willing to believe and imagine. Yet let us also remember that every prophet, even those with the power to do miracles, had no success changing what we believe and imagine. But academe being about politics allows us to believe that by following elaborate curriculums we are achieving enlightenment and becoming a more enlightened society. If so, however, why do we increasingly stand on the edge of destroying the world? How could this be the promise of enlightenment?

In the end academe only gives us the illusion of enlightenment. As with all illusions, the seduction is about us being spared of reality. Still, this one comes with a serious cost, the cost being that academe infantilizes us by fixating us on things that have nothing to do with anything. Academe diminishes and even warps our view of the world. So as the hegemony of academe deepens, so also does our peril.

28

ON CONFUSION

The legacy of colonialism can be amply seen in communication studies. At the foundation of communication theory, inquiry, and pedagogy is the belief that there is an intractable conflict between communication and confusion, and that communication emerges from the arresting, domesticating, removing, defeating, and conquering of confusion. Communication is the antithesis of confusion. Communication presumably arises from the conquering of confusion. The defeat of confusion is supposedly a good thing as communication fosters progress, civility, unity, and prosperity. Conversely, confusion presumably encourages chaos, disunity, and social devolution. We believe that communication is something we impose on the world. It is, again, how we achieve order, civility, and progress. Confusion is supposedly the world's natural proclivity. Thus the struggle for communication. In order to have progress, civility, and order, we have to conquer confusion.

What emerges is a narrative that views communication as being in an eternal conflict with confusion, and our survival and prosperity being dependent on us successfully defeating confusion. Communication is of evolution. The mastery of communication—acquiring superior means to conquer confusion—supposedly distinguishes civilized peoples from primitive peoples. Our supposed superiority can also be seen in the fact that we now have a discipline devoted to acquiring and stockpiling and disseminating the knowledge that allows us to defeat confusion. We also have the unparalleled rise of all manner of communication technologies that supposedly will now finally make for the end of confusion. Supposedly, communication is now ubiquitous. According to the narrative, we are now upon the end of confusion and thereby less susceptible to or at the mercy of the world's proclivity for chaos and ambiguity. We are, supposedly, at the end of history. Only progress awaits us. As a result of our conquering of confusion, we are now unbound. But as with all narratives, this is merely a story of how the world should *be*. Fortunately the world lends for other narratives, and even more constructive ones.

There shall be no conquering of confusion. It is a fool's errand, comparable to trying to catch the water from a waterfall with a cup. The world is laden with confusion. It permeates everything, defines everything, influences everything. Nothing of the world is devoid of confusion. Language, for instance, comes with a confusion that we can never completely remove. What words mean requires us to understand the relational, cultural, ideological, and historical context in which those words are located and situated. Yet those contexts are always changing. Then there is the problem of knowing a person's motives and intentions. There is simply no way to know exactly what a person means or is trying to mean. The complexity and mystery of our humanity make this kind of certainty impossible. As life reminds us again and again, determining or knowing even our own meanings is usually impossible. There is always confusion, and nothing about this confusion can be stopped. Our experiences and influences are always changing, and what these experiences and influences do to us can never be fully known. Confusion is inevitable. Then there is the confusion that comes from the world. Our resources are finite. There is only so much time we can spend with each other. Therefore there is only so much of each other we can come to know. Our understanding or knowledge of each other will never be complete. It will be always based on impressions, estimations, and perceptions. Our understanding of each other will always be laden with confusion.

Yet all of this confusion is heuristic. Without confusion, communication would be impossible. But to view confusion as integral to communication constitutes a fundamentally different understanding of communication, and ultimately, a fundamentally different understanding of what being human means. It all begins with viewing confusion differently, that is, ending our hostility to confusion, which really means changing our view of ourselves and the world. Again, we will never conquer confusion. Just as well, as there is simply no need to learn how to tolerate confusion. It is in no way a kind of nuisance that requires our tolerance. Instead what we need is a new temperament that encourages us to engage confusion, embrace confusion, and even celebrate confusion. It is only because confusion is inevitable that grace, empathy, compassion, mercy, hope, faith, forgiveness, tenderness, and all the things that make us human are possible. In other words, only by embracing, engaging, and celebrating confusion do we develop the capacities and capabilities that save us from our worse instincts and impulses. Embracing confusion enlarges our humanity and in so doing, also enlarges our understanding and experiencing of the world.

But our current worldview conspires in every way against confusion. We remain of the belief that defeating confusion is possible and desirable. So our war against confusion continues, with us never noticing that such a war is really a war upon ourselves. The fact is that our current models of communication are inherently dehumanizing. To seek to vanquish confusion (so as to presumably make for the rise of confusion) is to strip away all of the diversity, complexity, and mystery that make us human. What emerges as communication is nothing of the sort. This *communication* is devoid of any capacity to expand anything, enrich anything, enliven anything, redeem anything. In other words, this communication is devoid of any life redeeming qualities. With this communication, redemption is impossible. As a result, though this kind of communication is now ubiquitous, we are increasingly being ravaged by the forces of isolation, mystification, and alienation. What then is the value of this communication that aspires to vanquish confusion? Still, this is the communication that is status quo. This is also the communication that is increasingly displacing other models of communication. In sum, this is the communication that is increasingly ruling the world as colonization, under the guise of globalization, continues to take hold of nearly every corner of the world. Eventually, of course, this model of communication will implode and collapse. It is simply contrary to the natural rhythms of the world. But at what cost? That is, what are all the implications and consequences that could potentially come from a world that is devoid of human beings who have the capacity to exercise mercy, compassion, forgiveness, and all else that is vital to prospering in a world laden with confusion?

There is also the matter of epistemology. To view communication in terms of conquering confusion diminishes how we perceive and make sense of the world and each other. Communication merely becomes a means of sharing what we know and understand rather than a process that creates and shapes what we know and understand. Thus the common goal of communication is fidelity—the ability of communication to effectively and efficiently share our thoughts and emotions. This view extends also to language as we view communication as being inherently linguistic and symbolic in nature. For us, epistemology deals with mental, biological, and psychological processes. Communication, again, is merely the means of sharing what we know and understand. But in a world that is laden with confusion, what can we really claim to know? Also, the inevitability of communication makes fidelity an impossible mission. We merely have the illusion of fidelity. But in our determination to end confusion, what emerges is a knowledge that is hostile to confusion, a knowledge that supposedly gives us charity, reliability, and predictability. It is a knowledge that gives us the impression that we can somehow disregard the world's natural rhythms. Instead, confusion fosters doubt. Confusion being the natural order of the world means that communication is inherently epistemological—through communication we shape and frame our knowledge of the world. But rather than communication promoting exploration, innovation and imagination, our hostility to confusion leads to a model of communication that discourages these kinds of life-affirming processes. What emerges is a way of knowing and understanding that values reduction, prediction, categorization, and other discursive devices that make for the illusion of us conquering confusion. That is, a way of knowing—or a knowledge—that assumes to have a command of confusion, and accompanying ideology to this epistemology. This way of knowing and understanding makes for a fundamentally different way of organizing our society and determining how we use our resources. But for now, what should concern us most is the kind of humanity that comes out of this kind of civilization.

Confusion is merely a reaction to the world's boundless mystery. It is an admission of our inability to end this mystery. As such, being confused is a natural and even healthy reaction to this mystery. It reminds us that what is unknown will always exceed what is known. So nothing is fundamentally wrong with being confused and even remaining confused. To be of confusion is human. What really matters is our relation to confusion, as in being at peace with confusion. We have, unfortunately, come to a different relation. We believe we can spare ourselves the confusions, frustrations, and tribulations that come with confusion. We can get to heaven without having to die. We now view confusion as a kind of unnatural condition. We demand as a kind of entitlement a life devoid of confusion, and have set about to create a world that will make this so. Thus our obsession with information—the belief that with enough information the world will be devoid of confusion. We would have our perfect clarity. As a result of our aversion to confusion, what emerges is our own lack of psychological, existential, spiritual, relational, and communicational resources to deal with confusion. Confusion torments us, paralyzes us. We are perpetually afraid of confusion. We remain resolved to end confusion. We feel entitled to clarity and lucidity. But what good can possibly come from us remaining hostile and tortured by a condition that is so fundamentally human and even vital to being human? What becomes of us when the world refuses to submit to our entitlement to clarity, especially when confusion is vital to cultivating a temperament of charity, humility, restraint, caution, and inquiry? Without such a temperament, what kind of world are human beings capable of creating, what kind of world becomes inevitable?

Yet this hostility to confusion remains at the foundation of our conception of communication. To communicate is to dehumanize. We dehumanize each other each other in communication by always trying to remove all of the complexity, ambiguity, and mystery that comes with being human. This is what the conquest of confusion requires of us. But does communication really arise from this process? Indeed, as much as the process could possibly be dehumanizing, what if this is still the only way to achieve communication, to share our thoughts and emotions with each other? In sum, what if this is simply the price of communication? However, this view already assumes that communication should be about the sharing of our thoughts and emotions with others. But what if this is merely one definition of communication? What if this is merely one way of understanding and experiencing communication? In a world of boundless diversity, ambiguity, and mystery, there must no doubt be at least the possibility of other ways to value, define, and experience communication.

What makes these other ways impossible? Who gets to make this determination? Also, how did we come to assume that other ways of defining, valuing, and experiencing communication are simply less useful? The point being that behind our common conception of communication is an ontology or a set of foundational beliefs about what being human means and our relation to the world and each other. Simply put, our conception of communication belongs to a certain story of the world. We reinscribe this story by how we communicate and relate to each other. At the heart of this story, of course, is the belief that the world is in a perpetual conflict between a set of benevolent and malevolent forces, like that between life and death, order and chaos, meaning and ambiguity, communication and confusion. Presumably, life has no inherent purpose or meaning. We are to procreate and survive, and to do by any means necessary. Herein resides our determination to vanquish confusion. It impedes our survival and prosperity. To arrive at new ways of defining communication means also creating a new story of the world. Asking what is the purpose of communication means also asking what is the purpose of life. Of course there is no way of really knowing what or whether there is any purpose to life. Every theory is a story. But narratives matter, as this how we make sense of the world and organize our lives. Therefore what seems to be really at stake is whether we can create space for at least the possibility of a different story about the meaning and even purpose of life.

In reality, confusion is by no means the antithesis of communication. In fact, confusion vitalizes communication, inspires communication. Embracing confusion involves the development of a temperament that can at least save the world from much misery and destruction. It shows us with at least the potentiality to be of worlds that are rich in meaning and purpose. Instead of being merely a tool for sharing our thoughts and emotions, communication can potentially be our means of becoming human. What we commonly describe as communication problems are nothing of the sort. These are really problems of being human, such as our lacking the capacity to exercise compassion, empathy, forgiveness, tenderness, grace, hope, mercy, and faith. These are really the problems that cause discord and disharmony. These are also the problems that block us from understanding and collaborating with each other. So yes, communication can be defined in terms of sharing and exchanging our thoughts and emotions. But this is by no means the only definition of communication that the world permits, just as much as a bicycle is by no means our only definition of transportation. As much as we are capable of building and using bicycles to get from one point to the next, we are also capable of devising and embodying much more elaborate definitions of communication. The fact that our common definition of communication is of a story of the world that assumes that survival is our only purpose, and that communication was born out of evolutionary necessity is interesting, as this definition seeks to end confusion but actually undermines our survival and prosperity by undermining the temperament that is ultimately vital to saving us from ourselves and each other. So as much as the origin of communication could possibly be found in evolutionary necessity, as is commonly assumed, what is now evident is that our common definition of communication threatens us by continually dehumanizing us, by stripping away all our diversity, complexity, and mystery.

29

ON SEXUALITY

We need to stop using the language of sexuality to describe the identity of a human being. It is dehumanizing, meaning that to reduce a human being to a category is dehumanizing. It robs us of our complexity, diversity, mystery, and ultimately, our humanity. Our sexuality is merely a dimension of humanity. It is by no means the sum of our humanity or even the most important dimension of our humanity. Also, there is no way to extricate our sexuality from the many other dimensions of our humanity, such as our social, spiritual, existential, cultural, historical, ideological, and sensual selves. Our sexuality is phenomenally complex. As much as others may want to assume that our sexuality is the defining feature of our identity, many us would disagree.

Yet this is what we continue to do when we frame issues in terms of gay issues and refer to people as our gay friends. How did our gay friend become merely our gay friend? Who made the decision to strip away all the complexity and diversity of this person? Who made the decision that only the sexual dimension of this person should matter, and should matter most? But of course to strip away the complexity, diversity, and humanity of others is really to strip away our own complexity, diversity, and humanity. This is why the practice needs to stop. It is mutually dehumanizing. We need to find new ways of relating and communicating with each other that restore *all* of our complexity, diversity, and humanity. This is the only way we shall save ourselves from our worst instincts and impulses.

It is also a matter of politics. Again and again the case is made by many who support gay rights that homosexuality is found in the natural world. Thus, homosexuality is natural. This argument is made to counter the popular view that God (supposedly) only made Adam and Eve. But the latter claim means absolutely nothing. God also made many other natural things like tidal waves, volcanoes, earthquakes, desert storms, and hurricanes. We could just as well claim that in making these natural forces, which are responsible for the loss of so many innocent lives, that God has no regard for the innocent. That God made Adam and Eve only means that God made Adam and Eve. The claim means nothing. The origin of our sexuality is irrelevant. Yet this obsession with our sexuality perpetuates a politics that erases our complexity, diversity, and mystery. We need to strive for a new politics that will stop us from doing this to ourselves and each other.

We want to arrive at a politics that begins on the premise that the condition of our own humanity is bound up with the condition of the world. To harm others is to harm ourselves, and ultimately to harm the world. We are no doubt all entitled to life, liberty, and our own pursuit of what being happy means. But this is merely the beginning. For what does being entitled to life mean when the resources that are vital to preserving life are rapidly being depleted and polluted? Also, what does liberty mean when laws are increasingly being made to limit our liberty? Of course without life and liberty, being happy is impossible. For how could a person be happy in world devoid of life-sustaining resources, or where laws and rules are increasingly being enacted to limit what we can share, pursue, and experience?

Yet the United States claims to be founded on the premise that all human beings are entitled to life, liberty, and the pursuit of happiness. Our political and judicial systems are supposedly designed to protect this premise. But after 300 years of professing to be a nation that cherishes this premise, even in the face of slavery and Jim Crow, there is still no resolve to realize *all* of this premise. We are still quarreling about whether certain human beings should have the rights that other human beings already have, such as the right to marry and adopt. Why do we continue to be hostile to a premise that requires so little from us? That is, why do we remain determined to deny others access to a premise that already promises little? For again, what is the value of life and liberty in a world devoid of life-sustaining resources? Also, how were so many able to write so eloquently about life and liberty, yet all the while keeping human beings in slavery and bondage? Is this merely a matter of hypocrisy? This is what we are to believe. It was a failure of character. But this excuse diminishes the gravity of the abomination by allowing us to continue to believe that the founding fathers were still great men, and thereby still deserving of our admiration and emulation. This, after all, is what we continue to do with Plato, Aristotle, Socrates, and the other great Greeks who continue to frame and legitimize our ethics and politics. Presumably, nearly 300 years of slavery and Jim Crow were merely a stain on the character of the founding fathers. For if the problem is much more structural and ideological, what becomes of the sanctity of the Constitution, and all the political and judicial institutions that grew out of this document, and which were also responsible for preserving slavery and Jim Crow? What kind of life and liberty can such equality afford in such a world? As Frederick Douglass once said, no one can fasten a chain around the foot of another without also fastening that chain around their neck. Evidently, the founding fathers had no understanding of this reality. But what Frederick Douglass was seeking to remind us is that the condition of our humanity is bound up with the condition of other's humanity. There can be no life and liberty for merely some of us. It must be for all. Thus, what does it mean that after 300 years of being of this Constitution that promises us life and liberty, that certain persons, for merely and supposedly being of a different sexuality, must continue to struggle to be seen as human? Why must there be this enduring struggle to achieve what the Constitution promises, including our capacity to do as we wish with our bodies, such as being able to consume what we desire, being able to share our bodies with whom we desire, or even being capable to end our own lives with dignity and grace?

The problem begins with how we are defining life and liberty. Presumably, life is about being able to exist. We have a right to exist. Liberty is presumably about the ability to do as we wish with our own lives. But herein resides our problem. These definitions of life and liberty are shallow. Life is relational, communal, and ecological. We are intertwined with each other. We are intertwined with the world. To be entitled to life is about being responsible for the condition of others and the world. For what becomes of the condition of others and the world ultimately becomes the condition of our life. When the condition of others becomes perilous, our life also becomes perilous. Life is plural. But the dominant view is that life is singular. We are separate and outside of each other. We are bounded selves, ultimately responsible for the condition of our own lives. Our definition of liberty assumes that this is a world devoid of constraints. We supposedly have no obligation for the well-being of others or for the planet. For us, liberty means the end of restraint and intrusion. It means being able to determine our own fates, on our own terms, with our own resources. But this is actually a world of limits, and also of order. Our actions and decisions (and lack thereof) always come with implications and consequences. No action or decision is ever morally or ecologically neutral. Our actions and decisions either promote or impede life. Yet this in no way means that the latter is always negative. In the case of those who pose a real threat to others, sometimes we must impede life in order to promote life. The point being that liberty without responsibility is promiscuity. On the other hand, how did being happy become the purpose of life? To assume that pursuing what makes us happy is what matters most constitutes a shallow view of the human condition. It also distorts history by failing to recognize all that has often been forsaken and sacrificed to achieve outcomes that have nothing to do with being happy. Aspiring to be happy separates us from the world. It invites illusions. This is why no prophet sought to be happy. The pursuit is both juvenile and infantile. Our being happy does nothing for the condition of the world. It assumes, again, a world that is outside and separate from us. It also assumes a world devoid of order. For instance, consuming an abundance of unhealthy foods can possibly make us happy, but doing so does nothing to better the world. It is merely promiscuity masquerading as liberty. Ultimately, the world will determine what we can pursue and even what we should pursue.

In a world of order what matters is whether we are capable and willing to love. Put differently, in a world where we are intertwined, our actions and decisions must aid the well-being of others. This is why love matters. This is also why there is a moral imperative to love. But of course, to love is hard. Whereas simply being happy involves no obligation to others, love assumes a deep obligation to others. Love also involves resolve and fortitude. We must be ready to love in spite of deterrents, which means that tribulation, frustration, and confusion are inevitable. There will always be despair and misery and turmoil. But only through love does life flourish. Only through love does liberty escape promiscuity. In sum, only through love may we anchor ourselves at the center of the world.

So to love is our life's work. This is what we must be entitled to do. This is what we have to do in order to have a world that sustains life and liberty. Love promotes the totality of our being. It ends the separation, division, and fragmentation that put us at each other's throats. We come to recognize and appreciate the abundant complexity, diversity, and mystery that come with being human. Love reveals a world of order. It also reveals the possibility of a fundamentally different conception of being human. Out of this emergent conception appears our enduring obligation to each other. We are moral beings, as our actions and decisions always have consequences and implications. But most of all, love changes our ethics and politics. It undermines the moral integrity of the Constitution, as well as the institutions that are of this moral and ideological vision. Our Constitution embodies a moral and ideological vision born of a certain worldview that naturally sustains and legitimizes this vision. Also, as with any worldview, there are foundational beliefs about what being human means, our relation to the world, and so forth. With our Constitution, the foundational view is that human beings are autonomous selves, devoid of any moral capacity. Morality must be imposed upon us through laws, which involves the necessity of a variety of legislative institutions to enact these laws. Behind our Constitution is also the view that a civilized society is laden with laws and also effectively upholds these laws. Thus our conviction that our society is superior. We are supposedly the most dedicated to creating, administering, and upholding our laws.

But our own history undermines our view of ourselves. What of all the laws that made slavery and Jim Crow a reality for nearly 350 years? Or the laws that made the near demise of Native Americans? Or the laws that made for the legal subordination of women? Or the laws that made for the subjugation of persons of different sexual orientations? What also of all the laws that continue to make for the unparalleled incarceration of so many human beings for merely possessing and consuming various substances? In the face of all of this the moral integrity of the Constitution remains off limits. We simply assume that human beings are amoral and the Constitution offers the best set of protections. The primary quarrel—that is, the quarrel that our society is willing to permit—is merely about how to interpret the Constitution, with one side arguing for attention to context and the other side insisting on a literal reading. But there is absolutely no challenging or even questioning of the ideology that governs the Constitution. For both sides, this is heresy. The fact that many can actually insist on only looking at what the founding fathers meant is disconcerting. For jurists and legal scholars of this persuasion, the Constitution binds us to the moral and ideological vision of the founding fathers. If a problem arises, according to these jurists and legal scholars, our society should look at the words and writings of the founding fathers for clarification and direction. But what of the deeds of the founding fathers, as in the fact that these men, though insisting upon the creed of life and liberty, were holding other human beings in servitude and bondage? How did deeds become to matter less than words? But again, for all sides, slavery is merely moral failing that has nothing to do with the moral and ideological integrity of the Constitution. But this is also why the realization of a society that values life and liberty continues to elude us, and increasingly so. The ideology that governs the Constitution is dehumanizing. It impoverishes our conception of life and liberty by assuming a shallow conception of what being human means. The result is a society that in every way impedes our capacity to value life and liberty. So as much as laws opposing the full expression of different kinds of sexual orientations will soon come to an end, as the laws against African Americans and women were also certain to come to an end, life and liberty will remain in peril as the world's natural resources will continue to be depleted and polluted. Regardless of our celebrated differences, our demise is all but certain. For at the foundation of our society is a worldview that opposes love, and without love, separation, division, and fragmentation it will remain status quo. We will remain of a society, to use Erich Fromm's language, that is *necrophilic* (life negating) rather than *biophilic* (life affirming). The diversity we strive to embrace and celebrate will mean nothing. Without love, diversity is merely plurality, devoid of any life-affirming power. In other words, when separation, division, and fragmentation are status quo, diversity is impossible. We merely have the illusion of diversity, just as much as we have the illusion of life, liberty, and being happy.

30

ON SOCIAL WORLDS

Although social constructs matter as regards to understanding the social nature of human beings, we continue to mistake social contracts for social constructs. The common example that people tend to use to explain a social construct is currency. The point is made that currency is merely a piece of paper. The value of the currency is actually found in the social agreement between persons as to what the piece of paper means. Outside of this social agreement, the piece of paper means nothing. But this is actually an example of a social contract. Social constructs require no kind of social agreement. In this way, social constructs fundamentally expand our notion of social worlds, and in so doing deepen our understanding of ourselves as social beings who make social worlds.

Take the case of the person who professes to be a heterosexual. Such a view is purely social. Under anonymous conditions that person can be sexually aroused by both men and women, demonstrating or exposing the fact that this conception of ourselves as being only of a certain sexual category is purely social. We are no doubt sexual beings. But we are also sensual, spiritual, cultural, historical, ideological, relational, material, and existential beings. The totality of our humanity makes for a complexity, diversity, and mystery that undermines the stability and even legitimacy of any manner of social ordering.

This is no doubt a world of constraints, a world of order. But such constraints complement our social nature. Only because the world is of ambiguity are social worlds possible. In other words, in a world devoid of implications and consequences, meaning would be impossible. There would be no degrees of freedom. It is the world's order that invites meaning and forces meaning out of us. A world devoid of ambiguity would make no such demands, offer no such invitation. This is what being social means. It means that there is a place for us in the world. We can form our own conceptions and understandings of ourselves and our relations to each other. We can create our own social worlds. However, in order for our social worlds to be life affirming, our social processes must be in harmony with the order of the world. Social worlds that diminish life, including all life, will eventually perish. This includes social constructs, social contracts, and social norms that impede imagination and innovation, diversity and possibility, and evolution and liberation. The rhythms of the world will always oppose any social world that promotes tyranny and misery. Only social worlds that affirm life will strive and flourish. However, such social worlds can be—and will always be—of a diversity that is boundless, meaning of course that the diversity of social contracts, social constructs, and social norms that can be available to us are also boundless. Through our social worlds we marry the spiritual with the material, the existential with the ecological. This is why the quality and condition of social worlds matter. In being wombs, our social worlds fertilize and incubate life.

A vibrant social world is always encouraging the rise of new social constructs. We are always being encouraged to explore new ways of being human, including new ways of understanding and experiencing the world. In vibrant social worlds, exploration is a social norm. Change is also a social norm, which means that social constructs are fluid. Nothing is beyond a new interpretation and description. Everything is social in origin. Even our most prized truths are born of social forces. Of course the idea of truth being social in nature remains a troubling notion for many persons. Such persons simply believe that the world will simply be better off with absolute truths—ones that are unbending and unyielding, and will have no tolerance or patience with our nonsense. An absolute view of truth is about us devising a way to impose order on the world and upon ourselves. Such a truth is born out of deep suspicion and fear of ourselves. The mission of an absolute truth is to limit the world's ambiguity, our ambiguity. Such a truth releases us of the struggle of constantly figuring out the world, and also requires us to come to terms that our knowledge will always incomplete. In this way, an absolute truth stops communication, thereby also impeding exploration and imagination. In a world of absolute truths, dissent is unwelcome. Such truths protect the status quo. For in a world of absolute truths, obedience is the social norm. What else, after all, can mere mortals do in the face of such truths? What would be the purpose of communication, or the reason for imagination and innovation? Besides making for tyranny, such truths are always the tools of tyrants. The moral of the story is that absolute truths are of us. These truths are born out of our various anxieties, insecurities, and paranoia. No prophet speaks to these truths. If such were the case, God would be a tyrant. There would be no opportunity for us to help complete the world. Our existence would be purely for the sake of obedience. God would be a narcissist. As much as various scriptures lend for such a God, other interpretations are available to us. But the God we find will always correlate with our view of truth, and our view of truth has enormous consequences for what becomes of our social worlds. For instance, in a world of absolute truths, mercy is impossible, meaning that vengeance is status quo. This is the seduction that comes with absolute truths. Such truths appeal to our worst instincts and impulses. If God is unyielding and unbending, then we should aspire to be so. To do differently would supposedly invite chaos. To be just means strictly following the law (the truth). It means removing our supposedly fallible selves from the equation, and simply deciding the matter at hand by always trying to find the truth. We aspire—in at least in theory—to find and uphold the truth, regardless of the consequences. To do this is supposedly to do God's work. Upholding the truth is supposedly what makes us just and righteous. It is the measure of a human being. A society that is just and supposedly of righteous people is rigid and unyielding. Mercy is difficult to come by. Such a society is determined to uphold the truth, regardless of the fallout or consequences. The goal is to use truth to protect us from our fallibility, gullibility, and promiscuity—that is, to protect us from ourselves. The implication again being that without an absolute truth we will descend into chaos.

But a social conception of truth is much more heuristic than our common view of truth. No doubt, this is a world of truths. Mangoes will only come from mango trees, just as much as apples will only come from apple trees. But in a social conception of truth, God is truly great as our view of God can change and evolve. Also, in a society that is of such a conception of truth, mercy is compulsory. The social realm is the human realm, shaped by all the things that make us human, as well as the things that make us less so. The social realm is also laden with all manner of confusion, such as the confusion that is within us, between us, and around us. All of this confusion can be found in our social contracts, social constructs, and social norms. Clarity is fleeting. Consequently, our social worlds are laden with omissions, misperceptions, distortions, exaggerations, fabrications, and all manner of illusions and confusions. Our understanding of ourselves, each other, and the world is never perfect. We could always benefit from more communication. So in the social realm the human-making process is always ongoing. Our social processes are always changing. But this is good, as our social worlds are inherently ecological. We also change and evolve as our social worlds change and evolve. Our social worlds nourish us by providing us with the resources that are vital to becoming human. This is also why social constructs matter. Social constructs allow us to exceed the physical and material realm, fermenting imagination, innovation, and exploration. So as much as God probably only made Adam and Eve, the diversity of relations and social worlds that human beings can have with each other is nearly unbound.

31

ON DOUBT

No one warns you about the doubt that pervades everything, rattles everything, torments everything, threatens everything. Truth is supposed to save us from doubt. This is why we are supposed to hold on to our truths with all the conviction we can muster. Presumably, truth is the enemy of doubt. But then we go in search of truth and soon come to realize that extricating truth from doubt is impossible. Regardless of all we do, and all that we choose we believe, the bond between truth and doubt is inseparable. But what must we do now when doubt continues to pervade everything?

We can theoretically claim that doubt enriches everything. It makes us human by saving us from our worst instincts and impulses. Only by embracing doubt do we achieve humility and remain in awe of the world's boundless mystery and ambiguity. Without doubt, we would be nothing but beasts and savages. Without doubt, truth would have no capacity to evolve and change, which also means that we would have no capacity to evolve and change. Submission would be status quo. But embracing doubt is hard. Even Jesus Christ struggled with doubt. "Lord, why have you forsaken me?" That even Jesus Christ could struggle with doubt means that the rest of us will in no way be spared. It also means that our struggle with doubt is the most defining struggle.

But why even the metaphor of struggle? Why is this metaphor so popular with us? Why does it always seem the most natural description of our condition? But this is what metaphors have the capacity to do? When metaphors are done with us, believing that our view of the world is inherently metaphorical becomes really hard. Still, the metaphor of struggle allows us to continue to believe that truth is the enemy of doubt. This, again, is what metaphors have the power to do—shape and influence what we believe. Metaphors come from everywhere. But the metaphor of struggle comes from a primal place. This is arguably why this metaphor seems so natural and universal. Any society that promotes competition instills within us a worldview where struggle pervades. Thus escaping this metaphor of struggle is especially hard in a society that values this worldview. Also, the metaphor of struggle is seductive. In a world of struggle, one is either friend or foe. In such a world, everything is already determined, finalized, and figured out. We merely have to play our assigned roles.

Becoming human is a metaphorical matter. It is about changing the metaphors we use to describe and experience the world. It is also about heightening our awareness of the metaphors that surround us and which are also imposed on us. It is also about knowing which metaphors to resist, and also cultivating the capacity to resist these metaphors. It is about being open to trying on new metaphors, which means being willing to embody language differently. Yes, language is inherently metaphorical. But so also is being. As much as various metaphors can impede us, others can emancipate us. Language is a dimension of being. As much as we invoke metaphors in how we *use* language, we also invoke metaphors in how we *experience* language. Therefore as much as we have to be conscious of the metaphors that circulate in our language, we also have to be aware of the metaphors that shape how we experience language. For instance, why do we experience language as a tool? What does it mean to experience language as a tool? What manner of being does such a metaphor create? In what other ways can we experience language? Also, what metaphors can enlarge how we experience language? This common metaphor of language being a tool comes from our story of evolution. In being a tool, the metaphor would have us believe that language is merely an instrument. Its only goal is to help us get things done, and how proficiently so will depend on how masterly we wield this instrument that is language. So in this metaphor of language as a tool, our goal is to use language competently and proficiently. We aspire to gain mastery of language, just like how a swordsman aspires to wield a sword masterly. Just like a master swordsman, our goal is to make the instrument an extension of our being, to connect the instrument to our being so that there is no division between our intentions and the ambition of the instrument. The instrument must do our bidding. Anything less would invite chaos. So with language, our goal is practice, practice, practice. We aspire to master all the skills and techniques that will allow us to gain dominion over this tool.

But this is the problem with viewing language as a tool. This metaphor removes life from language. Language becomes merely an instrument. This metaphor diminishes our conception of life. With this metaphor, life is merely a canvas upon which we use language to impose our impressions and intentions. The focus is on us. We assume that the origin of language is purely for our purposes. It is for our survival and prosperity. Presumably, language has nothing to do with the condition of the world. It is purely our thing. We therefore tend to describe ourselves in terms of our linguistic and symbolic capacity. It is supposedly our superior linguistic and symbolic capacity that distinguishes us from other organic entities. Yet the Bible claims that God made the world out of language. By invoking the Word, the world was born. How then did language become merely our thing? What language did God use to make the world? What is that language? What became of that language? How did our language become cut off from that language and thereby lose the ability to create worlds?

The way we continue to use and relate and experience language is only bringing death and destruction upon the world. We invoke language to homogenize, normalize, civilize, terrorize, and categorize. We also use language to manipulate, separate, and assimilate. For us, the purpose of language is to serve the status quo, to impose order upon the world. Yet God evidently had no such intentions for language. The goal of language was to create. By invoking language the way God invokes language we are revealing to ourselves what being made in the image and likeness of God is all about. In using and embodying language in ways that create and celebrate life, we save the world from death and destruction. We also begin to recognize our connection and obligation to the world. But again, in order for all of this to happen, we have to realize a new relation to language that ends all manner of separation, division, and fragmentation.

32

ON BUREAUCRACY

In modernity the goal is to achieve rationality—to be rational human beings, acting rationally, ultimately realizing a rational society. For modernity, rationality is about the capacity to process reality without bias and prejudice. It is about suppressing our passions and inclinations, thereby being supposedly robust and rigorous in our decision-making. It is also about being completely committed to truth, clarity, and certainty. Simply put, rationality is about defeating the flesh, marginalizing the flesh, conquering the flesh. Rationality is about us waging war upon ourselves. This is modernity's gift to humanity.

Modernity assumes that without this conquering of the flesh, chaos and devolution will arise. Such is the origin of the fear that continues to torment us. This fear permeates everything, influences everything, shapes everything. Only by supposedly conquering the flesh will human beings achieve civility and prosperity. Rationality is supposedly the path to both. This is why rationality is vital. This is why, for modernity, rationality must be institutionalized—that is, constantly cultivated and propagated. But such is the origin of bureaucracy. Bureaucracy is the institutionalization of rationality, really western and European notions of rationality. It constitutes our determination to finally conquer the flesh completely and absolutely. For modernity, bureaucracy is inevitable. Without bureaucracy, civility and prosperity are supposedly impossible. Bureaucracy supposedly saves us from ourselves. By cultivating, propagating, and instituting rationality, bureaucracy constitutes an unrelenting war upon the flesh. But for modernity, this is a necessary war. Without this war, chaos will supposedly reign. This reasoning gives us the means to justify the fallout that comes with this war, including the savagery and cruelty. Make no mistake, this is a war, and as with any war, there is misery and carnage.

There are different orders of rationality in modernity. The first order of rationality and bureaucracy involves the creation and administration of knowledge. If human beings are merely bundles of selfish genes who are of a world that is in conflict with us, which modernity assumes, then our survival and prosperity depends on us creating a knowledge that will allow us to prevail in this struggle. This is presumably the only rational thing to do. This, again, is the *first order* of rationality that drives modernity. But this is only the beginning of the institutionalization of rationality. It is also only rational to devise means that will allow us to consistently appraise and discriminate this knowledge from other knowledges. This is the *second order* of rationality that drives modernity. It is eventually only rational to acquire, cultivate, and disseminate as much of this necessary knowledge as possible. Again, we presumably need this knowledge in order to survive and flourish. This is the *third order* of rationality that is of modernity. This is where bureaucracy begins to take shape. Our ways of defining, acquiring, appraising, disseminating, and purposing knowledge make bureaucracy rational (e.g., undergraduate curriculums, worksheets, and syllabuses). It is only rational to devise the most efficient and effective ways to disseminate this knowledge that limits the intrusion of the flesh. In other words, how else to avoid the dissemination of this knowledge from being corrupted by the flesh? This is the *fourth order* of rationality that is of modernity. But this rationality eventually evolves into another kind of rationality. Bureaucracy in turn promotes and cultivates a certain definition of rationality (curriculums and worksheets). This rationality controls and shapes the administration, organization, and production of knowledge (journal rankings, book publishers rankings, standards for promotion and tenure, publishing protocols, and manner of scholarly writing and arguing). This is the *fifth order* of rationality that is of modernity. This rationality of bureaucracy makes for a certain kind of human consciousness (the bureaucrat)—one that values hierarchy (command and control structures). This consciousness has an aversion to diversity, ambiguity, flexibility, spontaneity, and human ingenuity. Instead, this *sixth order* of rationality promotes conformity, commonality, homogeneity, stability, continuity, predictability, and safety. That is, a rationality with an aversion to chaos and disruption. The bureaucrat values being on task, suppressing passion and intuition, and being committed to processes (playing by the rules and working within the system) that stop any kind of chaos and disruption. So the bureaucrat's primary mission is to protect the integrity of the bureaucracy. For without following due process, as in diligently following all programs, curriculums, worksheets, and syllabuses, chaos will supposedly result. This rationality is seen when marginalized groups are encouraged to work within the system.

Finally, the rationality that gives rise to bureaucracy, and which in turn bureaucracy cultivates and promotes, makes for a society that perpetuates and prizes a certain model of rationality. This society circulates and recirculates this *seventh order* of rationality. In turn, this rationality reinforces a certain manner of being (ontology) that predisposes us to a certain way of understanding the world (epistemology). For instance, this rationality makes for a society that values markets. Markets are a product of modernity's rationality. In fact, markets are a natural expression of the epistemology that is found in modernity. Markets are (supposedly) fair, objective (devoid of flesh, and thereby have no regards for station, position, or orientation), robust, rigorous, and transparent. Markets also supposedly have the ability to organically determine what is fair and just. In the end, what seems obvious is that modernity cultivates rather then represents rationality.

Modernity's success can be seen in the fact that its various expressions of rationality now permeate everything. There is now near total control of the flesh. With the rise of a vast bureaucracy that controls the administration, organization, and dissemination of knowledge has come our unsurpassed capacity to produce, stockpile, and disseminate knowledge. The rise of this vast stockpile of knowledge concretizes our belief that modernity is delivering on the promise of an unrivaled progress and prosperity. Also, the fact that other civilizations are rushing to adopt a modernist worldview seems to objectively confirm its superiority. But there is much to be said about the rationality and bureaucracy that control the organization, administration, and dissemination of knowledge. What emerges from this bureaucracy is a knowledge that poses no threat to the status quo, and thereby no threat to us. This knowledge domesticates us by separating being from knowing. This separation comes from our determination to conquer the flesh.

But nothing escapes the flesh. The flesh is always present. Modernity merely achieves the illusion of absence and erasure. But there can be no separating of reason from passion, fact from fiction, truth from mystery, meaning from ambiguity. By waging an unrelenting war on the flesh, the bureaucracy that controls our organization, administration, and dissemination of knowledge only succeeds in disfiguring the flesh. For what are we to make of the striking omission of love, mercy, forgiveness, tenderness, grace, and compassion from the social sciences? What also to make of the fact that this bureaucracy that claims responsibility for the organization, administration, and dissemination of knowledge blatantly and systematically suppresses the asking of fundamentally new questions? What also to make of the fact that with the acquisition of this knowledge comes no moral evolution or expansion of our moral imagination? But this is what happens when the flesh is disfigured and terrorized. Yes, our knowledge is plenty, but how much of this knowledge is valuable?

There is a tragic irony about this situation. It is actually scholars and academics—those who are supposed to be the guardians and custodians of knowledge—that aim to protect this bureaucracy that makes knowledge impossible. Our efforts to acquire knowledge only take us further away from knowledge. There is no possibility of knowledge from this bureaucracy, the reason being that this was never the mission of this bureaucracy. The rationality that drives this bureaucracy ultimately seeks order. This is what modernity desires most. This is the purpose of bureaucracy—to deliver order. However, to achieve order, the flesh must be colonized. But again, as much as bureaucracy aspires to conquer the flesh, the flesh can never be entirely removed. So bureaucracy is always in conflict with the flesh, which means that bureaucracy is always fostering the illusion and impression that the flesh is responsible for our ills and problems.

33

ON JUSTICE

Philosophy assumes that any theory of justice must ultimately come from our own doing. We must look to ourselves rather than to the heavens for such a theory. Presumably, religion has nothing to offer, especially for a plural society. Philosophy also assumes that indigenous peoples have nothing to offer. So nearly every discussion of justice begins with Kant, Hume, Bentham, Mill, Dewey, Rawls, Singer, Nozick, and company. Apparently, women also have nothing much to offer.

 The most popular theory of justice claims that justice is about determining the greatest good for the greatest number. This theory shapes much of our political, legal, and economic frameworks. It intuitively seems the most just and natural approach of justice. It also seems the most elegant, as well as the most rigorous. Proponents also contend that this framework is progressive. It impedes tyranny and pushes us to find solutions that do the most good for the greatest number. Finally, proponents claim that this theory has no regard for station, persuasion, or orientation. It undermines bias and prejudice. It directs us to look purely at outcomes, and only support those outcomes that do the most good for the most number. Indeed, this theory comes under the heading of a rational choice theory as finding the greatest good, regardless of our position, persuasion, or orientation, for the greatest number is supposedly rational.

But what of the minority? What can the minority do when the majority has already determined what is the greatest good, or when what is the greatest good serves only the interest of the majority? It seems, after all, that what is in the interest of the greatest good is purely at the mercy of the will of the majority. Thus opponents of this theory of justice claim that with this theory nothing is inherently just, good, or even fair. It is all arbitrary. We are merely at the mercy of the will of the majority. This was the problem that John Rawls sought to fix in *A Theory of Justice*, a book that is now required reading in philosophy. If, according to Rawls, human beings can somehow be put in a situation that blocks our awareness of our station, location, and orientation, the rational thing for us to do would be to promote equality and liberty as doing so would serve our own self-interest. So, according to Rawls, promoting equality and liberty is rational, and as a result, inherently just, fair, and good. With the evolution of rationality comes justice. As such, the promotion of rationality is vital for the promotion of justice. Note also that for Rawls rationality means objectivity—the suppression of intuitions and passions. It also means self-interest. Thus according to Rawls, justice is about promoting equality and liberty, and what is just is also that which is good and fair. The onus is merely on us to be rational.

As with other rational choice models found in philosophy, economics, law, communication theory, and political theory, rationality is assumed to be of a universal and natural definition that transcends culture, history, and geography. Presumably, rationality means the promotion of self-interest, as doing so promotes our survival and prosperity. But the problem with rational choice models is that rationality is shaped by cultural forces. Many forces shape how we perceive and make sense of the world. Our experiences matter. Our circumstances matter. Our resources matter. That our experiences, circumstances, and resources will always be different means that our understanding of what is rational will always be different. Also, rationality is developmental. Our moral imagination shapes our view of what is rational. Thus what was rational for Martin Luther King was fundamentally different for what was rational for George Wallace. Rationality can mean sacrificing our lives for others who share no relational kinship with us. We are also by no means purely rational beings. We are also emotional, sensual, spiritual, relational, historical, and ecological beings. All of this complexity shapes for us what is rational. Finally, no human being can command all the information that is necessary to act completely or purely rational. All actions and decisions are made within a context that presents all manner of limitations. We make decisions based on what the context allows, and every context presents a different set of options and limitations. In sum, the definition of rationality found in rational choice models is illusory. Yet this in no way means that the notion is without value, or even that the diminution of the notion impedes our ability to achieve a just society. In fact, looking at rationality within the constraints I just outlined actually enriches our understanding of rationality. It means that determining what decisions and actions are rational—or just, fair, and good—requires us to look closely and carefully at a variety of variables, including the resources that are available to us, and the context that is before us. No decision-making occurs in a vacuum. Determining what is just involves much contemplation, reflection, and examination. Still, every decision is provisional, subject to correction, revision, and even nullification. This is what being rational should mean—being committed to possibility, even the possibility of being wrong. It should be about recognizing that our redemption actually resides in our limitations.

But let us begin again. Rawls's theory of justice begins with us having absolutely no awareness of our station, location, or orientation. That is, without any awareness of our circumstances, what would any person consider to be just? Of course this is situation realistically impossible. We are always conscious of our station, persuasion, and orientation, and our situations are always uneven and often in conflict with each other. Anyway, Rawls believes this kind of thought experiment is necessary to have a just society, one that promotes liberty and equality. For Rawls, the possibility of a just society depends on us abiding by an illusion. Such is what human beings must apparently do to have justice, and again, the most that can be had is equality and liberty. There is presumably no other way to rationally justify anything else. According to Rawls's theory, the promotion of liberty and equality leads to fairness. This is the measure of justice. Also, fairness leads to goodness, meaning that decisions that are fair are inherently good. The implication, as found in philosophy and Rawls's theory, is that such notions as love, mercy, compassion, and grace have no natural or rational location within any robust theory of justice. In fact, absolutely no mention of these notions appears in Rawls's *A Theory of Justice*. But again, this omission is based on a highly disfigured notion of rationality, and a no less disfigured view of justice. The moral of the story being that any theory of justice that begins on an illusion ends on an illusion.

To theorize is to imagine. Every theory of justice reflects a moral imagination. What we have the courage to imagine will shape how we perceive the world. However, what we can imagine can always change and evolve. It all depends on how much courage we are capable of exercising and exerting. It is also about what we have the courage to believe. Yes, believe. Every theory of justice asks us to believe something. In the case of the theory of justice that stresses the greatest good for the greatest number, we are to believe that nothing is inherently just. In the case of Rawls's theory, we are to believe that fairness is the most human beings can muster. The goal is always to convince us that a theory is merely a description of reality.

But a theory is really a description of our imagination. It reflects what we are willing to believe and even need to believe. This is the problem with philosophy—the lack of any expansive moral imagination. This is why our popular theories of justice are so deficient. On the other hand, this is why these theories are so appealing. These theories are in harmony with what we are willing to believe and imagine, meaning that nothing in these theories challenge what we believe and how we imagine the world to be. Instead, these theories rationalize and concretize what we believe. This, in fact, is what theories generally do. Much of theorizing is rationalizing. But eventually reality intervenes and even our most reliable theories become undone. Such is the case now with Rawls's theory of justice. Resolving the many problems and challenges this emerging world is presenting us with requires theories of justice that go way beyond the bounds of liberty and justice. We need theories that promote love, mercy, empathy, compassion, and grace so we can enlarge how we imagine and experience the world. Theorizing should be a process of becoming. It should be a process of describing our own emotional, historical, and epistemological limits and constraints. Or put differently, to theorize is to describe all the forces, resources, and experiences that make for our particular descriptions. We need to arrive at a way of doing theory that obligates to account for all of these forces, resources, and experiences, as well as the implications and consequences that come with our descriptions. That is, whose interests are best served by our theories and descriptions?

This is a world of unparalleled diversity. Our spaces and distances are collapsing and imploding. Our vital resources are also dwindling and disappearing. This situation is certain to make for increasing conflict, and increasingly all sides have weapons of mass destruction. In this emerging world any theory of justice that disregards or marginalizes the minority can face much misery and peril. In fact, the consequences can be dire. We need theories of justice that recognize that diversity is much more than diversity. Diversity is about disruption, even revolution. To look at the world differently is to understand the world differently. Diversity can never be about inclusion, assimilation, or toleration. For diversity to be really about diversity, communication, deliberation, and negotiation are necessary. We have to be genuinely committed to viewing the world from the perspective of others, and refraining from imposing our view of the world on others. In this emerging world what is just is fundamentally about our treatment of those who seem most different to us. This means the rise of theories of justice that can potentially view diversity as integral to the evolution and definition of justice.

Yet this recognition of diversity as a measure of justice is anything but new. The *Book of Hadith* (Sayings of the Prophet Muhammad) eloquently articulates a theory of justice that promotes diversity. After all, the Prophet was initially persecuted for merely being of a different religious or spiritual persuasion. The Prophet explicitly calls for no coercion in religion. We must respect each other's differences, even those differences—like our religious differences—that seem to most threaten to tear us asunder. The Prophet also explicitly calls for charity and generosity for *all* persons. We must even be charitable to those who take advantage of our charity and generosity. The Prophet also advises us to look within our own hearts to know what is just. We are capable of discerning right from wrong. This means that the Prophet calls us to respect the integrity of each other's personhood. Finally, and most importantly, the Prophet calls us to exercise mercy and forgiveness in ways that are boundless. There is simply no transgression that is beyond mercy. In fact, the exercising of mercy is our highest obligation.

Nothing in the *Book of Hadith* is contrary to anything found in the gospels of Matthew, Mark, Luke, and John. The story of Jesus Christ is also about diversity. It is also a story of persecution for being different. Jesus Christ says that only those without sin should cast the first stone. We are to refrain from judging and condemning others, especially those who seem most different to us. We are also to be most generous to the most vulnerable amongst us. We are also encouraged to love those who are most different to us, even those who seek to vanquish us. We are also obligated to be vulnerable to the humanity of others so as to hear what is often most difficult to hear. Only through this kind of vulnerability is understanding possible between different peoples. Then there are the calls to love and forgive those who trespass against us.

But philosophy would have nothing to do with the teaching of the Prophet or Jesus Christ. These are matters for theology, supposedly. But in reality these teachings have everything to do with achieving a just society out of peoples who are different. Note that neither the Prophet nor Jesus Christ calls us to tolerate, accommodate, or assimilate. We are to care, to forgive, and most of all, to love. There should be no illusions about diversity. Even prophets perish for simply being different. Yet this is the moral of the story—treating those who are most different to us as sacred, as deserving as the best of us. This is why diversity matters. It needs the best from us. In this way, diversity has really nothing to do with differences, or even with a person's persuasion or orientation. It is about our obligations to others, as in our redemption being bound up with the condition of others. There is nothing religious about this kind of obligation. Without mercy, all of us will eventually be blind. Without mercy, the past will be nothing but a prison. Without mercy, our moral clarity would be diminished. Finally, without mercy, our capacity to look at the world anew would remain paralyzed by the fears of others. In sum, without mercy, our evolution and redemption would be compromised. Thus mercy is fundamentally about necessity rather than religiosity. Similarly, love enlarges our moral imagination. It releases the mind from the ravages of hate and prejudice. It limbers the heart and soothes the soul. Also, love makes us less afraid of each other, and thereby less unwilling to consider different truths and modes of being. All of this that love affords is vital for the creation of a just society. For what is the possibility of a just society when persons are afraid and suspicious of each other? Or, what is the possibility of a just society when our minds are laden with hate and prejudice? Also, what is the possibility of a just society without empathy and compassion? How can apathy be a friend to any theory of justice? But just like love and mercy, compassion needs to be nurtured and cultivated. Just like love and mercy, compassion offers many important benefits to the creation of a just society.

There is simply no merit in the impression made by philosophy that the world's great spiritual scriptures are of no use in devising a theory of justice that is amenable to a plural and multicultural society. Yet philosophy continues to push this impression, even claiming that now, especially now, these scriptures need to be marginalized and even removed from the public realm. It is supposedly our religious diversity that now threatens us most. But there is nothing new about invoking religion to justify and mayhem. We have used religion and everything else, including philosophy. Of course philosophy gets away with this impression by simultaneously fostering the impression of being uniquely committed to rationality. But this claim is false. Most striking about the theories of justice that come from philosophy is the absence of rationality. Case in point, how rational is any theory of justice that never acknowledges our relation to our environment? How could any theory of justice only be about what is just in human affairs, and how could human affairs have nothing to do with the environment? How is this rational, meaning how could any theory of justice have no regard for what is just for the environment that provides all our life-sustaining resources? It would seem that any action that is unjust for the environment is also unjust for us. But in order to bring our ecological environment into the fold requires us to fundamentally expand our conception of the human condition. We have to adopt an ecological view of the human condition—a view that enfolds us into the environment and the environment into us. Such a view recognizes that our actions and decisions always have consequences for the environment and those consequences fall back on us. Nothing begins or ends at the human realm. There are always ecological costs, and eventually these costs must be settled. It seems only rational that any theory of justice should consider those costs in determining what is just. But to do so upsets the status quo. It would make for a completely new system of ethics, politics, and economics. We would have to be ready to look at ourselves anew, each other anew, the world anew, and this would mean substantially deepening our obligations to the world and each other. Simply put, significantly enlarging our definition of justice. But nothing less can a new theory of justice demand of us.

34

ON TECHNOLOGY

From the perspective of modernity, the proliferation of modern communication technologies is good thing. It means that the defeat of confusion, which also means the defeat of chaos. The proliferation of modern communication technologies is generally assumed to be making for the order that modernity long promised—an order that suppresses conflict, especially any that can disrupt the status quo. But there are consequences that come with the proliferation of these supposedly modern communication technologies. As much as these technologies are allowing us to shape the world in certain ways, these technologies are also in turn shaping us in ways that harmonize us with the world these technologies are creating. This is why the proliferation of these modern communication technologies also constitutes an insidious kind of neocolonialism. To introduce a foreign technology into a community is to introduce a foreign worldview into a community, and to incorporate that technology is also to take on that worldview. In many ways, the proliferation of various technologies is a study of colonialism. Yes, military and religious conquests are the hallmarks of colonialism, but the entry of foreign technology did much to help colonize the natives. Indeed, the introduction and proliferation of foreign technologies continue to function as a kind of trojan horse. In the case of these modern communication technologies, the threat is no less insidious, no less dangerous.

The promotion of these communication technologies has nothing to do with the promotion of communication. If communication is simply about the transaction of messages, as modernity assumes, then yes, these technologies do promote communication. But to define communication in terms of messages is comparable to defining transportation in terms of riding a bicycle. Yes, a bicycle is a kind of transportation, but on the other hand, riding a bicycle can hardly be defined as the sum of transportation. In fact, using a bicycle to define transportation actually distorts our understanding of what transportation can be. For why should transportation be simply defined in terms of moving from one location to the next? That is, why should transportation simply be about quantity and quality of movement? What about capacity, potentiality, and fecundity? For instance, no bicycle, regardless of the quality of the bicycle, can get us across an ocean, or over a desert, or over a mountain. Accomplishing these tasks would be impossible. These journeys, and all the experiences that come with these journeys, would be outside of our experiences. As much as we can define transportation in terms of moving from one point to a next, we could also define it in terms of journeying, and in so doing capture the fact that every mode of transportation reflects a view of the world, and that moving from one point to the next can potentially mean much more than physically moving from one point to the next. We have experiences as we move, and how we move and where we seek to move to shape our experiences. These experiences matter. Behind every definition of transportation is a view of what is possible.

All of this is true for how we define everything. We could define anything in numerous ways. Every definition is an ideological creature. It becomes a matter of which definition is the most heuristic—which one gives us the most to work with. Or, which one gives us the largest canvas. Nothing is inherently wrong with defining communication in terms of the transaction of messages. It simply constitutes a highly narrow definition of communication. It reduces communication to merely the sharing of messages, mostly speaking and writing. In reality, communication is a human-making activity, even a world-making activity. We also perform rather than merely speak a language. Language is never devoid of spirits. It is always ideologically laden. But all of this finds no place in our common understanding of communication that is driving the proliferation of modern communication technologies. For us, these technologies are promoting communication, allowing us to have much *more* communication. Again, as regards to quantity, this is the case. But potentiality is a different matter.

Potentiality deals with our capacity to be vulnerable to each other. Vulnerability is about the courage to believe, the courage to imagine, the courage to share, and ultimately, the courage to love. Modern communication technologies do nothing to enhance or enlarge such courage, such modes of being. In fact, these technologies undermine the formation of such courage by allowing us to avoid each other, especially in those situations that seem the most challenging, intimidating, and threatening. In other words, these technologies are allowing us to avoid all the experiences that are necessary for us to become fully human. Or put differently, these technologies are lessening the intensity of our experiences with each other. What remains is merely the illusion of relationships, as in the illusion of having friends, the illusion of being of community. Yet without friends, without community, isolation is what remains, and isolation is the end of us. Thus, by undermining vulnerability, modern communication technologies deprive us of the courage necessary to forge deep bonds of obligation and commitment. All of this comes with a price as isolation is by no means merely a physical isolation. Isolation disintegrates the human condition. It creates all manner of neuroses and psychoses. We need deep bonds of obligation and commitment to become fully human. However, without vulnerability, such bonds are impossible. This is why communication is a human-making activity. This is also how communication saves us from becoming beasts and savages.

The proliferation of modern communication technologies is helping to create a false sense of civility and prosperity. These technologies are in no way making us more humane. If anything, the opposite is true. Neither are these technologies making for a more democratic world. Again, if anything, the opposite is true. But in this case we seem bent on making perception reality. We credit these technologies for making possible new kinds of democratic movements that now seem to threaten the reign of all tyrants and monsters. We also credit these technologies for undermining modes of organization and administration that promote division, separation, and balkanization. We also credit these technologies for creating new and better democratic and participatory platforms, such as platforms that are much more dynamic, organic, and pluralistic. This is no doubt the impression. This impression also synchronizes well with the impression that modernity seeks forever to make—through our science and technology we will achieve an unsurpassed civility and prosperity.

But democracies have nothing to do with institutions. In fact, autocracies also have no origins in institutions. Democracy is a mode of being. It constitutes a certain way of being in the world with others. We become democratic by becoming more compassionate. This is why diversity comes with democracy. This is why equality comes with democracy. This is why peace comes with democracy. Democracy comes with our becoming fully human. So yes, the proliferation of modern communication technologies do seem to threaten the reign of tyrants, but autocracies can take a variety of forms, even pass for democracies. Indeed, many of what we define as democracies are anything but. We have reduced communication to participation and representation. But such processes, as history now makes plain, hardly ever challenge us to view the world from the perspective of others. We can remain dogmatic, narcissistic, and ethnocentric, and still profess to be democratic. Therefore defining democracy in terms of representation and participation neither enlarges our manner of being nor makes us less hostile to experiences that are different to our own. In this definition of democracy, determining the will of the majority is all that is necessary.

The proliferation of modern communication technologies can do nothing to curb our dogmatism, narcissism, and ethnocentrism. We will continue to connive and scheme to get the necessary majority to have our way. This is exactly what also happens in an autocracy. There is no empathy, much less any compassion, for the minority. The minority is always at the mercy of the majority, which means that the condition of the minority is always precarious. But the majority hardly benefits from marginalizing the minority. The lack of any obligation to be more compassionate narrows and even distorts our view of the world and each other. We only become more and more myopic, narcissistic, and ethnocentric. In a word, we become more autocratic. Our treatment of those who are different distinguishes a democracy from an autocracy. No doubt, the proliferation of modern communication technologies can help us amplify the perspective and even the plight of the minority. But this is all these technologies can really do. Democracy can only come from our doing. It can neither be imposed nor coerced. Also, the proliferation of modern communication technologies can do nothing to lessen the struggle that comes with achieving democracy. Compassion is difficult. It requires much effort and determination. But in all cases, it comes down to what the technology is doing to us. When the proliferation of modern communication technologies would have us believe that this process is promoting democracy and making for a new world order, what becomes of us in that process?

What does such a view of democracy do to us? What kind of capabilities and potentialities go unnurtured and unexercised? How in turn does the underdevelopment of vital capabilities and potentialities shape how we perceive and experience the world? For instance, if, as modernity assumes, communication emerges from the conquest of confusion, then it is only rational to avail ourselves to any and every technology that promises to help us vanquish confusion. There is no impetus to promote vulnerability. But without vulnerability, what becomes of us, especially when our unrelenting efforts to end confusion only promise to end in futility? What do we do with all the neuroses and psychoses that come with this futile quest? Simply put, what becomes of us in this war against ourselves, against the world? What becomes of us after communication ends? For this is what our war on confusion is about. To vanquish confusion is to vanquish communication, as without confusion communication is impossible. Confusion vitalizes communication. It inspires communication. Any technology that seeks to vanquish confusion puts us in conflict with ourselves.

35

ON METAPHORS

We commonly assume that language and knowledge are separate. We use language to articulate knowledge, share knowledge, acquire knowledge. We therefore also assume that knowledge is impossible without language, meaning that knowledge can never be outside of language, or anything outside of language can be knowledge. Language presumably makes knowledge possible. Language is also the measure of knowledge, which apparently means that knowledge can never conspire against language. As much as knowledge and language are separate, knowledge supposedly needs language more than language needs knowledge. Therefore in our world of knowledge, language defines knowledge, and also guides and influences how we engage and experience knowledge. Knowledge must always be amenable to the contours of language. It must be observable, verifiable, measurable, and ideally, quantifiable. After all, numbers too are a language. But what exactly is the nature of language? What is this thing that has so much control over knowledge, and how did this thing come to have such power over knowledge, as least the way we define knowledge? Also, how did we come to believe, and become susceptible to believing, that language and knowledge are separate?

We generally assume that language is merely a tool born out of evolutionary necessity. It is supposedly separate from being. Language presumably allows us to share our thoughts and emotions. It allows us to do various tasks that are vital for our survival and prosperity, such as allowing us to acquire, organize, and share knowledge. So without language, knowledge is presumably impossible, and without knowledge, life is presumably impossible. Our survival and prosperity supposedly depend on how much knowledge we can acquire and share. Besides being able to use language to share our thoughts and emotions, we also believe that language can capture and describe the world without bias or favor. It can be representational. This means we also believe that language is separate from the world. It also means that we believe that the world can fall within the scope and influence of language. It is merely, supposedly, a matter of training our language to be rigorous, which means striving to use language with precision, such as removing all the ambiguity from language. Supposedly, this ambiguity impedes the ability of language, and our own ability, to command the world. Through language we are capable of achieving this feat. Such also is supposedly the other great mission of language—to allow us to command the world. However, when we strive to separate language from the world, just as much as when we strive to separate language from being, we change our relation to language, the world, and ourselves. But again, how did we come to believe in these kinds of separations, and why does this belief appeal to us? Also, how does this belief influence how we experience language, the world, and ourselves?

There is no separation between language and knowledge. Neither is there any separation between language and being, and knowledge and being. Language is inherently metaphorical—always laden with metaphors.

On Metaphors

That language is metaphorical means that we live language rather than merely articulate language. Language emerges from the core of our being. It situates us in the world. It shapes our world. It influences our world. But this is all because of the metaphors that reside in language. Without metaphors, language would have no power to create anything. But quantity and quality of metaphors matter as regards determining what language has the power to do. Ultimately, the metaphors found in language come from us. But these metaphors in no way just come from us. Metaphors make for what Owen Barfield refers to as intercommunion—the coupling of different universes. In other words, metaphors allow us to enter different worlds. In fact, metaphors throw us into worlds unknown. This is why metaphors are integral to the cultivation of imagination. To say that life is like an ocean can lend for infinite meanings. But every meaning offers a different set of possibilities. This is how metaphors vitalize us and enlarge our worlds. It is also why metaphors matter. Metaphors make meaning possible. This is why language can never stay still. It always takes us into a different place. Metaphors mean that we can never fully command the meaning of language. What language means will always change as no metaphor will ever mean just *one* thing, which means that no human being will ever mean just *one* thing. With regards to language, there will always be ambiguity, multiplicity, and plurality. We will never have the capacity to exercise perfect control over language. There will always be surprises and occasions when language refuses to comply with even our best intentions. But this again is why metaphors are so important. Metaphors unsettle us, allowing us to change and evolve. Without metaphors, life would have no space to emerge. So metaphorically, metaphors are spaces—spaces where life happens. But metaphors are morally unequal. Some metaphors can diminish us and limit our worlds. But we cannot simply wash our language clean of these metaphors. These metaphors come from us and always reflect the condition of our own moral imagination. As such, what must concern us are the kinds of metaphors that are emerging from us, and why such metaphors appeal to us, as well as what are the implications that flow from our metaphors.

So what becomes now of knowledge? That language is metaphorical means that knowledge is metaphorical. But what to do about the fact that metaphors constitute knowledge? We can begin to identify the metaphors that constitute our own view of knowledge. What are the origins of these metaphors? What moral imagination gives life to these metaphors? Also, what are the implications and consequences that attend to these metaphors? But again, just like language, cleansing knowledge of various metaphors is difficult. These metaphors are of us. So what needs to concern us is how we can give rise to new metaphors that enrich rather than diminish life. How can we cultivate metaphors that promote innovation and imagination? What should we be doing spiritually, ecologically, and communicationally to cultivate such metaphors? But instead we have sought to banish the spiritual, ecological, magical, and supernatural. For this is what making knowledge amenable to the contours of language involves. Knowledge must become empirical, reducible to only what our senses can experience. This stipulation forces us to remove from language all those metaphors that exceed our senses. In so doing this stipulation depletes language and knowledge of metaphors that can fundamentally expand our moral imagination. Our language and knowledge become less magical and poetical, meaning that both become mechanical and technological—devoid of all the elements that make us human. Ultimately, of course, we become less human, afraid and tortured by our own magical, spiritual, and supernatural dimensions. With the end of imagination, all that remains is repetition, subordination, and submission. Enter the rise of machines.

Machines make us machines. Machines need language to function representationally, whereas human beings need language to function metaphorically. The world of machines and technology is inherently hostile to the world of the magical and poetical. For in the world of machines and technology, the goal is always to remove our magical, ecological, and supernatural dimensions so as to make way for the rational subject—the subject that claims to desire order, control, and hierarchy. That is, machines need subjects that desire what machines and technology can offer. But these subjects are really us being less and less human. This is us being separated from our humanity. This is us being separated from the world. This is us in the throes of alienation, lacking any capacity to bring meaning and beauty into the world. So as we become increasingly efficient and proficient in acquiring knowledge, or as these processes become increasingly technologized, our own lives are becoming increasingly bereft of meaning. As Owen Barfield asks, "How is it that the more able man becomes to manipulate the world to his advantage, the less he can perceive any meaning in it?"

But the machines are in no way responsible for our alienation. Neither is technology. Our alienation begins in our separation of language from being. Our alienation continues in how we acquire and organize knowledge. For what does being knowledgeable mean? It mostly means spending an enormous amount of solitary time consuming and processing knowledge. It has nothing to do with living and doing, and certainly nothing to do with living and sharing. It is an isolated activity, a passive activity. It involves no risking of life. It separates us from the world and each other. The activity separates us from ourselves by pushing us to be completely dependent on a way of experiencing language that is devoid of anything magical and poetical. For in a world of machines and technology, being efficient and proficient matters most. It is about how much knowledge we can acquire, produce, manipulate, and disseminate. There is no focus on being. Discussions of ethics and aesthetics must happen elsewhere. The mission of science is (presumably) to produce knowledge, which means devising the most effective means to do so. But as much as how we come to language is conspiring against us, so also is the way we come to knowledge. Such is the plight of modernity. The world we are complicit in creating is now exacting its revenge. The machines promise to make for our doing.

How did we come to separate language from being? Or, how did we become susceptible to forces that separate us from the magical, spiritual, ecological, and supernatural? Yes, modernism certainly took advantage of this susceptibility and separation. But this separation was there long before modernism. Still, what continues to make us averse to the magical and supernatural, the spiritual and ecological? What is the origin of the fear and suspicion? What is most striking is that our many problems and challenges never had anything to do with the absence of knowledge. It was never the absence of knowledge that made the Holocaust possible, or slavery, or Jim Crow. What therefore is the purpose of all this knowledge we are acquiring and stockpiling? What illusion is being served by all of this activity? It continues to be our failure to love, to forgive, to care, and to empathize that threatens us. So again, what illusion is being served by believing otherwise? But love, compassion, and mercy require action. In fact, these things require an extraordinary moral imagination. In a world of hate, prejudice, and all kinds of evils, imagination matters. To save ourselves from such a world requires us to be able to imagine worlds that abound with magic and poetry. However, in order to do so, we need to reclaim our best metaphors. We therefore need to end the separation between language and being so we can end all the other divisions and separations.

We do need knowledge. However, we need to finally get beyond the illusion that knowledge can ever be amoral, acultural, and apolitical. It is anything but. It is profoundly moral, and will always be such. For with any kind of knowledge, there will always be implications, and implications mean different kinds of possibilities. Our prosperity involves achieving a knowledge that offers the most possibilities, as in those possibilities that enrich rather than diminish life. This means locating us at the center of the project. We become the site of knowledge, the place where theory begins.

This means ending the separation between knowing and being. Realizing a knowledge that enriches life requires us to also realize the courage to love in ways that reflect the most imagination, those ways that reflect the boldest expression of the magical and supernatural. Any worthy project of knowledge must save us from the ravages of separation, division, and fragmentation. To realize knowledge is to become whole. Thus any worthy project of knowledge should always be understood as a moral undertaking that bears upon our moral imagination. We are always implicated. How much we can perceive is really about how much we can imagine.

36

ON THE END OF CIVILIZATION

What becomes of the possibility of civilization when human beings come to lack the constitution to deal with life's everyday confusions, frustrations, and tribulations? That is, what becomes of us as we become increasingly laden with all manner of neuroses and psychoses? Or, what becomes of us when our anxieties, insecurities, and paranoia become too much, and as a result, even the ability to function becomes impossible? Inevitably, communication becomes impossible, and all else that saves us from becoming beasts and savages. This is the *real* threat to modern civilization—the end of communication because of the many anxieties, insecurities, and paranoia that are increasingly overwhelming and paralyzing us. For as communication ends, all that is certain to rise is our increasing isolation and alienation, and all the ravages that come with such.

But this is now what passes as progress—the rise of all manner of devices and environs to allow for the privatization of the self. It is all pretention as claims of civility and collegiality are just ploys to mask the lack of both. There is no civilization. No civility. No collegiality. Only the pretention of such. For what cannot be made invisible is our increasing apathy and cruelty. Yes, relative to other kinds of blatant cruelty, our cruelty seems much different, even civilized. After all, a certain amount of cruelty is presumably necessary. It even feels natural, as what human beings ought to be doing in order to get things in order. But in the end, cruelty is cruelty, and regardless of all the pretention of civility, collegiality, and civilization, this cruelty will eventually make for the end of us.

But civilization marches on. The goal is progress and prosperity. Our conquest of the natural world now seems complete. We are presumably at the end of history. But only the illusion is so. Still, illusions matter. For what would be our pretentions without illusions? However, even the best of illusions must eventually come to terms with reality, and regardless of our best efforts, fall away and perish.

Most likely our weapons of mass destruction will eventually make for our undoing. There is also the possibility that our continuing destruction of the planet will do so first. Or perhaps the structural flaws within capitalism will eventually catch up with us and rid the world of laborers and consumers. All these scenarios now seem imminent. But for certain, no civilization can withstand the end of communication. With our increasing isolation and alienation, and the technology and pharmacology to sustain both, communication becomes less and less possible. Yet as communication becomes less and less possible, no amount of technology and pharmacology can save us from the apathy and cruelty that must inevitably follow from our increasing isolation and alienation. What should concern us is the civilizing and normalizing of this apathy and cruelty—that is, our everyday normal acts of cruelty. What should also concern us is how our claims of civility and collegiality, besides conspiring to smash dissent and diversity, work to civilize and normalize our cruelty and apathy. Such claims come with the pretention of being a superior civilization, one with supposedly great institutions of justice and democracy. How could such a civilization be possibly accused of cultivating and sanctioning cruelty? This is the civilization that values human rights and seeks the proliferation of our own supposedly great institutions of justice and democracy. Moreover, this is the civilization that seeks to bring progress and prosperity to all corners of the world. How could this civilization now be seen as something fundamentally different? What will this mean for us, especially those of us who are products of all the great institutions that are the hallmark of this civilization? What will become of civilization after the end of history, meaning, what will become of us?

It all seems unfathomable. What civilization could possibly come after our civilization? It all seems beyond our imagination. How could our prized and so universally admired civilization be destined for destruction? With the coming end of communication, there will increasing attempts to use regulation, legislation, and incarceration to achieve civilization. There will be no end to finding ways to police us. We will remain obsessed with finding new ways to monitor and control each other. The ever-increasing rise of deviancy and criminality that is certain to come as our civilization collapses will add only fuel to this obsession. There will be no arguing about the need for new kinds of regulation and harsher forms of incarceration. This is supposedly the price of civilization. But herein resides our demise. No amount of laws, regulations, and incarceration can save us from ourselves. We merely have the illusion of civilization, as well as the illusion of civility and decency. All these laws and regulations only mean that our situation is becoming increasingly dire. Moreover, these laws and regulations only make for the end of communication, and as always, without communication, isolation and alienation become reality. In other words, without communication, all that is certain to happen is our being increasingly tortured and paralyzed by all manner of neuroses and psychoses. We lose all capacity to deal with the rigors that come with democracy and community. These things require a vigorous moral constitution. Yet only democracy can save us from the ravages of autocracy—the autocracy that is certain to come as our civilization collapses. Without empathy and compassion, and all else that comes with a vigorous moral constitution, autocracy is all that follows. Democracy is by no means merely a political activity, or even the expression of a certain kind of political philosophy. It is, instead, the expression of a certain kind of moral constitution. We achieve democracy by becoming human, and achieving democracy makes us human. Without the ability or capacity to become human, civilization is impossible. Put differently, civilization is about becoming civilized, being capable of enormous empathy and compassion. It has nothing to do with our ability to regulate, police, and discipline each other through institutions. In fact, institutions harm our moral flourishing by impeding our capacity to encounter the world with passion, conviction, and imagination. Institutions institutionalize us, which only deepens the many anxieties, insecurities, and paranoia that come with our increasing isolation and alienation.

But as always, our civilization now promises us a fix to our many social and personal problems. This fix is pharmacology. We are now to believe that the cause of our increasing anxiety, depression, and despair is chemical and biological. Such ailments supposedly have nothing much to do with what is happening in our social, relational, ideological, and communicational worlds. We are released from looking critically, honestly, and courageously at the workings of our social, relational, ideological, and communicational worlds. We are also released from owning our own complicity in perpetuating these worlds, as well as any culpability for the many destructive consequences. But most of all, pharmacology succeeds by affirming the belief that the problem is us. We are supposedly of a defective nature. If civilization is going to be achieved, hierarchy is ultimately necessary. We must impose order by any means. The need to be happy functions ideologically. It masks other possible ambitions and aspirations. It relegitimizes the status quo, as in the promise of civilization to make our lives easy and happy. Thus the rise of pharmacology was all but certain. How else to handle the anxiety and misery that is increasingly torturing us without suggesting that something is fundamentally wrong with the order of things? Indeed, how else to deal with the fallout from all the isolation and alienation without altering the order of things? Supposedly, this kind of fixing is the best that our civilization can do. This is the age of fixing and patching. The cracks, which were always certain to happen, are now upon us. Yet there can be no masking of these cracks. These cracks reflect the foundational problems that are at the core of our civilization. Eventually, these cracks will tear our civilization asunder. So our fixing is merely prolonging the inevitable. Yes, our civilization has always shown an enormous capacity to adapt and co-opt. But these cracks that are now upon us will only deepen and widen. We can only offer fixes, but no amount of fixes will work. These kinds of structural cracks will only continue to widen, fermenting discord and strife, which will only heighten our anxiety and push us to call for more policing, monitoring, and gating. But these are nothing but fixes. However, what is really important is the illusion that our fixing sustains. It allows us to continue to believe that nothing is fundamentally wrong with the status quo. These illusions buy us time. But even the best illusions remain illusions. Eventually, no amount of policing, gating, and self-medicating will do. Such is the future of civilization.

But what would civilization look like with no isolation and alienation, and consequently, without all the neuroses and psychoses? It would be of a different social, political, ideological, and spatial order. This is why the rise of pharmacology matters. It protects the status quo and allows us to continue to view our increasing neuroses and psychoses as merely ailments. Only medication is supposedly necessary to get us back to full health. There is no indictment of the order of things. There is also no recognition of how our increasing neuroses and psychoses alter our view of the world, and how we relate and engage the world. Yet this is exactly the case. Our neuroses and psychoses would have us view the world as a dark and foreboding place, deserving of distrust, suspicion, and fear. This world is presumably always conspiring against us. We must therefore respond accordingly. We should be about our own survival and preservation, as in promoting a social, political, and economic order that favors our own self-interest. On the other hand, our increasing neuroses and psychoses undercut our capacity to act with passion, conviction, and imagination. Such conditions encourage us to perceive the world as always acting upon us. Our circumstances result from the workings of the world. We are complicit in nothing, and thereby have no responsibility to change anything. The world's order presumably results from natural forces, as in the strongest, smartest, and fittest rising to the top, and the rest falling to the bottom. This is supposedly how the world is and needs to be. So when the rich become richer and the poor become poorer, such is merely the natural working of the world. There is no onus on us to do anything. We are amenable to ideologies and theories that release us of any responsibility or complicity for the order of things. This is how these ideologies and theories seduce us, and reveals our own interest in promoting these theories and ideologies. So why a theory appeals to us really has nothing much to do with that theory to objectively explain anything. Theories are ideologies. We use theories to describe how we perceive and relate to the world and each other. No theory is outside or separate from an ideology. However, ideologies are in no way merely the sum of our beliefs, values, fears, and truths. Ideologies are also born of our anxieties, insecurities, and paranoia, meaning that ideologies are also born of our neuroses and psychoses, and in turn cultivate various neuroses and psychoses. The relationship between theory and ideology is inseparable and inextricable. Changing how we perceive the world involves changing how we experience the world. But now upon us are debilitative forces that are fundamentally limiting and disfiguring what we are capable of experiencing, and consequently, perceiving. This is why our increasing isolation and alienation needs to be of utmost concern to us. How we perceive the world shapes our knowledge of the world, which in turn influences how we organize our world. In the end, the condition of our humanity shapes everything, including what we value, define, and perceive as knowledge. No knowledge is outside of our own condition. This is why our increasing neuroses and psychoses need to concern us. They diminish how we define, relate, and value knowledge. In a world laden with neuroses and psychoses, we value the knowledge that seems separate and outside of us. This knowledge involves no looking at our insides and consequently, poses no threat to us. It is easy to consume and believe. Then there are all the things that would have us believe that this knowledge is supposedly outside of us. In turn, this knowledge allows us to believe that the world is also outside and separate from us, which of course allows us to hold to a narrow view of personhood, like the condition of our humanity supposedly having nothing to do with the condition of the world. There is therefore no compelling reason to care about the condition of the world. What becomes of the world supposedly has no bearing on us. This, again, is why this knowledge that is presumably outside of us seduces us again and again. It makes no demands on us, nor in any way threatens us. But how we perceive the world is by no means merely a matter of epistemology. We have to be emotionally, spiritually, and existentially amenable to perceiving the world a certain way. This, again, is why our increasing neuroses and psychoses need to concern us. What ways of perceiving the world are now becoming amenable to us? Or, how are our neuroses and psychoses shaping and legitimizing what we define and value as knowledge? On the other hand, what of the relation between our illusions and our neuroses and psychoses, such as the illusion that the world is separate and outside of us? What would become of all these kinds of illusions without our neuroses and psychoses? Such illusions, no doubt, would fall away. But, on the other hand, such illusions fuel our neuroses and psychoses.

We need a new knowledge. The world needs a new knowledge. The knowledge that now rules the world is putting us in peril. But no hegemony shows up without an army. There are always vast institutions, apparatuses, and structures to keep everything in place. But, for certain, this hegemony will eventually fall away as the world does have limits. However, what would a knowledge look like that began with us looking within, that is, looking honestly and courageously at all the forces and influences that shape how we perceive and experience the world? It would be, for sure, devoid of a conquering sensibility. There would be no pretention of generating grand truths that stand outside of history, or at least the pretension of truths that have no relation to human affairs. These kinds of truths make communication impossible. Then again, this was always the purpose. These kinds of truths were meant to conquer, to put down dissent and diversity, to foster order and control. These truths come from fears that come with being in a world that is of boundless ambiguity. The purpose of these truths is to lessen the intensity of these fears, even make these fears go away. Such is the origin of these truths. Only a people who are laden with these kinds of fears give rise to these kinds of autocratic and imperialistic truths. These truths have nothing to do with revealing the true nature of the world. This is merely a pretext. There is a psychological dimension to inquiry. We have a stake in protecting the methodologies that produce these truths, including being hostile to other methodologies. Yes, probably for the sake of diversity, we are willing to tolerate other methodologies, but this is the most we can do, and only for methodologies that pose no threat to the order of things. In the end, our fears require methodologies that promise hard and grand truths that will allow us to conquer the world's ambiguity.

Yet with all our complex methodologies and grand truths, our fears persist, even worsen. The world will continually remind us that ours is a fool's errand. Every grand truth is laden with ambiguity. What we are capable of perceiving and experiencing will depend on what we are capable of sharing and believing. This reality will make for democratic notions of truths. In this story of knowledge, the focus is on identifying those ideological, psychological, and material forces that limit what we are capable of sharing. This knowledge will in no way alienate us from the world and each other. This is the problem with our knowledge now. How we define and acquire knowledge alienates us from the world and each other. So as we acquire more and more knowledge, we become more and more alienated from the world and each other. A warped sense of knowledge emerges, as in believing that we can consume knowledge the way we consume food. This view of knowledge is also seen in how we assume a divide between truth and ethics. There is, of course, no such divide. Any pursuit of truth is a moral undertaking. There are always consequences and implications. However, every inquiry begins with beliefs, prejudices, and assumptions, things that are fundamentally human and laden with ambiguity. No truth can escape this human element. We all believe something. Any inquiry that professes to be rigorous needs to begin by looking at the beliefs that are setting everything in motion. What is the nature of these beliefs? What makes us susceptible to these beliefs? What are the consequences that come with these beliefs? Finally, what other kinds of beliefs can be potentially available to us? But now our alienation is as such that we believe that maintaining the illusory divide between truth and ethics constitutes rigor and good practice. But the illusion only works by saving us from the hard work that comes with looking deeply and honestly at all the forces that make us human and shape our view of the world. In reality, our pursuit of truth is anything but rigorous, nothing but self-deception. Its supposed success has nothing to do producing objective truths that will make for the foundation of a superior civilization. This is a mirage. It is what we need to believe, and what we need to believe is really what shapes our definition of civilization. Everything else is pretext and context. We live by what we believe rather than by our knowledge of things. Therefore in order to give rise to a new civilization, as in a life affirming civilization, we have to find a way to change what we believe and are willing to believe. This, again, is why the increasing deterioration of our psychological condition needs to concern us. It hardens and deepens our worst beliefs and impulses. It also makes us increasingly gullible to ideologies and epistemologies that alienate and estrange us from each other, the world, and ourselves. When fear consumes us, our imagination diminishes.

37

ON IDENTITY

We can define identity as simply the box a person checks. Or, the group we perceive ourselves belonging to. Either way, identity is about the resources—that is, the categories—that that are available to us. It is also about the kinds of normalizing and conforming pressures that are put on us to adopt a certain category. Finally, identity is about our experiences. What we experience and when, where, how, and with whom, also shapes how we perceive ourselves in relation to others. But why identity? Why the pressure to adopt a category? Is identity inevitable? In fact, is identity even moral?

History reveals that identity is primal. It characterizes every horror, every travesty, every abomination. For what would be the possibility of genocide without identity? Of course identity is by no means the cause of these abominations. But without identity, these abominations would be impossible. So identity facilitates the process. It gives us a way of organizing our destructive impulses and instincts. Behind every definition of identity is the primal impulse and instinct to distinguish friend from foe. Every category constitutes such a distinction. To choose a category is to declare who I perceive to be my friends, and who I perceive to be less so. But perception is a human thing. There are many things that shape our perception of ourselves and others. For instance, how we perceive ourselves influences how we perceive others. On the other hand, how others perceive us also influences how we perceive others. Further, how we perceive others is a matter of moral development. What categories we choose to adopt or whether we even choose a category, is about our measure of moral development. Our measure of moral development gives us the constitution to resist the many normalizing and conforming pressures that want us to distinguish friend from foe. We are in no way bound to any conception of identity that pushes us to distinguish friend from foe. We can exceed this reality, including all the ideologies and epistemologies that surround this reality. However, this is by no means easy to do. But this is why expanding our capacity to honestly and courageously engage the world's boundless ambiguity matters.

Identity cuts us off from each other. It limits our conception of ourselves, as well as our obligation to others. In a world of friends and foes, separation and division are inevitable. There is no genuine possibility for union and communion. There is always going to be distrust and suspicion of those we perceive to be of a different category. Yet many continue to call for the reclaiming of identity. Identity matters, presumably. We are to believe that diversity resides in our different identities. To get rid of our identities is to lose our diversity. Diversity is about differences. It is supposedly about the things that distinguish us from each other. Without identity, diversity will (supposedly) be impossible and homogeneity will rule. So by promoting identity, diversity emerges. This view assumes that identity is fundamentally an ideological and historical construct. No doubt, ideology and history do play a vital role in shaping identity. But identity is fundamentally developmental. Our measure of moral development shapes our view of ourselves and each other.

Viewing identity in terms of ideology and history also binds us to the past by insisting that our experiences control our perception of ourselves and others. Such control can be limiting. There is simply no way to achieve a complete and stable conception of ourselves. That is, there is no way to know how new experiences will shape our conception of ourselves and others. Our perception of ourselves can always change dramatically and unexpectedly. We also cannot control the conditions or circumstances that can always come upon us and alter our perception of ourselves. Our conception of ourselves reflects a narrow experiencing of ourselves. The ambiguity that comes with being human is simply too vast for us to ever command. But this is also what makes identity politics so dangerous. It fosters the illusion that we are capable of commanding the world's ambiguity and that doing so, even trying to do so, is a good thing. After all, what would be the possibility of diversity without identity? But what is really the possibility of diversity in a world of friends and foes? What is also the possibility of diversity when there is always distrust and suspicion of those we perceive of a different identity? Identity politics encourages us to find ways to lessen our distrust and suspicion of each other. We are also encouraged to find ways to bridge and tolerate the differences that come with our different identities. We should always be civil and collegial to each other. Evidently, the purpose of identity politics is merely to preserve the status quo. It maintains our distrust and suspicion of each other, thereby maintaining all the divisions, separations, and tensions that legitimizes the status quo us. It also cultivates self-interest, as in always encouraging us to pit the interest of our group against that of another. There is no encouragement to be genuinely selfless. This is why for identity politics tolerating and bridging are the best that can be had. Either strategy allows us to preserve our different identities. So as much as tolerance is increasingly recognized as a morally deficient exercise, for identity politics, the alternative is homogeneity and the end of our diverse histories and ideologies.

But this will never be the case, as identity has nothing to do with diversity. As much as identity politics touts the relation between identity and diversity, identity politics has no interest in identity. Putting all the posturing aside, identity politics is really about keeping us bound to groupings so as to preserve the status quo. It merely wants the inclusion of various groups, which, again, never poses any threat to the status quo. These groupings or boxes reveal nothing about what a person values, believes, or fears. This is how identity politics suppresses and limits our diversity. But this is also how identity politics distorts our conception of diversity. We can have identity without boxes. In fact, no amount of boxes can capture our diverse identities. Our identities will always be laden with ambiguity. As much as identity politics, as with any other politics, aspires to place our diverse identities into neat and tidy categories, only the illusion is so. Identities are inherently organic because we are inherently organic. As with anything organic, identities are always in flux, either evolving and changing or devolving and dying. Organic things survive and flourish by adapting to environs that are also always changing. In our case, our ambiguity gives us the resources to change and evolve. Without the ambiguity that is of us, there would no way for us to look at anything anew. The ambiguity that pervades the world makes sure that nothing is ever beyond the possibility of a new interpretation. There is always the possibility for a new meaning, a new understanding, a new reality, a new identity. That is, there is always the possibility for something new and different to come into the world and expand our conception of what the world can be, and even what we can be. This is what ambiguity gives us. It gives us life. Our identities must do no less. However, in order for our identities to bring life into the world, we must embrace ambiguity. What will emerge are identities that are permeable and vulnerable to new influences.

38

ON EVOLUTION

What is the location of evolution? Or, put differently, where does evolution really occur? What is also the purpose of evolution? Darwin, of course, assumes that evolution occurs at the level of our genes. It is about our genes doing all that is necessary to survive, reproduce, and propagate. We are supposedly merely survival machines—doing the bidding of bundles of selfish genes. Through competition for resources and mates, only the strongest, fittest, and smartest genes prevail and flourish. But Darwin's theory of evolution is merely *one* story of evolution. It is foremost an interpretation rather than a description of reality. It is therefore fallible and laden with ambiguity. In the case of Darwin's theory of evolution, there is a troubling communication problem.

With Darwin's theory communication is merely a tool to share our thoughts and emotions with others. It supposedly evolved out of evolutionary necessity so as to afford us superior forms of coordination and organization. In many presentations of Darwin's theory, communication is even defined as information processing and sharing, and organization constitutes the coordination of information. No doubt, communication can be experienced as a tool to exchange messages. But this constitutes a shallow definition of communication, as without communication becoming human is impossible. The negation of communication is isolation (death) rather than simply a lack of communication. Communication is life. Life unfolds and flourishes through communication. Darwin's theory misses this fact, this reality, this truth. On the other hand, Darwin's theory has no way to incorporate this emergent view of communication. To recognize that communication plays an integral role in shaping the human experience means also recognizing that human beings are fundamentally relational beings with a binding set of ecological obligations to others. Such obligations conflict with the mission of survival machines as articulated by Darwin's adherents.

To need communication in order to become human is to really need each other to become human. Without being ready and willing to do what is necessary to sustain communication, both sides succumb. Indeed, to recognize and appreciate all that comes with our relationality is to look differently at the mission of evolution. The mission of evolution is to promote life rather than merely propagate genes. To recognize and appreciate all that comes with our relationality is to find a different location for the origin of evolution. Evolution happens at the level of ecology. In being inherently relational, communication is inherently ecological. Without communication, evolution ends. So yes, communication, as Darwin's theory assumes, makes for superior kinds of coordination and organization. But before communication makes for any of this, communication makes life possible. That communication is ecological also means that communication shapes and influences what life becomes. As communication goes, so goes life. As such, to attend to communication is to attend to life. What improves the quality of communication also improves the quality of life. But what exactly improves the quality of communication?

According to Darwin's theory, anything that impedes the exchanging of messages diminishes the quality of communication. We measure the quality of communication in terms of noise reduction. Removing noise constitutes quality communication. But this is an impossible exercise as there will always be noise. In fact, the measure of life, as heard in storms, hurricanes, earthquakes, tornadoes, rains, and forest fires, is noise. Noise is life. Still, for argument purposes, let us pretend this exercise is possible. The end of noise has nothing to do with communication. We can, after all, efficiently and effectively exchange messages that hurt and harm each other and consequently, make only for peril and death. In this way, such communication cannot, at least in evolutionary terms, be defined as quality communication. Evidently, defining quality of communication in terms of the capacity of communication to increase our relational and ecological viability constitutes a much more heuristic definition of communication. That is, what communication practices enrich rather than diminish our relational and ecological viability, or what communication practices pull us toward each other, revealing our dependency on others for our survival and prosperity? Empathy and compassion exemplify such practices. Yet both are by no means merely examples of quality communication practices. These are ultimately life-affirming practices.

By increasing our relational and ecological viability, empathy and compassion actually promote evolution by enlarging our capacity to perceive and experience new things. This kind of vulnerability makes evolution possible. We happen to evolution as much as evolution happens to us. Ultimately, quality communication constitutes those practices that make us increasingly vulnerable. But there is much that comes with vulnerability. Vulnerability humanizes us by making us less violent and aggressive. Vulnerability also democratizes us by lessening our proclivity to impose our worldview on others. It impedes dogmatism, hegemonisn, and all racisms and tribalisms. Vulnerability also promotes equity by allowing us to experience the pain and misery of others. In sum, vulnerability undercuts the flourishing of our most destructive instincts and impulses. But this is also how communication promotes life. It removes the things that threaten life. This is also why evolution happens at the level of ecology rather than the level of genes. Regardless of the conniving, scheming, and plotting that evolution supposedly involves, no survival machine survives in any ecology that is doing things to end life. The condition of the ecology is foremost, and no entity survives by pretending otherwise. In other words, the condition of the ecology ultimately determines what becomes of life, and without a vibrant ecology, life cannot flourish. Darwin's theory assumes that evolution arises from our own doing, as in our own plotting, conniving, and scheming. Supposedly, evolution is driven by selfishness. By focusing on our own self-interest, collective interest emerges. Indeed, according to Darwin's theory, only by cultivating and rewarding self-interest is prosperity between different survival machines possible. But reconciling self-interest with communication is difficult. That communication is inherently relational and ecological means that the notion of self—as in self-interest—is an illusion. There are only relationships, and with relationships come obligations, and with obligations come consequences. We can, of course, always choose to deny this reality by continuing to pretend that there is this self that is acting independently. After all, such a view simplifies our view of the world. It also releases us from all kinds of obligations. On the other hand, a few advocates of Darwin's theory claim that through evolution competition eventually turns into cooperation, and selfishness into selflessness. Indeed, even communication could be evolutionary. But the fact remains that human beings need communication and there is simply no such thing as too much communication. Empathy and compassion demand selflessness—generously giving ourselves to others. Selfishness diminishes communication, and in doing so, degrades life. So regardless of whether selfishness turns into selflessness, the fact is that selfishness is death. By diminishing our relational and ecological vitality, selfishness impedes evolution. It also blocks us from developing the capacities and capabilities that are vital for the affirmation of new possibilities and realities. Without being able to generate either, life ends. In other words, life's prosperity depends on us enlarging our capacities and capabilities to experience new things. But such enlarging begins with communication. To view communication in terms of empathy and compassion is to recognize that communication is about being and becoming. The mission of communication is to enlarge us, to bring us to new kinds of being, that is, to bring us to new ways of perceiving and appreciating things. Communication is always displacing us, always moving us to new points. Yet how exactly communication will displace us will never be under our control. But this is also why vulnerability matters. Vulnerability is about releasing ourselves of expectations and preconceived notions. It also means being unafraid to use and experience language in new ways. Moreover, vulnerability means releasing others of our fears, anxieties, and insecurities. This means that nobody should feel judged or ridiculed, and thereby afraid to invite us to share new things. Vulnerability also means cleansing ourselves of devices and habits that suppress the open expression of conflict and thereby the privileging of certain interests and prejudices. Only by being vulnerable can we achieve the courage, patience, and resilience to deal constructively and heuristically with an ever-evolving and changing world.

There is arguably no other theory that plays as much of an integral role in shaping and legitimizing our worldview than Darwin's theory of evolution. On the other hand, this theory is also a product of our worldview. We believe Darwin's theory because we already believe what the theory implicates and assumes. We made Darwin because we needed a Darwin. In other words, Darwin's theory appeals to our most primal instincts and impulses because it is born out of our primal instincts and impulses. We need such a theory to legitimize everything we already believe. This is why Darwin matters. Darwin is the theory of the status quo. To look critically at Darwin is really to look critically at ourselves. But of course we must do much more than merely critique. We have to provide a more heuristic interpretation of the human experience and demonstrate the ability of this interpretation to make for a world with much less peril and death. In my view, communication gives us the beginnings of such an interpretation and possibility. But before any new knowledge can come forth, we have to at least be amenable to all that comes with such knowledge. We have to be willing to believe anew. Only by being willing to change what we believe is knowledge possible.

39

ON MORALITY

We generally assume that communication involves agreement. It is about what is mutually agreed, mutually shared, mutually understood. It is also about converging on a common meaning, a common understanding, a common action. No doubt, commonality is the status quo in communication theory. But our supposed communication problems have nothing to do with a lack of commonality. Such problems result from our own unwillingness to expand what we can recognize, value, sense, believe, share, appreciate, perceive, and experience. As such, how could communication be simply about what is shared, agreed, and understood? This means that communication is only about what we are willing to believe, to share, to perceive, to value, to recognize, to appreciate, to experience. This is also how communication as commonality favors the status quo. What we are generally willing to believe, recognize, value, and so forth is generally what others are also willing to believe, recognize, value, and so forth. We favor those persons who also share what we believe, value, recognize, appreciate, and so forth. After all, this kind of commonality is supposedly good for communication, and as a result, good for us.

So what becomes of communication where what we believe, value, perceive, appreciate, and recognize is different? We assume that communication would be difficult, even impossible. Achieving communication presumably involves cultivating commonality—that is, lessening the diversity between us. But communication really has nothing much to do with what we are willing to share, to value, to believe, to recognize, to appreciate, to perceive. It is rather about what we are unwilling to share, value, believe, and imagine. After all, this is where our communication problems begin. To view communication in terms of commonality is to view communication in terms of narcissism. Narcissism distorts our perception of ourselves and others. It also impedes our ability to learn and grow, evolve and change. Moreover, narcissism undermines our willingness to give and share. It promotes distrust and suspicion. In the end, narcissism puts us at each other's throats. It undermines the achieving of communication by turning us away from each other, especially those who seem different to us. Only by turning towards each other do we become human. Thus by turning us away from each other narcissism makes us less and less so. This loss of our humanity can be vividly seen in the fact that narcissism makes inevitably for all manner of racisms, tribalisms, and ethnocentrisms. Obsession with self means imposing our view of the world on others, as in a desire to impose our standards, values, principles, and truths on others, and a willingness to do so by any means necessary.

Narcissism impedes our ability to view the world from the perspective of others, meaning that narcissism impedes the evolution of empathy and compassion. This is how narcissism makes us less human. With narcissism, only our view of the world is valid, and consequently, should rightfully be the view that rules the world. With narcissism, diversity is impossible. So also is democracy. Tyranny is status quo. How else, after all, to impose our reality on others? How else to suppress conflicting truths and experiences? How else to deal with our lack of empathy and compassion? Narcissism makes violence inevitable. This is also how narcissism displaces communication. Unilaterally imposing our view of the world on others is violence. Violence means treating others as objects to be shaped, molded, and sculpted to fit our view of the world. It means removing the humanity of others, including the diversity that comes with our humanity. It also means removing our own humanity. Violence begins with our inability to recognize and come to terms with our own diversity, complexity, and mystery. Such is the peril of narcissism. It robs us of our humanity. It makes us less human by impeding the rise of all the things that are vital for us to become human, such as empathy, compassion, and most of all, communication.

Communication is about being physically, cognitively, emotionally, sensually, spiritually, and epistemologically available and vulnerable to others. It is a human-making phenomenon, a world-making phenomenon. We achieve communication by becoming human. We become human by enlarging what we are willing and ready to value, believe, assume, share, appreciate, recognize, perceive, and experience. Of course, there is no way for us to be vulnerable to everything. Learning to be vulnerable is a practice, even a sacred practice. We can only strive to be completely vulnerable. We do so by cultivating selflessness, that is, by practicing communication—striving always to appreciate what we are unable and even unwilling to appreciate, to recognize, to believe, to experience, to perceive, and so forth. Communication involves the expansion of our being. Enlarging what we are able and willing to value, to share, to believe, and to perceive enlarges what we are capable of being. Communication problems are fundamentally problems of being. Diversity is also the measure of communication. Diversity demands of us a willingness to go beyond what we are ready and willing to perceive, believe, appreciate, and experience. Without this willingness to push against our supposed limits, diversity is impossible. But so also is communication. So communication is always diversity-producing, diversity-generating. This, again, is why diversity is the measure of communication. *Communication is about creating spaces for the inclusion and accommodation of others.* This is why communication is inherently a democratic practice. Being committed to being completely vulnerable to that which seems most alien—and even threatening—to us makes us democratic and pluralistic.

Vulnerability is the *sine qua non* of democracy. This is how communication saves us from tyranny. Democracy is fundamentally about being—a communication practice. It constitutes the cultivation of a certain kind of being. But this is why viewing democracy in terms of institutions and even electoral participation represents a shallow conception of democracy. We can have such institutions and still have no diversity. Indeed, these institutions—as with all institutions—undercut communication by seeking to end ambiguity, which is vital to expanding what we are willing and capable of recognizing, believing, perceiving, experiencing, and appreciating. Institutions demand conformity, homogeneity, and commonality, and institutions achieve this by suppressing and removing ambiguity. However, as ambiguity is the lifeblood of communication, the end of ambiguity also means the end of communication and all that comes with communication, such as diversity and democracy. So institutions mean hostility to diversity and democracy, which also means that institutions mean hostility to communication. Case in point: over 350 years of our celebrated democracy did nothing to end slavery and Jim Crow. It also continues to do nothing to end our destruction of the planet and the unsurpassed proliferation of weapons of mass destruction. Communication expands our view of the world by enlarging what we are willing and able to recognize, believe, perceive, and experience. This expansion is what makes for the origins of democracy. We can only embody democracy. Democracy is also inherently ecological. It too must evolve and change, grow and learn, flourish and blossom. This is how communication functions as the lifeblood of democracy. Democracy evolves and changes by us evolving and changing, and this we do by pushing and stretching and challenging what we are willing to believe, appreciate, recognize, and so forth. Only through communication can we achieve and promote democracy, as only through communication can we achieve the kind of being that makes democracy possible.

40

ON REDUCTIONISM

There are a set of processes that are fundamentally responsible for driving and shaping western civilization. We segregate, discriminate, and categorize so as to reduce and even eliminate the world's ambiguity and complexity. This is what makes for our different disciplines—psychology, sociology, anthropology, communicology, biology, geology, mathematics, and physics. But this is only the beginning of the segregation, discrimination, and categorization that shape our social worlds. We segregated language into nouns, pronouns, verbs, adverbs, and adjectives. We segregated mathematics into prime numbers, odd numbers, and even numbers. We also segregated mathematics into addition, subtraction, division, and multiplication. We also segregated geometry from trigonometry. Biology begins with segregating animals from plants. We also segregated vertebrates from invertebrates, single-celled organisms from multicellular organisms, plants from trees, annuals from perennials. We segregated human beings into Mongoloids,

Caucasoids, and Negroids. We also segregated homosexuals from heterosexuals. In communicology, the segregating, discriminating, and categorizing continues. We have encoders and decoders, transmission and reception, verbal and nonverbal communication. We segregated nonverbal communication into optics, haptics, proxemics, paralinguistics, and so on. We also segregated communication into interpersonal communication, organizational communication, intercultural communication, political communication, presentational communication, and relational communication.

Yet our ability to reduce and eliminate the world's ambiguity continues to elude us. In fact, the world seems intent on becoming no less ambiguous and mysterious. For all our segregating, discriminating, and categorizing, still no truth is to be found that could save us from ourselves. The more we segregate, discriminate, and categorize, the more perilous our existence becomes. So as much as knowledge remains plentiful from our segregating, discriminating, and categorizing, wisdom continues to be scarce. But the segregating, discriminating, and categorizing continues to the hilt. However, what we are really doing as we segregate, discriminate, and categorize is tearing the world into pieces. We are ripping and tearing at everything that holds the world together. We are dismembering the world. There must no doubt be a price that comes with all of this damage. How much more of this ripping and tearing can the world bear? And where exactly did all of this segregating, discriminating, and categorizing begin? It probably began when we ripped ourselves away from the world, which made for the rise of such notions as heaven and hell, angels and demons, sacred and profane, God and the Devil. Then we ripped ourselves away from each other, becoming man and woman, believers and sinners. This is probably how Pythagoras, the supposed father of mathematics, came to profess that the world was divided into opposing forces, those that made for men, knowledge, and light, and those that made for women, ignorance, and darkness. Indeed segregating, discriminating, and categorizing ultimately to put us in conflict with the world, each other, and ourselves. This is how violence comes into the world.

So the more we segregate, discriminate, and categorize, the more violence we bring into the world. Such is the origin of persuasion. Nearly all of communicology is about the study of persuasion. We are to assume that persuasion is what human beings do, and that being vulnerable to persuasion is a good thing. We are to learn how to find the means of persuasion in any given situation. But persuasion is violence. Persuasion arises from us segregating senders (persuaders) from receivers (the persuaded). It also arises from our segregating causes from effects. Persuasion is presumably something that one does to another—that is, one who is supposedly outside and separate from us. It is about imposing our reality on others and reducing them to objects of our ambition. But who exactly is this other person who is subject to our persuasion? In reality, this person is us. Persuasion is about suppressing our own doubts, confusions, and turmoils. It is about trying to remove the ambiguity and confusion in ourselves. To persuade is to homogenize, to lessen the world's ambiguity, complexity, and mystery. Persuasion is narcissism. It is about shoring up the certainty of our position. Without this desire for certainty, persuasion is impossible. But there is always doubt, confusion, and ambiguity. No amount of persuasion can vanquish these states. On the other hand, what is left of our humanity without these states? How will new experiences and understandings arise without these states? How will we become vulnerable to new ways of being, and thereby become human? How will we change and evolve, grow and learn, without doubt, confusion, and ambiguity? How will democracy arise and thrive without our being able to be vulnerable to different experiences and understandings? After all, if our own position is without doubt or ambiguity, why the need for deliberation? That is, without doubt, ambiguity, and confusion, deliberation is impossible. It has no way to enter the world. However, without deliberation, democracy is also impossible. So in order for democracy, diversity, and deliberation to flourish, doubt, ambiguity, and confusion must also flourish. In this way, persuasion is the antithesis of democracy. It is the tool of tyranny. By impeding our ability to listen to ourselves, that is, to experience our own doubt, confusion, and ambiguity, persuasion impedes our ability to listen to others. Absence of democracy, absence of communication, all that remains is violence and tyranny.

Most of the violence we are increasingly bringing into the world is insidious. When we segregate theory from praxis, or ethics from politics, or the life sciences from the physical sciences, this is all violence because to reduce the world's ambiguity is to reduce our ambiguity and, ultimately, our own humanity. For instance, how could we possibly begin to segregate theory from praxis? What becomes of theory? It becomes nothing. Although we claim that theory describes our world, what exactly is this world that theory is describing? We are to assume that theory is describing a world that is separate and outside of us. However, theory can only inhabit the worlds we create, and the worlds we create shape what kinds of theory arise to describe these worlds. So what kinds of worlds we are creating is foremost, and what makes for the creation of worlds begins with how we view ourselves in relation to the world. If we begin, as we continue to do, by assuming that the world is separate and outside of us, we create theories that can only describe these worlds. These theories will have no generative capacity. In being born out of violence, these theories will also cultivate and encourage violence. This is why, for example, Darwin's theory is inherently violent. It pits everything against everything else. This is also why Freud's theory is inherently violent. It pits child against parent, us against civilization. In communicology, Berger's uncertainty reduction theory pits meaning against ambiguity, communication against confusion. In the end, these kinds of theories only help us to further segregate, discriminate, and categorize, and consequently, to merely become instruments of the status quo.

Either against the world or against each other, violence will make for our undoing. But what to do when even our disciplines of knowledge promote and cultivate violence? Such, again, is the insidious nature of violence. We continue to assume that violence comes with the world. It is both inevitable and necessary. So when Darwin claims that violence is integral to evolution, this intuitively makes sense to us. He gives us a way to rationalize violence. It is necessary for evolution. Without violence or the threat of violence, the rise of cooperation would supposedly be impossible. There would be no détente. In fact, more than being necessary, violence is assumed to be good. It supposedly saves us from those who would take advantage of our charity and generosity. This, again, is why Darwin appeals to us. He gives us a way to rationalize and legitimize our investment in violence. Nothing about what Darwin claims threatens the status quo. We always desired to believe that violence was good for something. Darwin never told us anything that we were reluctant or unwilling to believe. This is also the case with our other theories. When communicology theorizes that confusion impedes communication, this is by no means news to us. We always knew that confusion had to be vanquished. It is supposedly one of those malevolent forces that torment the world.

To save ourselves from violence requires creating worldviews that have no origins in violence. This means creating worldviews out of love. Love, rather than peace, is the antithesis of violence. Whereas violence comes into the world by us segregating, discriminating, and categorizing, love embraces all the world's ambiguity, mystery, and complexity. It recognizes the relationship between all things. Love celebrates the union and communion amongst all things. That everything is related means that the well-being of one thing is related to the well-being of everything else. To care for one thing commits us to care for every other thing. Love enlarges us. It challenges and pushes our bounds of empathy and compassion. It diminishes the ego, thereby cultivating charity and generosity of mind, body, and spirit. This generosity allows us to hear the fear and confusion in others. For to listen, to genuinely listen, involves owning our doubt and diminishing our ego. Listening requires a certain kind of being. It is an act of generosity, such as being able to focus on others rather than ourselves. Listening is an act of love. We listen because we recognize that much of our humanity resides in others, including others who are yet to come into our worlds. Love recognizes and embraces this reality. That much of our humanity resides in others means that the limits of our humanity are limitless. There is no way to fully know what we are capable of being and becoming. There is always ambiguity and mystery. But most of all, there is always possibility, as in the possibility to come to new ways of understanding and experiencing something. Being human is about being human with others. This is how the well-being others becomes our concern. To care about the well-being of others is to care for our own well-being.

Love ends the segregation between ontology, epistemology, and axiology, meaning that love dissolves the division between mind, body, and spirit. What we perceive, define, and value as knowledge is about what we are willing to perceive, define, and value as knowledge. That there is no division or separation between mind, body, and spirit means that theories of mind must also be theories of body and spirit. What we perceive, define, and value as knowledge is about our own willingness to love. By influencing what we have the courage to believe, love also influences what we have the courage to perceive. Love is the measure of knowledge. Our willingness to love shapes our knowledge of the world, how we engage the world, and ultimately, how we experience the world.

We have to come to knowledge on our own terms. We cannot impose knowledge on others. Neither can any amount of theories and methodologies produce any kind of knowledge that is of value to us. Outside of love, knowledge is impossible. Of course we can always point to our endless libraries and supposedly great universities as proof of our vast bodies of knowledge, and our ability to capture and share this knowledge. But in the end what is the value of any knowledge that only brings more and more violence into the world and makes our existence more and more perilous?

4 1

ON CIRCULARITY

There is a relation between doubt and diversity that contains much beauty. This means that our determination to diminish doubt is bound up with our determination to end diversity. Doubt means ambiguity. Doubt means that what will be unknown will always exceed what is known. Doubt means humility. To know is only to know what I will never know. Through doubt spaces organically open for the inclusion and consideration of other meanings and interpretations. This is how doubt promotes diversity. Yet a deep aversion and hostility to doubt remain at the center of our worldview in the west. We seek to end doubt. But to end doubt is to end diversity.

The world's diversity is increasingly being erased by our actions. We are now losing a language every seven days, acres of virgin forests every few minutes, and are rapidly depleting all the fish in the world's oceans. Darwin's theory of evolution is playing a particularly important role in this vanquishing of diversity. Survival of the fittest means that the decisions and actions of those who are perceived to be so are inherently just. Such persons should command leadership positions, thereby possessing the power to control the fates of others. The rise of Darwin is about our continuing struggle to end doubt, especially doubt in what being human means. Darwin promises us a calculus that will fully and rigorously explain what being human means. The end of doubt is now without doubt. This is the continuing seduction of Darwin. This is also what explains the continuing rise of Darwin, as seen in the rise of new disciplines like sociobiology, psychobiology, anthrobiology, and communicology. All these new disciplines claim that Darwin makes for a much more exact knowledge and ultimately, a much more exact society. We now use Darwin to explain everything. Never before has Darwin been so popular. Yet on the other hand, never before has diversity been in such peril.

Of course correlation has nothing to do with causation. But Darwin's theory is inherently circular. Presumably, the fittest, strongest, and brightest survive and flourish by being the fittest, strongest, and brightest. So again, why only do the fittest, strongest, and brightest survive, by simply being the fittest, strongest, and brightest? But of course other kinds of survival machines also flourish. Still, why is survival the measure of success and prosperity? That is, why is the ability to reproduce and propagate our genes the measure of success? In Darwin's theory, we are to assume that life is about survival of the fittest, and survival means replicating our genes. From the perspective of Darwin, those survival machines that have achieved the means to reproduce are the fittest, strongest, and brightest. Conversely, those survival machines that have no capacity or ambition to do so are presumably less fit, strong, and bright. This is the circularity that pervades Darwin's theory. We must simply assume from the beginning that our primary mission is to replicate our genes. By anchoring us to this assumption, Darwin gives us no way out of this circularity.

This circularity allows Darwin's theory to maintain the pretension of being able to explain everything. Darwin's theory becomes a theory of everything. There is no need for another theory. Welcome to the end of doubt. But what to do with those survival machines that have no ambition to reproduce? What also to do with altruism? Darwin's theory, as even its staunchest proponents admit, still has no reliable way of explaining altruism, especially the highest levels of altruism, such as the sacrifice of our own lives for those who have no biological relation to us. But who would call John Brown, Martin Luther King, and Sojourner Truth fools? The theory of everything becomes the theory of hardly everything. It can only explain the world from which it comes. It in no way lends for a different story of the world. In this way, Darwin's theory limits our imagination by limiting what we can conceive and perceive. No consequence could be more damaging. This is how Darwin's theory conspires against diversity. By keeping us bound to a self-filling and self-perpetuating narrative, Darwin traps us within a closed system, which of course is always certain to collapse and implode. But this is how Darwin conspires against doubt. There is no place for doubt in closed systems. Closed means closed from doubt, closed from diversity, closed from possibility. Closed also means closed from disruption, transformation, and even revolution. Closed means discouraging, marginalizing, and excluding anything that could threaten the status quo, or anything that could challenge us to view the world in new ways. Yet how could this possibly be a good thing or something we will ever want to promote and encourage?

But the attraction, as seen with Darwin, is elsewhere. In presumably saving us from doubt, closed systems save us from all the anxiety that comes with doubt. There is no natural proclivity to doubt. Doubt is hard. Doubt is disorientating. Doubt invites anguish and despair, torment and tribulation. So the world imposes doubt on us. It forces us to own and harbor doubt. For doubt is life-affirming. Doubt means humility. Doubt means that even our most prized truths will never completely explain everything. Neither will others ever possess such truths. In a world of doubt, diversity is inevitable. Diversity is about recognizing that our truths will always be inherently incomplete. There is always doubt, which means that there is no need to worship our truths as gods, including the means of arriving at these truths. No truth is beyond revision. Doubt collapses any divide between the world and us. That the world is laden with doubt means that we are also laden with doubt. To own our doubt is to recognize that there is virtue in doubt. Doubt impedes our dogmatic, militaristic, and ethnocentric instincts and impulses. It promotes curiosity and generosity of spirit. But most of all, doubt cultivates humility. In doing all of these things, doubt promotes diversity. So without doubt, diversity is impossible. That the world will always be laden with doubt, regardless of our own determination to end doubt, means that any mode of theorizing that assumes differently only serves to limit us. Such theorizing only gives us the illusion of knowledge. Eventually doubt will rise, and the theories that are born from such theorizing will implode, as will the hegemonies that nurture and legitimize these theories. Doubt is how the world keeps us in place. There is much beauty with being human. To realize this beauty means coming to peace with our place in the world. This means recognizing that there is nothing fundamentally wrong with any knowledge that begins or ends in doubt. Doubt is no foe of knowledge. In fact, doubt vitalizes knowledge. Without doubt, knowledge is impossible. As much as sociobiology, anthrobiology, psychobiology, and communicology are cast as the coming of a new knowledge that will finally make for the end of doubt, such disciplines offer no new knowledge. Nothing about this knowledge challenges what we already assume, believe, and value. Its goal was always to vanquish doubt, thereby deepening our conviction that Darwin's theory was really a theory of everything, and thereby deserving to be the theory that shapes how we organize our lives and distribute our resources. This is a case of politics masquerading as theory. Of course the political is always bound up with the epistemological. But in this case the political is driving everything. There is a sense that the barbarians are at the gates, threatening to dismantle the great institutions that are the crown jewels of western and European civilization. The supposed natural aristocracy and hierarchy that guide this civilization are apparently now under assault from those coming from supposedly backward civilizations. Capitalism is also under threat from the increasing many who are presumably jealous and envious of the few who are getting all the spoils by merely being the fittest, strongest, and brightest. In all the scenarios, either protecting the integrity of our natural hierarchy, or justifying the increasing disparity between rich and poor, Darwin seamlessly connects and explains everything. It is the only theory the status quo needs to justify everything.

But Darwin's theory is only describing the world it is already assuming. This is why the theory seems so capable of eloquently and seamlessly describing everything. However, with such circularity comes the end of doubt and diversity. Also fueling this circularity is our model of theory. A good theory should presumably describe a world that is separate and outside of us. This definition of theory pervades all sides of the political spectrum. Most of postcolonial theory, feminist theory, critical theory, critical race theory, and queer theory use this model of theory. The fact that nearly all persuasions are generally using the same model of theory means that all sides are of the same epistemology, which in turn means that though certain persuasions give the impression of wanting revolution, nothing could be further from the truth. Revolutions require new epistemologies rather than merely new theories and methodologies. So this is why in the face of postcolonial theory, feminist theory, and so forth, Darwin's theory continues to rise and increasingly shape how we organize our lives and distribute our resources. There is no threat from a new epistemology. This is also why academe continues to be fully complicit in maintaining the order of things. It promises no threat of a new knowledge, including new ways of defining and experiencing knowledge. Any possibility of revolution will therefore have to come from some place other than academe, even be ready to conspire against academe.

The new trend in academe is to claim to be against theory. We should commit to praxis through and through. But this trend makes no sense. We still have to generate knowledge, define knowledge, and share knowledge. Theory is inevitable. We will always be in the theory business. Rather than being against theory, we should be against how we continue to define theory, experience theory, and assume about theory. All of this begins with changing our relation to theory. That we will always be doing theory means that we will always be seeking to know. But what should we be seeking to know, and how, and from where and whom? Yes, know thyself and know the world seem plausible places to begin. But somewhere something went terribly wrong. For how did so many years of diligently acquiring and stockpiling this knowledge culminate in all the great horrors of the last century and our own continuing destruction of the planet? We are to believe that all of this carnage and destruction has nothing to do with the nature of our knowledge. It is instead about how we use knowledge. We are to assume that knowledge is devoid of ideology and history. It is supposedly this neutral thing. Like any tool, which is also a common metaphor for knowledge, we can use knowledge to build or to destroy. It all depends on our motives and decisions. This is the standard story of our knowledge being innocent. The fault is purely with our intentions and ambitions. But this story assumes a divide between knowledge and us. There is no such divide. No knowledge is yet to fall out of the sky, or come out of the earth like plants. We bring knowledge into the world. Therefore what about us brings this knowledge into the world, especially a knowledge that is so inherently destructive? Why did not so many other peoples bring such a knowledge into the world? But there are other divides at work other than that between knowledge and us. There is also the divide between the world and us, life and death, animals and plants, mind and body, force and matter, theory and praxis, life sciences and social sciences, and many others. Division and separation are the hallmarks of our knowledge. This is why our knowledge is inherently destructive.

But why this obsession with all this division and separation? The guesses are probably endless. Nevertheless, what now seems plain is that all of this division and separation is limiting our imagination. To do theory differently means doing away with all of this division and separation, beginning with the division between the world and us. This is the only way a new knowledge will arise.

42

ON DESIGN

What is the purpose of design? Where does design come from within the human experience? The popular answer is functionality. The purpose of design is supposedly to increase our capacity to function efficiently and effectively. After all, what else is the purpose of a table, a chair, a car, a pen, or nearly any other artifact of design? This is also supposedly the catalyst that drives design in the natural world. But how and why did functionality come to have such a hold on our understanding of design? Functionality assumes that human beings are of a world devoid of any mystery. The purpose of design is supposedly to extend our capacity to survive by helping us control and command various elements, resources, and forces. The measure of functionality is efficiency—being able to do more with less. Utility also matters. But good design achieves maximum productivity with minimum resources. Functionality captures and complements the view that a good life is productive, defined by our accomplishments and achievements. We are always encouraged to be productive, to be always setting and achieving our goals. Good design presumably enhances our productivity. It helps us to attain a quality life by enhancing our productivity.

This is productivity functioning as a master trope—a seminal rhetorical device that organizes our social world. But productivity is also an expression of ontology. It reflects a certain view of what being human means. So our designs are always encouraging us to be productive and to experience the world in terms of productivity. This is also how design functions ideologically. No design is completely divorced from ideology. This is also how design functions as an insidious kind of colonialism—invisibly yet powerfully reshaping how natives and indigenous peoples relate and perceive the world and each other.

That the goals of design are functionality and productivity means that our focus is always on finding new and better designs that will increase our own productivity and ultimately our quality of life. How much productivity we can achieve, and thereby how much quality of life we can attain, is now dependent on how well we can design. Design becomes paramount in determining our quality of life. Functionality makes for productivity, which in turn makes for quality of life. The equation also means that design becomes everything. We have to be always designing, always trying to increase the functionality of our designs. There must always to be 2.0, 3,0, 4.0, 5.0, 6.0, 7.0, and every new version needs to arrive quickly. Features also matter. There must always be new and better features. Features mean functionality, as in our increasing capacity to do a number of new things. Presumably, features mean progress. Good designing is about increasing the features that are available to us. Every new design comes with promises making many new exciting features available to us. We seem to be convinced that of all these new features will make our lives better. We can now do things that we once could have only imagined. This, again, is progress. It is supposedly our increasing our capacity to be productive.

Every new design means discarding and disposing of another design. Disposability emerges prominently in our consciousness. Attachment impedes progress. We must always be ready to adopt the new design and learn the new features. Only by doing all of this will the quality of our lives be improved. So with each new design, even the promise of a new design, comes much excitement and anticipation. How will this new design improve the quality of our lives? In what new ways will this new design expand and increase our productivity? What will we now be able to do faster and better? We are still in the age of excitement and anticipation. We continue to believe that every new design will make our lives better. Manufacturers of course have no interest or incentive to have us believe otherwise. In fact, many stakeholders have a vital interest in deepening our own belief about the power of design to make our lives better, and thereby fueling all the excitement when news comes of the arrival of a new design.

But eventually this age of excitement and anticipation will come to pass. Eventually no new design will do anything to either enhance or improve our quality of life. This illusion will come to an end. It is inevitable. We will eventually have to find a new story of design, which means finding a new purpose for design, a new way of defining good design, and a new way of relating to design. The problems with viewing design in terms of functionality and productivity are now insurmountable. We are simply running out of the natural resources necessary to sustain this kind of design. This story of design has always put us in conflict with the world. But now all sides of the problem are converging and promising to make a perilous ending. We are also running out of the natural resources necessary to sustain the production of every new version. Also, operating these new designs are making demands on our natural resources that are simply unsustainable. Finally, disposing of old designs is taxing our natural resources. We still have no way of reintegrating the resources that make for our designs back into the natural world and in harmony with other resources.

No solution to any of these problems is on the horizon. Of course, these problems are in no way new. But such is also the power of ideology to sustain illusions, in this case, our capacity to pretend that this day of reckoning will never be upon us. We could just continue manufacturing, using, and discarding without end, like the planet had no limits or that human beings were released from these limits. This is the problem with our current story of design. It has no regards for the natural world, reflecting our own disregard for the natural world. For us, the natural world is merely a repository of resources. In the end, what emerges from our current story of design is a determination and obsession with design to achieve a level of functionality and productivity that will make for a perfect life that is unbound from the natural world. This obsession is of course being driven by our perception that new designs are actually making our lives better, and consequently saving us from all manner of tribulations. But what of the misery and despair that are increasingly ravaging our lives, and which are coming from our increasing social isolation?

A mission of design is social connectivity—to link and connect us with many other human beings. However, as our social connectivity rises, so also rises our social isolation. Yet for us, the problem is still one design, thereby demanding a design solution. Our story of design assumes that the natural world is outside and separate from us. Besides constraints of resources, there are presumably no other kinds of limits. Productivity is unbound, which means that design is also unbound. We can supposedly design our way out of any problem. We are released of any moral or ecological constraints. We can design to the hilt, as long as the resources are available for us to do so. Lately, our goal is to make our designs increasingly connective to each other. But herein is a problem with our story of design. Isolation has nothing to do with connectivity. Only machines suffer from a lack of connectivity. Isolation is a human problem, specifically a problem of constitution, or lack thereof. Vulnerability saves us from isolation. That is, getting beyond the ravages of isolation requires of us the capacity to form and sustain honest, nurturing, and affirming relationships. Only through vulnerability such relationships are possible. Vulnerability is the path to authenticity. However, vulnerability is really about the courage to be vulnerable, to be ready and willing to reveal our humanity to others in ways that hopefully are met with empathy, compassion, and affirmation. We need vulnerability. Vulnerability makes us human. It enlarges our humanity. It mellows the spirit and soothes the mind. Vulnerability speaks to a different story of design. No amount of functionality and productivity can get us to vulnerability. The problems that are increasingly upon us have nothing to do with a lack of functionality and productivity.

We are dealing with problems of vulnerability. Designing for vulnerability requires a different story of design. It means recognizing and appreciating a different story of what being human means. We are ecological beings. Our humanity is bound up with the natural world, which means that the condition of the world is bound up with our own condition. Consequently, design is always moral and ecological, as well as cultural and ideological. Good design should heighten our moral and ecological sensibility. Put differently, good designing should enlarge our moral and epistemological imagination, and accordingly, enrich and expand the human experience. This is a fundamentally different way of conceiving of design theory. It also constitutes a different way of teaching design. Most of design pedagogy focuses on mastering the skills and techniques that make for good designing. Indeed, design theory does get a fair amount of attention in various curriculums, including the politics of design. But the focus of most curriculums is on skill acquisition as design is still about commanding and manipulating elements and materials. This kind of skill is no doubt important. But design is also about understanding and appreciating the design that is already happening in the world. A river is always design. So also is an ocean, a forest, a lake. There is always design. This is what life does. This is how life emerges in the world. This is what life does. The world will never be devoid of design. No doubt, there will still be the contention that most design curriculums acknowledge as much. We would be advised to also note the new designing that is promoting and lending for ecological sustainability.

Many will also contend that functionality is driving all of this designing in the natural world. Functionality, again, is about using resources efficiently and effectively. Indeed, functionality matters. But this is by no means the goal or the sum of design. What about the emancipatory capacity of design, such as the power of design to enlarge how we perceive things and what we are willing to experience? What also of the capacity of design to enlarge how we relate to and experience each other? In sum, what of the capacity of design to promote possibility? What now passes for functionality in the natural world has nothing much to do with functionality, meaning that what we perceive as functionality is possibly a product of our own ideological standpoint. Design is possibly evolutionary, is about life unfolding and emerging. As life is about possibility, to nurture life is to nurture possibility. When life is thriving, so too is possibility. Thus rather than promoting functionality, the story of design is probably about liberating possibility. Take the case of a bird nest. We can certainly look at the nest in terms of functionality. But what would be the possibility of new life without the nest? How would life come into the world and flourish without this design? So yes, functionally, the nest is impressive as design. But just as impressive is how this design is nurturing life and promoting possibility. This is design being moral and ecological. Our challenge now is to arrive at a new story of design that promotes possibility.

43

ON DISCRIMINATION AND HARASSMENT

How does a society become infantilized and what does such a trend poses for democracy? Put differently, what becomes of dissent, diversity, and conflict in an infantilized world? No doubt, such a society will aim to suppress these natural life-affirming forces, as engaging these forces requires high levels of mental, emotional, and spiritual maturity and resiliency. Democracy requires resolve, fortitude, patience, and, most of all, moral courage. We achieve and practice democracy. But again, how does a society become infantilized and consequently, impede democracy? A case study is in order.

NON-DISCRIMINATION AND ANTI-HARASSMENT IN EMPLOYMENT POLICY STATEMENT[2]

------------ University has a policy of employing, advancing in employment, and otherwise treating individuals without discrimination or harassment on the basis of race, color, creed, religion, sex, gender, national origin, citizenship, ethnicity, marital status, age, disability, sexual orientation, gender identity and gender expression, veteran status, or any other status protected by applicable law to the extent prohibited by law. The University prohibits any such discrimination or harassment.

Under this policy, harassment is verbal or physical conduct, or written or electronic communications that denigrate or express hostility or aversion toward an individual because of his or her race, color, creed, religion, gender, national origin, citizenship, ethnicity, marital status, age, disability, sexual orientation, gender identity and gender expression, veteran status or any other status protected by applicable law to the extent prohibited by law, and that:

- Has the purpose or effect of creating an intimidating, hostile or offensive work environment; or

- Has the purpose or effect of unreasonably interfering with an individual's work performance; or

- Otherwise adversely affects an individual's employment.

- Harassing conduct includes, but is not necessarily limited to:

---

2 This is an actual Non-discrimination and Anti-Harassment policy.

- Epithets, slurs or negative stereotyping.

- Threatening, intimidating or hostile acts.

- Denigrating jokes.

- Written or graphic material that denigrates or shows hostility or aversion toward a group or an individual believed to be part of a particular group.

- Written or graphic material that is placed on walls or elsewhere on University premises, or is circulated in the workplace.

- Using electronic equipment to distribute, view, or otherwise disseminate materials or messages that are abusive, profane, threatening, defamatory or offensive.

- Conditioning employment terms on submission to harassing conduct, sexual advances, requests for sexual favors, etc.

- In addition, no person will be subject to discipline, retaliation, intimidation, or any other adverse treatment because he or she makes a complaint of discrimination or harassment in good faith or has participated in the investigative process in any way. Employees who believe that they are being discriminated against and/or harassed should promptly report such harassment to any one of the following:

- His or her immediate supervisor, the supervisor's supervisor, or a dean;

- Office of Human Resources staff including:

- The Assistant Director of Employment Practices and Equal Employment Opportunity;

- The Recruitment and Diversity Specialist;

- The Manager of Staff Relations and Recruitment;

- The Director of Resolution Processes and The Sexual Harassment Officer; or

- Any other member of the Office of Human Resources.

Upon a report of discrimination and/or harassment, the University will conduct a prompt and thorough investigation of the allegations. Upon completing the investigation, the University will take appropriate corrective action consistent with the results of the investigation. Disciplinary action, up to and including discharge, may be taken against employees who violate this policy.

This policy applies to all applicants, employees, and outside vendors and consultants during the course of business with the University. The University also maintains a separate Sexual Harassment Prevention Policy, and a separate Non-discrimination in Employment on the Basis of Disability Policy. Policies related to prohibited behaviors apply in the workplace and in any work-related setting outside the workplace, such as during work-related trips, work-related meetings and work-related social events.

Policy Administration

- Human Resources

- Links to Procedures and Related Information

- Non-Discrimination and Equal Opportunity Policy Statement

- Non-Discrimination, Equal Employment Opportunity and Affirmative Action

- Non-Discrimination on the Basis of Disability Policy Statement

- Non-Discrimination in Employment on the Basis of Disability

- Non-Discrimination/Students with Disabilities Policy

- Sexual Harassment Prevention Policy

- Sexual Harassment Procedures

Amended: August 2005
Amended: November 2007

But who determines what constitutes harassment? That is, who determines, and by what cultural norms, what kind of conduct and communication denigrates or expresses hostility or aversion towards a person because of his or her race, creed, gender, and so forth? Also, how does one determine whether a person was purposely intending to create an intimidating, hostile, or offensive work environment? Again, what cultural norms are being used to make this determination, and why these norms rather than others? Moreover, who determines, using what cultural norms, what conduct or communication can "otherwise adversely" affect others? Indeed, according to the University, "as long as [a person creates] an environment in which a person feels extremely uncomfortable learning or working, then it is actionable [a complaint can be filed]." But again, what cultural norms are being used to make this determination? What also of the moral, ideological, and psychological forces that play into this determination, as well as what constitutes discomfort? In sum, this seemingly progressive policy seeks to remove our cultural, moral, ideological, and spiritual diversity. It constitutes an insidious attempt to such diversity. There are simply no conduct or messages that are universally perceived as threatening, defamatory, or offensive as everything has a cultural context. Culture matters. If diversity is to mean anything, culture has to matter. The University is supposed to know that culture matters. This is the purpose of anthropology. So what explains this erasure of culture, and how did such erasure become so easy?

But what exactly is the purpose of this harassment policy? The University, of course, would claim that the purpose is inclusion. The University is creating a safe space for diversity. But this goal of inclusion is nothing but ideology. First and foremost, no university is truly and genuinely committed to the promotion of inclusion. As the policy states, the University is only committed to the inclusion of certain groups of peoples, and thereby a diversity that begins and ends with race, gender, sexuality, creed, and so forth. There are all manner of diversity, such as our religious diversity, that the University has absolutely no intention of including, accommodating, and celebrating. Yet how the University decided what diversity should be included and excluded was arbitrary. This is purely a creature of ideology. Even the goal of inclusion is ideology. We are to assume that inclusion is inherently good. It is moral. But for diversity, inclusion is a problem. Inclusion depoliticizes diversity. It reduces diversity to a category, or as a category to be included. We are reduced to our race, ethnicity, sexuality, creed, gender, and so forth. We are to assume that these groupings determine our diversity and thereby fundamentally shape our identity. Our full diversity, complexity, and mystery are erased. This again is seen in how the harassment policy erases the moral, cultural, historical, spiritual, ideological, and geographical forces that shape how we perceive and experience the world.

The University is first and foremost an institution. It values stability, conformity, continuity, and predictability. No institution can genuinely promote diversity. Diversity means dissent, conflict, disruption, and even revolution. The supposed inclusion demands the emasculation of diversity. What emerges is anything but diversity. Plurality masquerades as diversity. That is, what emerges poses no threat to anything. This, again, is how diversity is depoliticized. We merely have the illusion of diversity. In reality, the harassment policy is merely another way the University, in being an institution, suppresses dissent, conflict, and ultimately, the threat of revolution. The policy constitutes the co-opting, and thereby the neutralizing, of diversity. In many ways, this new ploy was inevitable. With every institution having to deal with a world that is increasingly multicultural as our spaces and distances collapse and implode, institutions had to find a way to neutralize this threat. Unable to eliminate the threat, co-opting the threat was all that was left. The success of this co-opting is on full display in the harassment policy. We now actually believe that through this policy we are promoting diversity. This policy presumably constitutes our commitment to diversity. Our resolve is also found in our commitment to enforce this policy vigorously. There must supposedly be no tolerance of any conduct that impedes diversity. However, all that emerges in the end is an institution that is increasingly hostile to diversity. Such is the irony that now characterizes the modern university. Of all the institutions, the one that is supposed to be committed to knowledge and liberating us from the ravages of ignorance is actually the one most hostile to diversity. It will tolerate no dissent, no disruption, and the sanctions for even being accused of doing otherwise are often harsh. According to the University, we only teach democracy. The practicing must apparently happen elsewhere. This hostility to democracy is also on full display in the harassment policy.

There is no recognition that meaning is always fluid. Nothing lends for only *one* meaning, *one* interpretation. We are to assume that there is an intractable conflict between diversity and democracy. Promoting diversity supposedly requires curtailing democracy, such as prohibiting the use of certain words and phrases, ending the expression of certain values and beliefs, and suppressing various kinds of dissent and conflict. However, without democracy, diversity is impossible. Democracy means the cultivation of sedition. In a democracy, nothing is inherently sacred as nothing is ever devoid of ambiguity. There is the possibility for a different meaning. Democracy aims to safeguard that possibility. Thus in a democracy nothing is beyond discussion and deliberation. No interpretation is ever final. Nothing is inherently sacred because humans are cultural, historical, and ideological beings. We will always perceive and experience the world in different ways. A democracy recognizes our diverse rationalities, sensibilities, spiritualities, histories, and modalities. Such differences are inevitable in a world laden with an ambiguity that no meaning can vanquish. However, without such differences, our ability to evolve, mature, and change would be impossible. A democracy pushes and challenges us to engage and contemplate even that which we perceive as despicable and abominable. Through this pushing and challenging we enlarge what we are capable of perceiving and understanding. This is, ultimately, how democracy makes us human.

To sacrifice democracy for diversity impoverishes both. So what happens when a person feels uncomfortable or harassed? According to the harassment policy, this person should promptly report the matter to a supervisor or one of the many offices dedicated to promoting diversity.

There will then be an investigation, and depending on the findings, disciplinary actions will be taken, including the possibility of termination. The burden is on the accuser to show unequivocally that no discomfort or harassment was intended. Those conducting the investigation will then determine whether the explanation suffices and therefore whether the conduct or communication was purposely intimidating or harassing. No exercise is as precarious, as ultimately one person is seeking to look into the heart and soul of another human being. But this is what has now become of the modern university—it encourages us to look into the hearts and souls of others. We are all mystics now. Do these institutional processes enable and nurture democracy? In other words, does encouraging a person who feels harassed to make a prompt complaint enable and nurture democracy? What about first encouraging the person to engage the other person and to identify and explain what conduct or communication is making the person feel uncomfortable or harassed? Simply put, what about encouraging the person to be courageous? Why encourage the person to assume that the other person is malevolent and unrepentant? Why also encourage the person to assume that only institutional apparatuses can solve our problems with others? How did community and solidarity come to have no capacity to solve these problems? Why encourage this belief? But such is what institutions must do, that is, make us seem helpless. This is how institutions seduce us, by promising to save us from doing things that are hard, like exercising courage. However, without courage, what becomes of the human condition? We need courage to believe, to mature, to love. Through courage we acquire the muscularity and resiliency that make a democratic consciousness inevitable. Conversely, without courage we become fragile and infantile, in the grips of all manner of neuroses and psychoses. But most of all, we become myopic, autocratic, and narcissistic, unable to recognize our own hegemonisn, chauvinism, and ethnocentrism. Who could, after all, argue with the intent to establish a policy that prohibits discrimination and harassment? It seems like the only right thing to do. For who would want to encourage or tolerate harassment? This is also why the policy erases culture by simply assuming that what is harassing conduct or communication is outside of culture. We supposedly all know what constitutes such conduct and communication, and also concur with how such transgressions should be handled. As such, the University allows for no dissent or conflicting views. It also allows for no other course of action when dealing with supposed transgressions. Anything other than decisive corrective action apparently constitutes complicity. So again what is most striking about this harassment policy—in addition to the Sexual Harassment Policy and the Non-discrimination in Employment on the Basis of Disability Policy—is its overt hostility to diversity. Such irony cannot be underscored enough. A policy that aims to promote diversity conspires in every way against diversity.

44

ON TEACHING

Teaching is act of love. This is what our educational institutions have yet to understand. We can certainly teach our students how to do certain things. But we cannot teach our students anything profound. That is an illusion. All we can do is love our students, and hopefully by doing so they will find the courage to be vulnerable to themselves, each other, and the world. This is the most that teaching can do, and all that teaching should aspire to do. Anything else is violence. There can be no learning, or at least the learning of anything profound, outside of love. Before we can learn, we must believe, and what we believe will influence what we learn and understand.

So what must we do now? How do we teach in the face of apathy, despair, and cynicism? In fact, how do we teach in a world hostile to love? Yet no other institution than education has probably done more to making the world so. This is the tragic irony that is now upon us. Our educational institutions have nothing to do with education. The goal of these institutions is to domesticate us. This is why violence pervades these institutions. Mandating that students take certain courses is violence. Forcing students to learn certain things is violence. Demanding that students conform to certain norms of civility is violence. We have no qualms about all of this violence. In fact, our syllabuses come with many pages of threats and warnings. Every possible violation has a penalty. We simply cannot imagine doing education without violence. For how will our students know what courses to take, or what to learn, and thereby know what is important? Apparently, our students have no capacity to act responsibly without the threat of violence. Thus in order to save the world from chaos and anarchy, violence is presumably necessary. It presumably saves us from our worse instincts and impulses. In this way, our institutions play a vital role in instilling in us a deep fear of chaos and anarchy, that is, a deep fear of ourselves. We deny our students the ability to act maturely, responsibly, and most of all, courageously. Our educational institutions infantilize our students by robbing them of what is necessary to mature and become human. Our students lose the ability to act creatively and imaginatively, as in being able to determine on their own terms what is important and worthy of study and learning. Besides allowing us to dictate to our students what is important, our curriculums come with endless mandatory courses that allow for no diversity and innovation, and also pose no interest or challenge to our students. Our students have no passion to learn anything, and neither are they willing to make any effort to do differently. They merely want to know what is going to be on the test, or what do they need to know in order to complete the course and graduate. We then complain about our students' apathy and unwillingness to learn anything, especially anything that requires strenuous effort. But what of our own complicity in the making of this reality?

So what kind of human beings are our educational institutions producing? That is, what kinds of human beings come from being exposed to so much violence? We become what we have become. Our apathy is rampant. Our belief in the veracity of violence is without question. We care only for ourselves and our own well-being. Though we are much more educated, we are much less learned. We know much more about more things, but much less about what is really important. What we lack is the ability to create, to imagine, and to act purposefully on the world. What we also lack is the ability to look honestly and courageously at the forces that shape us and influence how we perceive and relate to the world. Most of all, we lack the courage and fortitude to love.

There are certain questions that we should ask before we teach. What is knowledge? How do we acquire acknowledge? Why knowledge? What is the purpose of knowledge? What eventually becomes apparent is that how we define knowledge, acquire knowledge, and relate to knowledge begins with what we believe. Also, what we believe and are willing to believe deal with matters of the heart, the soul, the spirit. Therefore in order to learn, that is, to acquire a fundamentally new understanding of something, we have to be ready or willing to change what we believe. Teaching is about challenging the workings of a person's mind, body, spirit, and heart. Every prophet has challenged us this way. Demands were placed on every dimension of our being. Yes, every prophet brought a teaching, but every teaching challenged every dimension of our being, beginning with what we believe. Indeed, every prophet sought to embody a teaching. This is why no prophet left anything in writing. Knowing these teachings word by word is secondary. We are to embody these teachings. We are to struggle. We are to do that which we are unwilling to do, even afraid to do. This is how we acquire knowledge, through struggle. We must be ready to challenge every dimension of our being. This is why Moses parted the ocean and Jesus Christ raised the dead. What we believe was being challenged. Knowledge is about faith. What we come to know and understand ultimately depends on us being ready and willing to believe in things that are seemingly impossible, such as the possibility of us parting an ocean or raising the dead. Whether these things are possible is secondary. What matters is what is involved in believing in these extraordinary things. How do we come to believe these things? What must we do?

There is power in belief. This is really where our power resides. This, again, is why the prophets put no emphasis on quantity of knowledge. It is what we believe that matters. This will ultimately determine what becomes of us. Thus challenging what we believe should be the mission of education. Instead, our focus is equipping our students with information, and finding the most effective means to do so. But what is all this information doing for us? Does the world have less peril? Do our students have less neuroses and psychoses? Indeed, what is the value of any education that in the end cannot even help us save our own souls? The mission of education should be about encouraging our students to love. Through love we enlarge what we perceive and how we relate to the world and each other. But to encourage our students to love also changes the role of the teacher. In the current mission the teacher is the objective dispenser of knowledge. We are responsible for equipping our students with all the necessary information. We also sometimes profess to teach our students how to view the world critically, such as when we help them to understand the insidious workings of ideology. In both roles the teacher is aspiring to be detached and morally neutral. We are still assuming that knowledge can be acquired through learning and studying. But no teacher is ever objectively detached and morally neutral. We bring all of our humanity into the classroom, just as much as our students do. That we bring all of our humanity into the classroom means that we also bring our hopes, fears, beliefs, values, and biases into the classroom. How we ourselves are defining, acquiring, relating, and experiencing knowledge reflects our own moral, spiritual, and ideological constitution. Knowledge is always laden with politics. We are active agents in the classroom. Our own understanding of knowledge has consequences for what becomes of the world.

Yet our own moral, spiritual, and ideological constitution is never exposed and critiqued, which means that how we ourselves are defining, acquiring, and experiencing knowledge is never exposed and critiqued. Thus what to make of our own teaching of ideological criticism when our own ideology is never critiqued? The point, again, being that ideology means consequences. To view education in terms of cultivating love recognizes this reality. Encouraging our students to love involves us loving our students. Through love we enlarge what we ourselves are capable of perceiving, understanding, and experiencing. In other words, through love we collapse the false divide between teaching and learning, theory and praxis, and other such schisms that only limit what our students and we can become through education. Through love education becomes emancipatory.

45

ON THE GOOD LIFE

Gary Gutting, a professor of philosophy at the University of Notre Dame, agrees that the core message of Jesus Christ's moral code is love. He also agrees with Aquinas that to love is "to do what we can to see that a person has a good life." But then comes the confusion. "But what is a good life? We might, thinking of the core message of Jesus, say that it's a life of loving others. But this response just takes us in a circle. Jesus tells us that to lead a good life we should love one another, but loving one another requires helping one another lead good lives. Unless we first know what it is to lead a good life, Jesus' law of love gives us little guidance on how to live." For Gutting, "This is no mere abstract worry. There are many competing conceptions of a good life. Utilitarians like John Stuart Mill think it is one that maximizes the pleasure of mankind as a whole. Others, like Immanuel Kant, think it is a life of virtue for its own sake, even if this requires renouncing pleasure. Followers of Aristotle think it requires flourishing through various intellectual, psychological and social virtues.

How a life of love for others should be lived depends on which conception of a good life is correct."

Gutting claims that the Sermon on the Mount "does not offer a clear view of what makes for a good life." Moreover, "Jesus does not explicitly or decisively endorse central contemporary values like democratic government, the abolition of slavery and the equality of women. Proponents of these values have found inspiration and support from his morality of love, but Jesus' words alone do not push us in their direction." According to Gutting, "None of this is to say that the Sermon on the Mount is not a source of profound moral truth. But this truth is accessible only by reading the sermon in the light of 2,000 years of interpretation and development. Much of the history of Christianity consists of trying to develop a viable way of life from Jesus' puzzling sayings." However, Christian Churches have been "central in sustaining the traditions of thought and practice that transformed Jesus' passionate but enigmatic teachings into coherent and fruitful moral visions." Thus to "profit from its wisdom we need to understand it through traditions of thought and practice within or informed by Christianity."

Gutting is taking issue with the increasingly popular view that Jesus Christ's teachings need to be separated (really, emancipated) from the institutional church. He believes that that "to forget the church is to forget Jesus." But when one looks at all the blood that is on the hands of the church, it was the church that forgot Jesus, and continues to forget Jesus. Thus the real question is why does the church continue to forget the teachings of Jesus Christ? What about the traditions of the church has made for so much blood and misery, and thereby the continued forgetting of Jesus Christ?

But let us begin at the beginning. Gutting claims that Jesus Christ's moral code gives us no definition of the good life. If so, what to make of the teachings to forgive those who trespass against us, to give up our riches and material possessions, to be a servant rather than leader, to be generous to the most vulnerable amongst us, to be peacekeepers, and so forth? The church only corrupts Jesus Christ's moral code, the reason being that the church is born out of a distortion of the moral code. There is nothing in this code that supports the creation of the church. The church constitutes hierarchy, and hierarchy impedes diversity. When Gutting writes about Jesus Christ's moral code needing traditions of thought and practice, this is hierarchy. But this is also how hierarchy impedes diversity. Traditions mean stability and continuity. Traditions mean status quo. Traditions mean hostility to diversity. Traditions mean a privileging of the past. That Jesus Christ brought a New Covenant shows plainly that Jesus Christ had no regard for traditions. Indeed, Jesus Christ was persecuted for threatening and upsetting the order of things, such as his refusal to allow a woman to be stoned for adultery. Jesus Christ's moral code is to be inclusive rather than exclusive. It will never conform to the demands of the church. This is why the church tends to have such a corrosive effect of the code. If Jesus Christ's moral code were to truly flourish, the church would certainly perish.

The good life that Jesus Christ's moral code speaks to is about deed. We will know a tree by the fruit it bears. This is also how a Christian is known. Is the person seeking to love others the way Jesus Christ loved us? Does the person refrain from judging others and so forth? A Christian is known by deed rather than belief. Any person can profess to believe in anything, but deed is a different matter and Jesus Christ calls us to do things that are really hard. However, everything that Jesus Christ calls us to do is meant to save us. This is why Jesus Christ's moral code is no different to the moral codes found in Jainism, Buddhism, Hinduism, and Judaism. We have long known what is the good life and why such a life matters. Such knowledge was never only the domain of the church. The good life is fundamentally about us recognizing that our redemption ultimately resides in our relation to each other. Heaven or hell will come from our own doing, or lack thereof. In this regard, the good life that Jesus Christ describes is pointing us decisively in a certain moral direction that does contain a vision of a good society. How could war be ambiguous when Jesus Christ's moral code calls us to be peacekeepers? How could the equality of women be ambiguous when Jesus Christ's moral code involves loving others as much as we love ourselves? How could the abolition of slavery be ambiguous when Jesus Christ's moral code involves loving others as much as Jesus Christ loved us? How could democracy be ambiguous when Jesus Christ's moral code advises us to be pure in heart? Ultimately, Jesus Christ's moral code is about how to live so as to create a society that promotes life. It is as much a moral as a political code. It challenges us to live in ways that undermine any status quo that is against peace, equality, diversity. There is nothing "puzzling" about Jesus Christ's moral code. However, according to Gutting, because of "Jesus' puzzling sayings," Christians have had to use pre-Christian scholars like Plato and Socrates to understand "the law of love" and other scholars like Kant and Mill to attain "a plausible explication of Jesus' teachings." But again, what exactly is puzzling about "Blessed are the merciful, for they will be shown mercy?" What "plausible explication" is missing from "Blessed are the peacemakers, for they will be called sons of God?" What about the law of love needs further explication? Besides the teachings of Jesus Christ, there is also the life of Jesus Christ for us to look to for direction, explication, and inspiration. As such, what exactly about the life of Jesus Christ is puzzling and confusing? What seems to be missing? In reality, nothing is missing. Yes, Jesus Christ said nothing about slavery. But slavery would never be found in world where we were genuinely embodying Jesus Christ's teaching to love others as much as we love ourselves. Between Jesus Christ's teachings and life, the moral code is properly explicated. What remains missing is our own lack of courage to do as the moral code commands us to do. To claim that the code is puzzling is nothing but an excuse for our own lack of conviction. Of course, there is always ambiguity with any text, which means that our interpretations will always differ. But this again is why we have both the life and teachings of Jesus Christ. We are no doubt entitled to our different interpretations, but such differences do nothing to release us from the fact that only through love is our redemption possible.

46

ON DEATH

No doubt, death is all that is certain. But what would life be without death? How would life find meaning? Death puts everything in perspective. It speaks to our mortality. We will never be gods. Everything we create and achieve will eventually expire, collapse, or implode. Dust to dust, ashes to ashes. Death exposes our insignificance and any false sense of importance. It devalues everything we value. It mocks us, belittles us, makes fools of us. We can do nothing about death. Its inevitability is truly inevitable. But death only mocks us because we continue to deny its inevitability.

We perceive and experience death as a negative force. We therefore aspire to vanquish death. We want what we create and achieve to defy the gravity of death. We believe that our prosperity depends on us defying death. So everything we create must be rigid, durable, and enduring. Nothing must succumb or perish easily and quickly. Anything less than defiance and resistance is weakness. This, again, is how death comes to mock us. For regardless of all our resistance and defiance, death will prevail. This much is certain. Yet we persist in our hostility to death. What is the origin of this hostility? How did this come to be culturally, ideologically, and epistemologically so? Moreover, why do we persist in doing something that is so inherently destructive? In persisting to conquer death all we continue to do is bring more and more misery into the world.

Death is a redeeming force. It cleanses the world by eventually removing everything that stops the rise of something new. Death undermines every status quo. That nothing can last forever means that change is inevitable. A new order will eventually arise. Because death is inevitable, change is inevitable. Moreover, because death is inevitable, diversity is inevitable. That is, without death, as in forest fires, volcanoes, tsunamis, hurricanes, and earthquakes, diversity is impossible. Death liberates diversity. It also brings spontaneity into the world. For death is both inevitable and unpredictable. Thus death forces us to embrace the moment that is before us. It could well be our last. However, what of those persons who by apparently embracing death have no qualms of murdering the innocent? Where is the virtue in such embrace of death? In reality such persons embrace murder rather than death. Their supposed embracing of death is used only to become a weapon to maim and murder. It is about using death as a means to an end. To truly embrace death is to embrace the inevitability of death. Attachment is misery. It means the illusion of permanence. It means lacking the courage to let go. Attachment also means our unwillingness to accept the world on its own terms. Death is inevitable. Everything will eventually expire. Nothing is meant to be permanent. "This too shall pass." Attachment puts us in conflict with world's natural rhythms. It puts us in conflict with ourselves by stopping us from evolving and changing. It impedes the rise of new states of being and consciousness. In other words, attachment, by putting us in conflict with death, stops us from being born anew. For only through death is life possible. We only begin to live by coming to peace with death. Death vitalizes life. It brings out all of life's beauty, vitality, and fecundity. Without death, life is nothing. Its creative and generative capacity comes from death. Attachment robs us of life. It diminishes us. Attachment means lack of imagination, as in our unwillingness to look at the world anew. It means a lack of courage. It reflects our unwillingness to die, and thereby our unwillingness to change and evolve. To live well, that is, to live honestly and creatively requires courage. Only by embracing death do we acquire the courage to love, and only finding the courage to die do we achieve the courage to live. As such, attachment means deception, deceit, and duplicity, beginning with our own self-deception. By embracing death we acquire the courage to live in ways that make us fertile to all that is possible with the world. This is the virtue of death. It promotes possibility. It pushes us to reimagine what is possible.

But how did we come to oppose death, to be hostile to death? This hostility pervades everything, shapes everything, defines everything. We desire a knowledge that will conquer death. Our goal is a world devoid of diseases and maladies. We aim to achieve such a world by gaining dominion over the body. We will know everything, and as a result will be able to anticipate and manipulate everything. That we aspire to know everything means that we are willing to do anything to know everything. After all, our survival is presumably at stake. Only by knowing everything we will be able to save ourselves from death. So our quest is unrelenting. Nothing less than an absolute and complete knowledge will do, that is, a knowledge that will allow us to control and predict everything. This is our plan for conquering death. We aspire to use knowledge as a weapon against death. Through an absolute and complete knowledge we will vanquish death, including all the things that are supposedly of death, such as chaos, ambiguity, and confusion.

But life is nothing without death. Both dwell within the bosom of each other. To be hostile to death is to be hostile to life. Our war against death is nothing but a war against life. This is why this absolute and complete knowledge we seek is demonstrably so destructive and responsible for so much misery. What other knowledge system is comparably destructive? But of course we continue to perceive death as being hostile to life. How do we begin to end this division and hostility? How do we begin to create a new knowledge, for only a new knowledge will save us from the peril that is now upon us? In communicology the divide between life and death is that between communication and confusion, meaning and ambiguity. The knowledge that forms communicology aims to vanquish confusion and ambiguity. We assume that through the vanquishing of confusion communication will arise and all will be well with the world. But of course, as much as there is no divide between life and death, there is no divide between communication and confusion, meaning and ambiguity. There is always confusion and ambiguity, and without either, communication and meaning would be impossible. But within communicology the quest continues to vanquish confusion and ambiguity. What results is an impoverished understanding of communication that robs us of endless capability, such as the ability to flourish in a world of boundless diversity. Without the means to engage each other honestly and compassionately, all that remains for us is a world increasingly fraught with peril and misery. As we become more proficient in amassing and disseminating communication knowledge, we have also become more isolated, separated, and disconnected. Neither our increasing propensity for aggression nor our growing isolation is life-affirming by any standard. Where therefore is the life that this knowledge is supposed to promote? Where also is the progress that this knowledge is supposed to make possible? In reality, neither life nor progress has come from this knowledge. Yet we refuse to indict this knowledge. We continue to believe that our knowledge is ideologically neutral. The fault is presumably with us and how we chose to use this knowledge. So the origin of the Holocaust was presumably political rather than epistemological. But how is the Holocaust or Jim Crow epistemologically different from our destruction of the planet and the world's biodiversity?

The fact is that this knowledge has an inherent aversion to diversity. It perceives diversity as an expression of death, such as our fear that linguistic diversity impedes unity and progress. It assumes that diversity invites chaos and disunity. This is why all our embracing, valuing, and even celebrating of diversity eventually amounts to nothing. Epistemologically, diversity is the wrong side of the divide. It is on the side of death. Homogeneity is on the side of life, supposedly. But of course our divide is wrong. Diversity is life. It is also the measure of life. Our diversity problem cannot be merely fixed by putting diversity on a different side of the divide. We have already put homogeneity on the side of life. Therefore the best we can now do is manage diversity, accommodate diversity, and tolerate diversity. But this diversity can pose no threat to the status quo. That this diversity is being managed, accommodated, and tolerated means that this diversity is bound by the dictates of homogeneity, commonality, and similarity. Consequently, all that can be had is merely the pretense of diversity, plurality passing as diversity. It is diversity in appearance only, devoid of any life-affirming potentiality.

A different conception of diversity requires a different knowledge system. Diversity is about relationships. Everything is related to everything else. Diversity is about the building of new relationships. It is about increasing the quality and density of our relationships. The world achieves diversity through the creation of new relationships. In order to understand diversity we therefore have to understand relationships. Relationships mean that our potentiality really resides in what is between us rather than what is within us. Through our relationships we realize our capacities and capabilities. Relationships mean that our own potentialities are bound up with the potentialities of others, and that our fates and destinies are also bound up with the fates and destinies of others. Diversity therefore requires an integrative approach to the world. Everything bears everything else. There are always consequences and implications. But most importantly, diversity implicates us in the affairs of the world. What we do, either purposely or otherwise, bears on the condition of the world. Being human is fundamentally about being in a relationship with the world, which means that our own diversity is bound up with the world's diversity. That we are ending the world's diversity in our pursuit to vanquish death bears on our own diversity and prosperity. This is the moral story of diversity—our prosperity is bound up with the world's diversity. Any knowledge system that jeopardizes the world's diversity also jeopardizes our prosperity.

Yet this is exactly what our knowledge continues to do. This hostility to diversity is, again, seen in communicology. We assume that through convergence we achieve communication. Anything that impedes convergence presumably invites discord and disharmony. Convergence means commonality, similarity, and homogeneity. It also means agreement and compromise. But most of all, convergence means fear, specifically fear of divergence. Supposedly, divergence is discord, disharmony, and ultimately, death. Communicology insidiously propagates this fear of death (and diversity) by defining communication in terms of convergence. We are to assume that without convergence death will be upon us. We must therefore be willing to agree, compromise, and assimilate for the sake of life. Without being willing to converge, such as agreeing to share a common symbolic and linguistic system, communication would be impossible, making harmony and discord no less impossible. So for the sake of life, convergence must prevail. This is the case that communicology makes for communication. Communication is a means to an end. It makes good things—like democracy and community—possible, which also means that convergence is necessary to achieving good things. But what of the possibility of communication being an end rather than a means? In other words, what of the possibility of communication having nothing to do with communication?

Communication assumes that we are separate and outside of each other. Communication connects us by pulling us towards each other. It gives us access to each other's minds, which in turn is supposedly vital to achieving coordination and organization. Because communicology assumes that communication is inherently a linguistic and symbolic process, we are to also assume that we achieve access to each other's minds through language and symbols. The notion of mind becomes a linguistic and symbolic phenomenon, and the study of mind and language becomes inextricable. But again, what of the possibility of communication having nothing to do with communication? We can begin to imagine this by recognizing that there is no separation between us. There is therefore no separation of our minds. That there is no separation between us means that there is also no separation for us to exceed through communication. It also means that there is no need for convergence, which in turn means that there is no need to cultivate similarity, commonality, and homogeneity. It also means that there is no need to promote symbolic and linguistic commonality, or even the supposed indispensability of language to communication. Mind becomes something different. It is between us, amongst us, within us, and all around us. Mind is found in relationships. Viewing mind in terms of language limits our conception of mind. That mind can be found in any relationship means that mind is boundless. It exceeds language. It also means that as much as mind shapes our relationships, our relationships also shape our minds. So again, by associating mind with language, we limit what mind is and what we are capable of minding. This is our predicament. We are of a knowledge that limits what we are capable of being. We are of a knowledge that lacks the most elementary of things, a good understanding of us.

47

ON MORAL PHILOSOPHY

I am surprised that moral philosophy continues to be taken seriously. That is, I am surprised that we continue to believe that moral philosophy can tell us how we should live and what constitutes the good life. Its understanding of the human condition is fundamentally wrong. We are anything but rational beings. Moreover, moral philosophy has yet to fully acknowledge that rationality is shaped by cultural, historical, and a myriad of other forces. Yet every dominant perspective in moral philosophy begins on the premise that we are rational beings or should aspire to become so. So Kant wants to us to do what is just regardless of the costs and the circumstances. Mill wants us to always do what is best for the majority. Rawls wants us to maximize both liberty and equality by pretending we have no knowledge of our circumstances. Nozick wants us to promote liberty to the hilt, regardless of whether the heavens may fall. Now Parfit wants us "to follow the principles whose universal acceptance everyone could rationally will." Which of us can even barely sustain any of these different commands, or should even be trying to do so?

Moral philosophy assumes that our redemption resides in us being rational. Yet moral philosophy offers different and conflicting definitions of rationality. For example, what Rawls views as rational is different to what Nozick views as rational. Still, moral philosophy wants us to be rational. We must pretend that cultural, historical, developmental, and epistemological forces play no role in how we engage the world, or that these forces adversely affect how we engage the world, or that we are capable of removing the influence of these forces. Moral philosophy continues to deny our boundless complexity and ambiguity. We must all be equally and universally rational. We must all agree to value the same things and in the same ways. However, where is the evidence that we are capable of consistently embodying Kant's perspective, or that of Mill, Rawls, and company? Moreover, where is the evidence that by adopting any of these perspectives the world will be spared of war and ecological disaster? Where is even the promise? Indeed, none of the prominent perspectives in moral philosophy assumes that we are ecological beings. Yet it is now demonstrably true that our own condition is bound with the condition of the world. Any model of rationality that has no regards for this reality will ultimately make for peril and misery. Such is the case with all the prominent perspectives in moral philosophy. There is no recognition that we are ecological beings. What is good for us must also be good for the world. At the very least this what being rational should mean, as anything else puts our survival in peril. This is also where moral philosophy needs to begin.

We could, of course, continue to deny the fact that our own well-being is bound up with the world's well-being. But eventually the world will impose this reality on us. It comes down to what price we are willing to pay to finally recognize this reality. How much more misery are we willing to endure? How much more peril are we ready to entertain? We can come to an understanding of what is just and good by merely asking what is best for the world—what actions and decisions promote life, or what actions and decisions promote possibility? Ideally, doing so would be best for us. But we are complex beings. Most likely we will continue to do differently and foolishly. However, that we are inherently ecological beings means that our poorly conceived actions and decisions will never go without consequences. Our foolishness will always come with a price. As much as we can choose to deny our relation to the world, the world will never release us of the consequences that come with doing so. In many ways, this is a good thing.

I am also yet to understand how moral philosophy continues to have no regard for anthropology. How could any serious and rigorous quest to understand what is good and just involve no consideration of what different peoples across the world view as good and just? How could such a quest begin and end with only the likes of Kant, Mill, Rawls, Locke, Hume, and Nozick? How could such a blatant racial, cultural, and civilizational bias remain so firmly in place? No doubt, all peoples and cultures struggle with determining what is good and just. Many civilizations have been doing so even before the dawn of European civilization. Yet moral philosophy would have us assume otherwise. We therefore apparently have nothing to learn from other peoples. But what does this abject failure in rigor reveal about the seriousness of our quest to understand what is good and just? Is this merely a problem of rigor, or a reflection of our own racism, narcissism, and ethnocentrism? The pervasiveness of the omission in moral philosophy would suggest the latter.

Finally, what of the omission of the world's great spiritual teachings in moral philosophy? All of these teachings deal with understanding what is good and just. Moreover, most peoples look to these teachings to know what is good and just. The omission of these teachings in moral philosophy would have us believe that these teachings have no relevance in any serious quest to understand what is good and just. Yet moral philosophy never reveals how and where these teachings are deficient. We are to simply assume that Kant, Mill, Rawls, and company have more profound ideas about what is good and just than Jesus Christ, Mohammed, Siddhartha, and company. However, what does this reveal about moral philosophy's view of all the peoples who use these spiritual teachings to understand what is good and just, even after studying Mill, Kant, Rawls, and company? How can moral philosophy have no regards for this reality? Moral philosophy would no doubt prefer that these spiritual teachings be confined to theology rather than philosophy. But this separation is arbitrary. It makes no sense outside of moral philosophy.

Theology and anthropology end moral philosophy. Both expose moral philosophy as having no real interest in knowing what is good and just. Both also reveal the many prejudices that encumber moral philosophy. Moral philosophy reminds us that epistemology is always bound up with ideology. No knowledge is free of what we believe and value. Moral philosophy would have us believe that we are genuinely and objectively trying to know what is good and just. But we are actually only willing to accept a certain kind of answer to our inquiry. This is how and why moral philosophy was born. We want an answer to what is good and just that will pose no threat to anything. Neither theology nor anthropology can do this for us. But this is what Kant, Hume, Mill, Rawls, and company give us. We are to assume that the perspectives these persons give us are different. But such is hardly the case. Also, none of these perspectives challenge the status quo, meaning that none challenge our own ways of being in the world. In fact, all give us a narrow view of what is good and just. But this was always we sought. Any other kind of knowledge could possibly turn everything upside down. So the mission of moral philosophy was always to sustain the status quo. It does so by limiting how we perceive the human experience. If human beings are rational beings, then what is good and just will be found within this realm. However, if human beings are relational, ecological, existential, spiritual, cultural, and historical beings, then determining what is good and just becomes a much more complex and ambiguous matter. The mission of moral philosophy is to save us from this complexity and ambiguity because ideologically we want to be saved from complexity and ambiguity. Until we achieve the courage to fully engage the world's boundless ambiguity and complexity, we will continue to believe things that limit how we perceive and make sense of things, such as what is just and good.

48

ON LIBERTY

We are to assume that the relationship between liberty and capitalism is inextricable. Capitalism promotes liberty. This is presumably the moral case for capitalism. Through markets we acquire and determine what goods and services we desire. We can also determine the price of these goods and services. Moreover, because there will always be needs and desires for different things, there will always be markets for these things. The beauty of capitalism, according to advocates, is that no government entity is dictating our needs and desires. We are presumably doing so of our own accord. In other words, capitalism is organically democratic. Through markets we are democratically determining what is good and fair and even decent. Thus, for advocates, to impede capitalism is to impede our ability to democratically determine what we should value. To impede this process is to rob us of our dignity. For advocates, in promoting liberty, democracy, and our dignity, capitalism is foundational to all that is good with us. This is presumably why capitalism is our natural condition. That no full-blown capitalist nation has yet gone to war with another full-blown capitalist nation is apparently further proof of the truth of capitalism. Moreover, capitalism prizes efficiency. It aspires to use resources efficiently as doing so makes markets vibrant. Advocates claim that capitalism gives us the most compelling vision of liberty. It disassociates liberty from promiscuity by tying liberty to democracy, and gives us a way to efficiently use our resources.

How now to claim that capitalism is a nemesis of liberty? But such is the case. Theoretically, at least, markets strive for efficiency. Efficiency means using, allocating, and pricing resources that minimize cost and maximize profit. It is about achieving the greatest disparity between cost and profit. Achieving this disparity involves minimizing the cost of labor. This effort to reduce the cost of labor is unending and unrelenting. However, success in this endeavor undermines liberty. For what becomes of liberty when, either because of low wages or no wages, we are unable to purchase what we need and desire? What becomes of our dignity? Moreover, what becomes of the democracy that capitalism promotes when we are unable to influence the direction of markets because we lack the resources (wages and earnings) to participate in the workings of markets? In tying liberty with resources, what happens when resources (such as wages) go away? This is the crisis of capitalism. It professes to value liberty but is constantly working to end the resources that are necessary for the exercising of liberty. However, within capitalism resources never really disappear. Seeking to maximize the disparity between cost and profit means that by reducing the cost of resources, profit increases. So as labor is losing liberty, wealth is gaining liberty by possessing more and more resources to influence the direction and workings of markets, as well as the political context that surrounds the workings of markets. Thus what is certain within capitalism is the widening gap between rich and poor. However, this inevitable widening is much more than an economic widening. It is fundamentally a gap in liberty and also constitutes the erosion of democracy. Ultimately, this is capitalism turning upon itself. But without liberty and democracy, what becomes of the dignity that capitalism prizes? In reality, capitalism is always degrading our dignity by constantly seeking to lessen our own resources, either by deskilling jobs, automating jobs, moving jobs to places with low wages, or simply ending jobs for any manner of reasons. But the gap between rich and poor, the few and the many, can only become so wide before everything implodes. Yet there is no way for capitalism to reconcile liberty with equality, and thereby stop the widening gap between rich and poor. Even theoretically, the task is impossible. Thus what is now upon us is the full-blown implosion of capitalism.

For advocates of capitalism, liberty is about the ability to control our fates. It is about being able to shape our lives by our own means. Liberty is about doing us. But this is a myopic and narcissistic view of liberty. This view of liberty assumes that our humanities are outside and separate from each other, meaning that my life has no bearing on your life. This, of course, is false. Even psychology now recognizes the intertwined nature of our minds. However, what is seductive about the liberty that capitalism promotes is that it releases of our obligations to each other. It allows us to believe that we can do our own thing without having any regards for others. We can create our own lives purely on our own terms. We merely have to be willing to get up and get. Liberty supposedly levels the playing field. We all have the liberty to make our lives valuable. Advocates of capitalism like to point to the relation between liberty and responsibility. We are to take responsibility for our own mediocrity. Our lack of success is presumably of our own doing, or lack thereof. We supposedly always had the liberty to do differently. But note how advocates use the language of responsibility. Liberty is about being responsible for our lives. Our success presumably comes from only our own doing. Advocates use responsibility to keep the focus on us. Our success apparently has nothing to do with anything else but our own doing. We should therefore never begrudge the success of others. We supposedly all had the liberty to succeed. So the language of responsibility challenges us to look at only ourselves. But this view of responsibility is no less myopic than our view of liberty.

As our own humanities are bound up with the humanities of others, what is our responsibility for others? Moreover, because the condition of our humanity is bound up with the condition of the world, what is our responsibility for the planet? But how did liberty become such a celebrated notion? Was serfdom a problem of liberty, specifically the lack thereof? Was slavery? The Holocaust? We all would probably like to be able to create our own lives and shape our own fates. But in a relational and ecological world this means something completely different to what we have been made to believe. This means embracing our obligation to each other, as well as our obligation to the planet. It means recognizing that our actions and decisions have consequences for others and the world. Liberty is a false notion. It is born out of our need to avoid our obligation to each other. This is how Thomas Jefferson and company could write so eloquently about liberty, and still remain fully involved in slavery. Liberty is meant to pose no threat to the status quo. We are to assume that what slaves were really deprived of was liberty. By achieving liberty, all is now supposedly to be well. However, giving slaves liberty posed no threat to the status quo. The reason being that slavery had nothing to do with liberty, or the lack thereof. It was about our unwillingness to recognize our humanity being bound up with the humanity of others. Liberty is a diversion. That we continue to invoke the language of liberty when addressing our treatment of various peoples only further underscores how effective is this diversion. For what threat to the status quo is posed by the supposed giving of liberty to various peoples? Why then all this commotion over liberty? Does liberty promise to end our increasing isolation, or our reckless plundering of the planet's natural resources?

There are no problems that have origins in the lack of liberty. We are always dealing with problems of obligation. However, fully embracing our obligation to each other involves changing our worldview and everything else. We have to begin viewing ourselves differently. A relational and ecological view of the human experience comes with enormous demands and challenges. Liberty saves us from this struggle. In promoting liberty we reinscribe the idea that we are responsible for only our own well-being. Our only obligation is to avoid infringing on the liberty of others. We are to live and let live. Presumably, all the resources we need to live well already reside within us. We have no need for each other, and thereby should be left alone to do our own thing. Liberty would have us believe that all is well with the order of things. Success, again, merely requires us to take advantage of our liberty. We should strive to stand on our own feet and profit from only the sweat from our brow. We must owe nothing to anyone. Indeed, the narrative of liberty is seductive. It gives us an easy way to understand what constitutes the good life. It also in no way challenges us to disrupt anything. Liberty is all that we need to live well. Thus, "give us liberty, or give us death." But this liberty that capitalism promotes is nothing but promiscuity. Promiscuity means having no regards and obligations for others. What turns us on is purely our business. We owe no account to anyone. We presumably have an inalienable right to do as we please, as long as we never violate the ability of others to do likewise. Liberty assumes that only by being able to do as we please will we become happy and our lives be worthwhile. So for liberty life is about being happy. It is our only obligation. We are presumably entitled to be happy. It is the promise of liberty. But why should being happy be the ultimate pursuit of life? What prophets concur? Indeed, what is so compelling about being happy? Anything, after all, can make us happy. Inflicting pain on others can make us happy. Exploiting others can make us happy. Being with only our kind can make us happy. Killing animals can make us happy. In sum, being happy comes with no moral calculus. Only those things that infringe on the liberty of others are off limits. Everything else is fair game. Being happy is about pursuing what makes us so. It is satisfying our supposed inalienable entitlement to be so. But such entitlement fosters narcissism, as in our complete disregard for how many natural resources we continue to use to achieve our own happiness.

A relational and ecological world comes with a moral compass. There are always constraints and consequences. The pursuit of happiness makes no sense in such a world. What is good for us must ultimately be good for others and for the planet. In a relational and ecological world, selflessness matters. We are to become much larger than ourselves so we can perceive the world and others from outside of ourselves, meaning from outside our own egotism, tribalism, narcissism, and ethnocentrism. This constitutes an enormous struggle, sometimes even an impossible struggle. But such struggling reveals that life is about finding purpose and meaning, and as Viktor Frankl observed, the most profound meaning is found in love.

49

ON INTERCULTURAL COMMUNICATION

Intercultural communication texts, courses, and discourses generally assume a common set of definitions for intercultural communication. *"Intercultural communication generally involves face-to-face communication between people from different national cultures." "Intercultural communication occurs when large and important cultural differences create dissimilar interpretations and expectations about how to communicate competently."* We therefore generally assume that intercultural communication is communication between peoples of different cultures. As such, intercultural communication texts and courses generally focus on introducing us to the features and attributes of different cultures. We are to learn the distinct features that allow us to distinguish masculine from feminine cultures, high-context from low-context cultures, and so forth. We are to assume that these differences matter. Lack of this knowledge presumably impedes intercultural communication, thereby threatening the possibility of strife and conflict. So knowledge of different cultures is supposedly vital for the cultivation of *good* intercultural communication.

Popular definitions of intercultural communication also assume that communication is a medium through which different cultures interact with each other. It is a kind of drawbridge between islands. Intercultural communication is about both sides keeping the bridge down and encouraging both sides to use the bridge. Both sides should also use the bridge with consideration for the other side. This means that both sides should obey and respect all the necessary regulations and conventions so that there are no accidents and congestion. It also means knowing all the laws and norms that govern either side of the bridge. To translate, this means knowing how the other side uses words, symbols, and language. We should know what different behaviors and actions mean. We should also know the meanings behind various customs and traditions. Once again, knowledge is presumably vital to *good* intercultural communication. Therefore intercultural communication texts and courses devote considerable attention to how different cultures use words, symbols, and language. The goal is to save us from ignorantly saying or doing something offensive. Ultimately, the goal of intercultural communication is to achieve harmony between peoples of different cultures. This harmony will supposedly save the world from strife and conflict.

What intercultural communication texts, courses, and discourses are assuming is no different to what the rest of us are assuming. We also believe that strife and conflict will arise without achieving harmony between our differences. Every intercultural communication text promises to give us this knowledge to achieve harmony. This is the mission of intercultural communication—to (supposedly) use communication to lessen the threat of our differences. It is about knowing what, when, where, and how to relate to and communicate with peoples of different cultures so as to avoid tension and confusion. Intercultural communication texts and courses promise to supply us with this knowledge, and accordingly, help promote peace and stability. We read that "*The world is experiencing new forms of conflict . . . Some of these are overt military actions and some of them are covert statements of protest. Many of these conflicts arise from cross-cultural tensions, cross-border political goals and tensions arising from multi-ethnic, multi-religious populations. To date, neither mainstream media nor scholarly debate has successfully addressed the issue of how modern conflicts affect intercultural communication both at the theoretical level as well as at the level of specific case studies. In order to curb the flaring up of conflicts or for conflicts to come to sustainable, creative endings, it is important to bring to public attention the key uses and contributions of intercultural communication.*" We also have intercultural communication seminars with titles like "*Communicating in a Cross-Cultural Environment—Skills for Working and Living in a Multicultural World*" that come with the following descriptions: "*How do cultural differences create barriers for effective communication? What cultural values do we have that affect how we interact with others, especially those from differing cultural backgrounds? What skills are useful when working with people from different cultural backgrounds? What is the role of these cultural differences in addressing interpersonal conflicts? Our interactions with the world are shaped by our cultural values and understandings. This workshop will seek to address the above questions through a broad analysis of cultural values and understandings, and a focus on identifying barriers that prevent effective cross-cultural communication. Emphasis will be placed on developing and practicing skills that will aid in decreasing the effects of these barriers.*" Finally, there are the headlines that cast our differences as the cause of strife and conflict. "*Mobs of South Africans shout: "Who are you? Where are you from?*" In the end, whether in texts, courses, or headlines, the belief is reinforced that without finding effective ways to deal with our cultural differences, strife and conflict will arise and throw the world into chaos and mayhem. We must therefore strive to harmonize our differences, which means that for intercultural communication the goal is convergence, as in both sides agreeing to tolerate and bridge each other's differences. So, ultimately, the mission of intercultural communication is to find the most effective means to neutralize our differences.

But is such a focus valid or even valuable? That is, are our differences really the cause of strife and conflict between different peoples? Did the slaughter of the Tutsis by the Hutus arise from the differences between these peoples? Did the Holocaust arise from the differences between Germans and Jews? Did slavery and Jim Crow arise from the differences between Whites and Blacks? Did the Rape of Nanking arise from the differences between the Japanese and Chinese? What ideology do we perpetuate by continuing to assume that strife and conflict result from our differences, specifically our apparent failure to neutralize these differences? Why do we seem so susceptible to this belief? Arguably, this belief appeals to our most primal instincts and impulses. To view the world in a primal way is to view the world in terms of friends and foes. We find friends in things and persons that give us cognitive stability, making for an obsession with similarity, commonality, and homogeneity. Foes are things and persons that threaten our cognitive complexity, thereby perceived as different and threatening. Moreover, friends are perceived in terms of order, stability, and safety, whereas foes are perceived in terms of chaos, disruption, and conflict. Evidently, to view the world in a primal way is to divide the world into opposing forces that are inherently hostile to each other. We supposedly have no choice but to vanquish the malevolent forces. We have been futilely trying to do so for hundreds of years. We now seem to have resigned ourselves to managing and tolerating these forces, thus the rise of intercultural communication and the mission of managing and bridging our differences. However, our primal distrust and suspicion of diversity, chaos, and disruption remains firmly in place as our ideological and epistemological bias remains with the forces of similarity, homogeneity, and commonality. This is why ultimately the mission of intercultural communication is to neutralize our differences. Presumably, without favoring and privileging similarity, commonality, and homogeneity, chaos, confusion, and disruption will arise and make communication and civility impossible. So intercultural communication insists that both sides abide by a common set of norms and regulations. Enter speech codes and various prohibitions against the use of "offensive" and "threatening" language. In the end, a deep distrust and suspicion of our differences remains firmly in place. Though many have no qualms about warning of a coming clash of civilizations, others who claim to be progressive and liberal also have no qualms imposing all manner of arbitrary laws and regulations to sustain a certain normativity of civility and collegiality. Both sides fear that without taming and neutralizing and normalizing our differences, chaos and strife will arise and throw the world into death and mayhem. So behind all the posturing and pretending to be of fundamentally different politics, both sides are actually cut from the same ideological and epistemological cloth.

We perceive differences. Differences are social concepts. Yes, there are no doubt differences between us, but how we define, perceive, relate, and experience differences comes from us. We can be other than primal in how we perceive, relate, and experience others. We can be moral. We can strive to find our humanity in others. Instead of fear, suspicion, and distrust, we can view each other with empathy, compassion, and mutuality. We can be generous in our interpretation of each other. We can also be ecological in our view of others, viewing our well-being as being intertwined with the well-being of others. Moreover, why should our unwillingness to bridge and engage each other's differences lead inevitably to strife and conflict? Why is this inevitability being assumed? What about live and let live? What is inherently wrong with this politics? Simply put, intercultural communication gives us no compelling reason why intercultural communication is necessary. Why should we be compelled to neutralize and compromise our own differences? Why also should we be coerced to harbor a fear of chaos, death, and confusion? After all, intercultural communication would be impossible without this fear. There would only be communication. Through communication we shape how we perceive others. Through communication we shape how we perceive ourselves. Through communication we create and shape our social worlds. Communication is a human-making practice. Communication is a world-making practice. Communication is bound up with ideology and epistemology, meaning that communication is never separate or outside of ideology and epistemology. Through communication we are always doing something to our relation to the world. As communication changes, our relation to the world changes. Consequently, communication is inherently cultural, political, and epistemological. But most of all, communication is inherently moral as there are always consequences and implications that come with it. So why intercultural communication? When is communication ever devoid of culture? What makes us susceptible to this illusion, and thereby willing to accept the shallow definition of communication that constitutes intercultural communication?

Intercultural communication has nothing to do with communication. It is merely another invention to help neutralize and compromise our differences. This is why intercultural communication needs speech codes and prohibitions against certain kinds of language. We use intercultural communication to impose an ideological and epistemological normativity that suppresses diversity, dissent, and disgust. In reality, the purpose of intercultural communication is to end communication, as diversity, dissent, and confusion are actually the lifeblood of communication. Communication, rather than being the negation of confusion, produces confusion and is even vitalized by confusion. We find confusion in the fact that language is laden with ambiguity. There are always diverse and multiple meanings. We can do nothing to end this reality, and any attempt to do so only impedes communication. Indeed, communication flourishes when confusion flourishes. The notion that through intercultural communication we engage and bridge our differences is no less an illusion. Through communication we generate difference, achieve difference.

There is no difference outside of communication. In communication, difference is inevitable. Difference is that other meaning, that other interpretation, that other understanding that the world's ambiguity makes inevitable. Communication harbors no hostility to difference. There is no need to neutralize and compromise difference. Difference will always be inevitable. Without difference communication would perish. So in order for communication to flourish, difference must flourish. We should therefore always strive to promote communication, so as to perpetually increase the diversity of our differences so that no position (difference) ever achieves a position of hegemony. It is the hegemony of various differences, or the ability of such differences to coercively suppress the rise of other differences, rather than any difference per se, that really puts the world in peril. When communication is robust and vibrant, hegemony is impossible. No one meaning, nor one interpretation, nor one understanding, nor one Truth, nor one reality can achieve hegemony. There is always the possibility for something new, something different.

Communication is ecological. It is life-generating, life-affirming. Meanings and interpretations are always emerging, changing, and evolving. Such is the flow and rhythm of life. Everything is always in flux, always laden with possibility. When communication is robust and vibrant, the possibility of violence diminishes. Violence comes from hegemony—institutions, structures, and practices that have the power and resources to impede the rise of new meanings, interpretations, and understandings. This is also how communication organically lessens the threat of our differences. There will always be differences that aim to suppress other differences by any means possible. But this can only happen by impeding communication. Communication and hegemony can never mutually coexist, and without hegemony violence is difficult to generate. We use violence to achieve hegemony, and hegemony to legitimize violence. Therefore by impeding the formation of hegemony, communication impedes the rise of violence. This is why communication matters, especially in a world where our spaces and distances are rapidly collapsing and imploding. It saves us from violence.

However, for supposedly the sake of achieving peace, intercultural communication insists that we neutralize and compromise our differences. We must pledge to be civil and kind to each other so as to promote an atmosphere of inclusion and tolerance. There shall be no offensive or threatening speech. This is presumably what is necessary to have peace and security. Neutralizing and compromising our differences is supposedly best for all sides. This politics assumes that peace is elegantly impossible in the face of our diversity. We have to fudge and compromise our way to peace. But what is the value of this peace that intercultural communication seeks? It is a peace that assumes that strife and conflict ultimately arise from our differences. It is a peace that assumes that peace is the negation of war. It is a peace that assumes that communication is merely a means to achieving peace. Ironically, this peace also assumes a suspicion of peace. Conflict is supposedly our natural proclivity. It is also supposedly the world's natural proclivity. There can presumably be no peace without the constant fear and threat of war. This peace is supposedly the best that can be had. However, to even have this peace requires both sides to be always readying themselves for war, which means always improving our capacity to kill and destroy each other. For instance, upon receiving the Nobel Peace Prize, the President of the United States said that he could not be guided by only the examples of Martin Luther King and Gandhi. "I face the world as it is, and cannot stand idle in the face of threats to the American people. For make no mistake: Evil does exist in the world. A non-violent movement could not have halted Hitler's armies. Negotiations cannot convince al Qaeda's leaders to lay down their arms. To say that force may sometimes be necessary is not a call to cynicism—it is a recognition of history; the imperfections of man and the limits of reason."

But this is a false dichotomy, as being committed to peace has nothing to do with standing idly by as peril looms. This dichotomy distorts and trivializes what promoting peace involves. It makes believe, although the President professes to know better, that there is weakness and naiveté in the lives and creed of King and Gandhi. Presumably, persons involved in promoting peace believe that evil is merely an illusion and a non-violent movement could have put an end to the likes of Hitler and al Qaeda. Our naiveté can also be supposedly seen in our apparent failure to recognize the harsh truths of history, our imperfect nature, and "the limits of reason." But which proponent of peace is so naïve? The President of the United States gives us no names, points to no examples.

To promote peace is to oppose violence, especially the everyday and ordinary violent practices that ultimately give rise to all manner of racism and terrorism that makes war inevitable. War is an ultimate outcome. The mission of the peace movement is to end all the practices and conditions that cultivate and legitimize violence. Without violence, war is impossible. To cast peace as the negation of war is fundamentally misleading as doing so fosters the impression that peace is the absence of war. But of course this is false, as slavery and apartheid could have been found in places where war was absent. To promote peace is to cultivate practices and conditions that undermine the possibility of violence.

For proponents of peace, the harsh truth of history is that violence makes war inevitable and justifiable. We lessen the possibility of war by impeding the conditions that promote violence. Thus there is simply no such thing as a morally just war. To accept the premise of a just war is to mask all of the violence that ultimately makes war possible. For proponents of peace, this is the height of naiveté. No less naïve isbelieving that in a world increasingly laden with nuclear weapons, that any war, regardless of however just and moral, is winnable and even survivable. Also, no less naïve is failing to recognize from history, as in our own wars in

Vietnam, Afghanistan, and Iraq, that determining which wars are morally just is fraught with peril and uncertainty.

Still, our new Nobel Peace laureate claims that "the plain fact is this: The United States of America has helped underwrite global security for more than six decades with the blood of our citizens and the strength of our arms... We have done so out of enlightened self-interest—because we seek a better future for our children and grandchildren, and we believe that their lives will be better if others' children and grandchildren can live in freedom and prosperity." Indeed, such sacrifices should be duly noted. But what about the endless violence, terrorism, and destruction that the U.S. is also responsible for by toppling legitimate governments around the world, propping up cruel and murderous dictators, and proliferating all kinds of weapon systems and hardware that heighten local conflicts? What also of our reckless plundering of the world's natural resources and the attending ecological destruction that now puts the planet in peril? Who is naïve to believe that all of this violence begets no violence, and a world tortured by endless wars?

But of course, the President makes no mention of our own culpability in burdening the world with war, misery, and peril. No mention, also, about our violent subjugation and oppression of African Americans and Native Americans. We have merely made "mistakes." For our new Nobel Peace Laureate, "our challenge" is to reconcile "two seemingly irreconcilable truths—that war is sometimes necessary, and war at some level is an expression of human folly." But this is another false schism as war will always reflect a lack of moral imagination. Again, this reality is amply seen in the fact that any future war involving nuclear weapons, regardless again of however just and moral, will most likely vanquish us all. What then is the value of planning and resourcing for such a war?

We can embrace other challenges. We can challenge ourselves to remove all the practices and conditions that promote and legitimize violence. These challenges require much more than simply adhering to international standards governing the use of force, and the others that the President outlines that pose no threat to the order of things and ultimately save us from each other's indifference and violence. For proponents of peace, there are no illusions about our capacity and even proclivity for evil. On the other hand, there is no certainty either. We value the sacrifices of both John Brown and Martin Luther King. For us, the challenge is removing all the ideological, social, and material conditions that excite, encourage, and legitimize violence, such as ending our own incarceration of so many peoples for non-violent offenses, lessening the growing gap between rich and poor, ending poverty and despair, reconfiguring our relation to the planet so as to lessen our impact, exposing the futility of war and all forms of retribution, encouraging self-determination for all peoples, releasing peoples from the structures and forces of imperialism and colonialism, fostering cooperation between different peoples, and doing everything we can to lessen the threat and suspicion of our differences.

We understand well the case for just war, and the anguish that comes with supporting such wars. But no war, regardless of our capacity and proclivity for evil, evolves out of an ideological and material vacuum. This, for us, is "a plain fact" and "a hard truth." We believe in peace and oppose violence because we recognize only too well our abundant and stubborn capacity to create misery and wage war, and that peace rather than violence ultimately constitutes a more constructive path to our survival and prosperity. What then is the value of this peace that intercultural communication assumes? How did this become the only peace that can be had or is within our potential? In sum, why is there supposedly no elegant and rigorous mainstream theory of peace?

To look at history anew is to find that our differences had nothing to do with the Holocaust or any of the abominations that stain us. Our differences merely function as context and pretext to mask our unwillingness to do other things. These abominations are born of our unwillingness to do what every prophet asks to do to: love, share, forgive. This, according to all the scriptures, is the only path to a robust and elegant peace. But intercultural communication allows us to avoid our blatant hypocrisy as well as our own complicity in impeding this kind of peace. Our problems presumably reside in our differences, specifically in other's differences. This is why the world is in peril. We are faultless. The fault presumably resides with others. If only those differences could go away, or even be degraded, all would supposedly be well with the world. This is the sentiment that pervades intercultural communication. This is also why intercultural communication is obsessed with taming and neutralizing our differences. By fixing this problem of our differences, intercultural communication promises to save us from strife and peril.

But as our differences pose no such threat, what exactly is intercultural communication seeking to accomplish? In fact, what exactly can intercultural communication really accomplish by focusing on something that has nothing to do with anything? Intercultural communication is nothing but a distraction. However, as the world is now fraught with so much peril, this is a distraction that nobody can really afford. Intercultural communication reinscribes a view of the world that seduces our most primal instincts and impulses. Nothing about this worldview can be salvaged. We need a worldview that promotes communication, as communication makes us moral by pushing us to own the consequences of all our actions and lack thereof. With communication there are always consequences, and these consequences are never even. Still, communication is the womb of possibility. Without communication, nothing happens, meaning that nothing can live, change, evolve, even die. We become human only through communication. We create and shape our social worlds through communication. We would also have no way of creating and experiencing our gods. In fact, without communication, nothing can be sacred. We perceive and experience the sacred through communication. Through communication the sacred dwells. Thus in a world that diminishes communication, there would be no recognition and appreciation of the sacred. Everything will be reduced to the workings of natural and biological processes. We would be nothing but survival machines. Information would be the status quo, and networks, rather than relationships, would rule the world. A world devoid of the sacred means that there is no onus on us to treat anything with care, love, and reverence. We will abuse and violate everything. Trash the environment. Exploit each other. Nothing about any of this will cause us any qualms. This is what happens when nothing is sacred. The consequences are never good. This is also what happens when communication is eroded. Communication brings the sacred into being by pulling us toward each other. Communication is a social, spiritual, and ecological practice. Without the generous support and involvement of others, communication degrades and devolves, and as this happens communication loses the ability to nourish possibility. So what exactly is sacred or should be sacred? It is life. No communication flourishes in a vacuum. Communication requires a sharing of ourselves, a giving of ourselves. Without such generosity, communication perishes. Isolation emerges, but of course isolation is death. It erodes the mind and smashes the soul. So communication encourages the sharing of ourselves. It cultivates an ethics of care. For without empathy, communication implodes. Without vulnerability, communication devolves. We attend to the needs of each other through communication, and only through communication. We nurture each other through communication, and only through communication. We attend to the needs and concerns of life through communication, and only through communication. In other words, because life dwells and flourishes in communication, to attend to communication is to attend to life.

But what exactly is life? It is possibility. When we enlarge what we are capable of sharing, meaning, and understanding, we are also enlarging what life is potentially capable of being and becoming. This is how communication promotes possibility. The sharing and generosity that communication requires of us enlarges our humanity, making us vulnerable to new experiences and new realms of possibility. This is the case for communication. It promotes life. This is also why attending to communication—even the teaching and theorizing of communication—is a sacred matter. As communication goes, so goes the world. Our destiny is bound up with what becomes of communication, which really means that our fates—regardless of our differences—are intertwined.

50

ON THE NATURE OF THOUGHT

Language does influence how we perceive, conceptualize, and relate to the world. This means that as much as language influences our thought system, our thought system influences our language. Behind our thought system and language system is our worldview, which shapes both systems. Our worldviews infuse both systems with ontological, epistemological, historical dimensions. Thus our thought systems have dimensions of power, meaning, and purpose, which means that these systems are really systems of being rather than products of cognitive processes. Our thoughts come from our being and also shape our being. Changing our thoughts therefore involves changing our being.

So there is an inseparable relation between language, being, and our thoughts. That each influences and shapes the other means that changing one also involves changing the other. It also means that the other will make change difficult, sometimes even impossible. But what else to do when our thought system is making for our demise? This is was David

Bohm's project. According to Bohm, our thought system chops up the world into pieces. It splinters the world. It separates and divides everything into conflicting pieces (meaning versus ambiguity, order versus chaos, ignorance versus knowledge, male versus female, life versus death, matter versus energy, and so forth). What emerges is a thought system that assumes a world laden with conflict, a thought system that puts us in constant conflict with the world, a thought system that torments our being with all manner of unnecessary and unhealthy conflict and tension, and a thought system that infuses all of this division, separation, and fragmentation in our language. Ultimately, what comes forth is a thought system, a language system, and a manner of being that together only makes for death and destruction.

We have arrived at a thought system, language system, and manner of being that separate us from the world. But what cannot be underscored enough is the death and destruction that comes from these different systems of thought, language, and being. There would be no Holocaust, no apartheid, no Jim Crow, no slavery without these systems. Indeed, all our sciences, especially the physical, natural, and social sciences, are premised on the belief that our thought system is merely a cognitive process that deals with inputs and outputs. It reflects, when operating optimally, fully developed analytical, computational, and mathematical processes. This is what presumably constitutes rational thought, and ultimately a rational being and a rational society. But in reality there is no division between the social and natural, the spiritual and material, the cultural and ecological. These divisions begin in the retardation of being—limiting our conception of being by separating being from the natural world. What emerges is a being that is divorced from the natural world, and thereby without any obligation to the natural world. This being is increasingly separated from other beings, and thereby also without any obligation to other beings. But eventually this being is socially and increasingly physically isolated, and consequently, tortured by all manner of neuroses and psychoses.

However, this increasing isolation is also being driven by a thought system that encourages isolation and undermines our obligation for others and the natural world, that is, a thought system that undermines the evolution of community, solidarity, and mutuality. Out of this thought system comes a world that deserves suspicion. This is supposedly a world of competition, selfishness, and greed. This thought system assumes that this world requires a manner of being that is always suspicious, calculating, and cold, thus hostile in every way to the demands of community. What becomes of language as this thought system unfolds always serves to compound our social isolation. Language becomes increasingly separated and divorced from being. Now language is reduced to words and symbols. In most cases, these words mean nothing. There is no obligation to be honest. Language becomes a tool of deception and manipulation. The goal is to learn how to use language skillfully rather than honestly, compassionately, and courageously. In a world of division, separation, and fragmentation, deception, deceit, and duplicity are the status quo. Vulnerability is impossible and isolation inevitable. We cannot therefore view the rise of our social isolation as merely a psychological condition that is making for increasing neuroses and psychoses. It is also a political condition, an epistemological condition, and an ontological condition. It is a crisis of being that increasingly threatens the world.

This world needs a new knowledge system. We need new theories, methodologies, and epistemologies. We need epistemologies that come from modes of being that aim for communion rather than fragmentation, integration rather than separation, union rather than division. We need to end the illusion of the objective observer, the neutral theorist, the apolitical scholar. We also need to move beyond theories, methodologies, and epistemologies that profess to have no relation to being. The fact that the knowledge which now rules the world is bringing nothing but death and destruction is all about the kind of being that is creating such knowledge. There is simply no separation between being and knowing.

The consequences and implications begin with what is lost in our increasing lack of obligation to the world and each other. It is the increasing loss of obligation rather than merely the division, separation, and fragmentation that makes for our undoing. To lessen our obligation to the world is to lessen our potentiality. In other words, besides distorting and narrowing our conception of what being human means, the loss of obligation releases us from doing and exercising all that is necessary to nurture the well-being of the world and each other. It diminishes our humanity by releasing us from the responsibility to find ways to care for the world and all that is of the world. In a word, such a loss of obligation undermines our capacity to love. It was Erich Fromm, whose life was dedicated to understanding the origins of the Holocaust, who compellingly pointed to the negative relation between love and fragmentation. Union, communion, and integration make us biophilic (of ideologies that encourage to appreciate, care, and love all life), whereas division, separation, and fragmentation make us necrophilic (of ideologies that make us hostile to all life). According to Fromm, the latter fuels hate and violence by putting us at each other's throats. However, on the other hand, only through love and loving do human being overcome division, separation, and fragmentation. For Fromm, who barely escaped the Holocaust, love was a manner of being rather than a kind of emotion that a person selfishly reserves for only a special person. It is about our capacity to selflessly love the world and all that is of the world. To love means to take responsibility for the condition of the world and each other. It constitutes the boldest expression of our obligation to the world and each other. To love is also about the courage to love, as in being of the fortitude and resolve to love. Those who desire certainty and safety, according to Fromm, lack the courage to love. To be of an obligation that involves the willingness to love the world and all that is of the world therefore requires of us the most courage, the most resolve, the most fortitude, that is, the highest expression of being human. But only through such a love do our ways of perceiving the world unite and integrate everything, removing all of the illusions and distortions that come from our division, separation, and fragmentation. We therefore need a knowledge that is born out of love, and accordingly obligates us to love. Only through love we will come to a knowledge that unites and integrates everything, that makes everything whole. Such a knowledge will have no ambition to destroy or exploit anything. We would come to recognize that to do anything to harm the world ultimately involves harming ourselves. For again, what will always be most apparent is that there is no separation between us and the world. We will always become what becomes of the world.

Besides how we define knowledge, epistemology also means how we relate to knowledge, share knowledge, and what we do with knowledge. But behind every epistemology is a vision of the world that makes us think about the world in certain ways, and also shapes and influences how we use language to think about the world. However, everything begins with the human condition and our imagination or lack thereof. What we perceive and imagine the world to be begins with what we are ready to believe the world to be. Knowledge is an expression of being.

EPILOGUE

The essays in this book constitute *one* story of the human experience. There are, of course, many other narratives. But this is exactly the point. We continue to believe that there is and probably should be only one story, and we should be about trying to promote and institutionalize this story. But no one story will ever have the means to command all the world's ambiguity, complexity, and mystery. This is epistemologically impossible, meaning humanly impossible. Still, some narratives are much more heuristic than others. In this book I sought to introduce *another* story, and demonstrate this story's heuristic promise. This is how I believe we should approach and assess different narratives. Which narratives most expand our realm of possibility and thereby most contribute to a politics of possibility? Understandably, this is merely one way of looking at different narratives. There are possibly better ways of performing this task. But for now at least, this method works as regards saving the world from further misery and suffering.

The world desperately needs a new set of narratives or a reclaiming of narratives that have long been marginalized. With new stories come new possibilities. This is why stories matter. Every story gives us a different vision of the world, a different way of imagining what is possible. This is why we all have a stake in the cultivation of stories. If theories capture the world's truths, stories create the worlds that house, nurture, and legitimize these truths. There simply can be no theories without stories. In fact, there can be no facts, no truths, no gods without stories. In the end, life is about us and our stories. Yet our stories are all that we need. We simply now need much more heuristic stories. That is, those can at least lend for the possibility of a much better ending than what now seems to await us. Of course our goal should be in no way to go out and look for stories that will give us the ending we want because we are unable to deal with the ending that now seems inevitable. We have always been made to believe that certain endings are just inevitable. Such endings are supposedly already written in our nature and in the world's natural order. But every story is born of a certain imagination that reflects something we are already willing to believe. This is why all that we have are our stories. Every story begins and ends with what we are willing to believe, to imagine. However, what we are willing to believe can change, and thereby what we are capable of imagining can also change. The matter is merely one of courage. Do we have the courage to challenge and enlarge what we are willing to believe? What we have the courage to believe will shape what we have the courage to imagine. Einstein's theory of relativity is an act of imagination. So also is Darwin's theory of evolution, and Freud's theory of dreams. We are no doubt capable of imagining other theories and stories. Indeed, why should we limit ourselves to only what Einstein, Darwin, Freud or any other human being is willing to believe and capable of imagining? Why should such narratives be the end of our own imagination? Where is such an order written?

Most compelling about the human experience is that there is no end to our stories, which also means that there is no end to our worlds. We simply have to find the courage to believe, to imagine. The power of any story is predicated on what we have the courage to believe, to imagine.

Every story, as with any theory, asks us to believe something, to imagine the world a certain way. This, in the end, is what should concern us. What is a theory asking us to believe, to imagine? This is how a theory achieves prominence, by appealing to what we are already willing to believe and imagine. Of course we are to assume that a theory only achieves its well-deserved prominence by its truthfulness, which has supposedly been proven through elaborate methods and rigorous procedures. But such is merely another plot of the story. No theory can violate the integrity of the story that brings it into the world. So our attention is misplaced. Rather than focusing on the veracity of any theory, we should focus instead on the story that is creating and casting the theory. What is this story asking us to believe and imagine that is appealing to us? What is the seduction? Such is the success of Darwin's theory. It is of a story that is deeply seductive. This story was destined to give us a Darwin character. There was always going to be a Darwin character in this story. It was inevitable. So there is nothing much we gain by arguing over the veracity of a theory. What is more valuable is for us to look at the archeology and architecture of a story. For instance, what is a story asking us to believe, to imagine? Why do certain stories seduce us? On the other hand, what other stories are we capable of imagining and even realizing? This book is about *one* of those stories.

REFERENCES

Aitchison, J. (2000). *The seeds of speech: Language origination and evolution*. Cambridge: Cambridge University Press.

Bohm, D. (1998). *On creativity*. New York: Routledge.

Corballis, M. C. (2002). *From hand to mouth: The origins of language*. Princeton, NJ: Princeton University Press.

Crawford, M. (2009). *Shop Class as Soulcraft: An Inquiry into the Value of Work*. New York: Penguin Press.

Dyson, G. B. (1997). *Darwin among the machines*. New York: Helix Books.

Dyson, F. (2000, May 16). *Progress in religion*. Edge. http://www.edge.org/documents/archive/edge68.html

Dyson, F. (2010, February 25). Silent quantum genius. *New York Review of Books*.

Hanh, N. T. (2006). *Understanding our mind*. Berkeley, CA: Parallax Press.

Hewes, G. W. (1992). Primate communication and the gesturial origin of language. *Current Anthropology*, 33, pp. 65-84.

Kuhn, T. S. (1996). *The structure of scientific revolutions*. Chicago: University of Chicago Press.

McCrone, J. (1991). *The ape that spoke: Language and the evolution of the human mind.* New York: William Morrow.

Weinberg, S. (1992). *Dreams of a final theory.* New York: Pantheon Books.

Weinberg, S. (1995, October 5). Reductionism redux. *The New York Review of Books,* pp. 1-6.

Weinberg, S. (1999). A designer universe? *The New York Review of Books,* pp. 1-9.

Weinberg, S. (2000, January). Five and a half utopias. *Atlantic Monthly,* pp. 1-6.

Weinberg, S. (2001a, May 31). Can science explain everything? Anything? *The New York Review of Books,* p. 19.

Weinberg, S. (2001b, November 15). The future of science and the universe. *The New York Review of Books,* pp. 1-10.

www.ingramcontent.com/pod-product-compliance
Lightning Source LLC
Chambersburg PA
CBHW071108160426
43196CB00013B/2500